PERFORMING POPULISM

Performing Populism

Visions of Spanish Politics from 15-M to Podemos

RUBEN PEREZ HIDALGO

VANDERBILT UNIVERSITY PRESS

Nashville, Tennessee

Library of Congress Cataloging-in-Publication Data

Names: Perez Hidalgo, Ruben, 1981– author.
Title: Performing populism : visions of Spanish politics from 15-M to
    Podemos / Ruben Perez Hidalgo.
Description: Nashville, Tennessee : Vanderbilt University Press, 2023. |
    Includes bibliographical references and index.
Identifiers: LCCN 2023031046 (print) | LCCN 2023031047 (ebook) | ISBN
    9780826506092 (paperback) | ISBN 9780826506108 (hardcover) | ISBN
    9780826506115 (epub) | ISBN 9780826506122 (pdf)
Subjects: LCSH: 15-M (Organization) | Podemos (Political party) |
    Populism—Spain. | Spain—Politics and government—21st century.
Classification: LCC JN8395.A2 P47 2023 (print) | LCC JN8395.A2 (ebook) |
    DDC 320.56/620946--dc23/eng/20230727
LC record available at https://lccn.loc.gov/2023031046
LC ebook record available at https://lccn.loc.gov/2023031047

A mi padre, que me enseñó a sentir el pensamiento.
A mi madre, que me enseñó a pensar el sentimiento.

CONTENTS

ACKNOWLEDGMENTS

Writing a book is a lonely enterprise that ironically can't be done without the help of many people. First, I want to thank the peer reviewers whose very helpful and detailed comments have immensely improved the quality of all my arguments. I also need to acknowledge the help of Vanderbilt's acquisitions editor, Zack Gresham. Without his ongoing support, this book wouldn't have seen the light of day. Equally, without my colleagues' support in the Department of Spanish and Latin American Studies at the University of Sydney, I couldn't have survived the many ups and downs involved in the writing of my first book. More broadly, it is at Sydney University and specifically in its School of Languages and Cultures, that I have been made to feel like I belong to a vibrant intellectual community. That feeling carried me through moments of self-doubt when I thought I didn't have the wherewithal to finish writing a chapter, or I didn't know how to accept fair criticism, or I simply felt like an impostor who had a lucky run that was about to end. And last but in no way least, I must acknowledge my wife's contagious laughter. The daily sound of her laughing has been the fuel of my writing. Her vibrant energy and constant positive view of life is the anchor for everything I do. Without that, I simply wouldn't know how to be.

Introduction

Populism is the Poetry of Common Sense.

—SANTIAGO ALBA RICO

If one had to begin recounting how the idea of populism was popularized in Spain, the 15-M movement, also known as the Indignados, that emerged during the spring of 2011 in response to the global financial crisis would undoubtedly mark the start of such a story. Those of us who experienced it felt like a new collective common sense was blooming. And as the epigraph to this book advances, poetic language was oftentimes needed to convey the emotional impact the movement had in Spanish politics.[1] As Bryan Cameron has suggested, the 15-M was a moment of "emotional liberation" that obliterated the "outmoded affective attachments that have linked Spaniards to hegemonic parties (PP, PSOE, etc.)."[2] But leaving aside momentarily the realm of political affections to gain some historical perspective, the relevance of the 15-M lies in what has been commonly regarded as the movement's unparalleled force to challenge "the standard Transition [from Francoism to democracy] narrative and the promotion of an isolated cultural sphere floating over our capitalist dystopia."[3] That's why Óscar Pereira-Zazo and Steven L. Torres called it "a second Transition."[4] This was a new stage in Spanish politics that implied a "re-politization process [that] opened the gate for a new cycle of social mobilization in Spain."[5] Nevertheless, scholars working on the movement initially found themselves having to defend its significance against voices in Spain's political commentary that characterized it as, at best, a fleeting, internet-fueled protest.[6] Partly as a direct response to that critical mindset, partly because the movement's importance demanded it, within less than a year, one of the most prominent and most popular collection of essays, Guillem Martínez's *CT o la cultura de la Transición*, was published. The book was inspired by the 15-M's own forceful proposal that the movement was a fundamental historical rupture with the cultural and political consensus established since the country's democratic transition more than three decades earlier.[7] The passing of time has granted the 15-M its status as a "real social movement" that brought about a new political era; the once seemingly indestructible two-party system was gone in a matter of four years (when the political party Podemos, the so-called inheritor of the 15-M, became the third biggest electoral force in the Spanish Parliament).[8]

Social movement scholars who investigated the 15-M's political genealogy have since qualified some of the most enthusiastic analyses of 15-M's unprecedented political break (and Podemos's subsequent tour de force in Spanish politics) by debunking the myth of its novelty and spontaneous nature, arguing otherwise for the historical and long-lasting ties of the main organizers in the 15-M with Spanish autonomous movements (e.g., squatters, anarchists).[9] Whether or not it supposed a complete break from the past, the movement's most important aspect was its ability to allow for a more expansive notion of the political to be popularized, one that understood cultural representation as a mode of political articulation as part of a political culture: "the values, conceptions, and behaviors that are oriented toward the political sphere, and which configure the subjective perception of a group of people toward the system of power."[10] What is more, the movement opened the door to a new political imagination that, at minimum, created a "tendency towards populist positions" and would quickly put the term *populism* at the center of Spain's political culture.[11] And thus Spanish populism acquired its force through its "daily linguistic circulation," which ultimately gave the concept an unparalleled ability to create a new, popular common sense in culture for a new era in politics.[12]

With that in mind, this book goes back to the very first days when the 15-M began to take hold in the Spanish imagination, in order to investigate how the everyday conception of populism originated in practice (e.g., in the occupied squares, in its implicit dialogues with mainstream media, in documentaries) and would later (d)evolve around the Podemos phenomenon. To such end, this book doesn't look at how different intellectuals, spokespeople, or political leaders originally theorized Spanish populism. On the contrary, the focus is on the many and heterogeneous cultural manifestations that in one way or another had the concept of the people— of populism—in the praxis of their meaning-making processes. That is, this book pays a great deal of attention to moments when the politics of populism can be better understood by way of culture, especially popular culture. More importantly, these moments are encapsulated in an array of cultural artifacts, ones that saw and performed the new political time that was inaugurated by the 15-M in 2011. Much attention is paid to the visual and the performative character of populism, whose diverse political practice mirrors its equally diverse cultural manifestations.

Because of such heterogeneity, the political events and cultural products discussed in these pages are organized in narratological fashion around the story of how populism in Spain began with the 15-M, grew in immense popularity when Podemos burst onto the scene, and then suddenly declined until finally disappearing, coinciding with the party's loss of influence. This is a political narrative that will be told from several angles of cultural interpretation: through protest imagery on the internet, through nonfiction film and its varied translations to cinematic fiction, through the viewpoint of mediatic political leadership and its different audiovisual iterations, and through the collaborative power of online prosumer visual culture. These are different sides in the geometry of the Spanish people that serve to visualize the populist version, "the people," which is ultimately the main protagonist in this book. And the people's journey undoubtedly began with the irruption of the 15-M.

The 15-M was the spark that ignited a political culture popularizing alternative ways of doing politics that competed and challenged established ways of understanding the political. The country's political culture was shifting from one in which citizens were uninvolved in politics, as the political was perceived as extraordinary and antithetical to people's everyday experiences, to a "participant political culture" that made politics a matter of the citizenry's ordinary lives.[13] One of the most immediate consequences was that the political lens on everyday life dramatically expanded. It was not only that a new political culture sprang up but also that an (audio)visual culture accompanied it. For instance, television programming became crowded with "politainment" (political entertainment) on prime time, from the daily four-hour political *tertulias* like *Al rojo vivo*, *Las mañanas de cuatro*, or *El programa de Ana Rosa* to the equally long, heated Saturday-night debates in *La sexta noche*, the Catalan *FAQS* in TV3, or the blockbuster docuseries *Salvados*.[14] The political was broadened not just quantitatively—in terms of the sheer increase in the number of people who appeared to be politically engaged on television as well as the upsurge of demonstrations since 2011—but also qualitatively, as many different types of cultural expressions became vessels for political change, seen and performed on screens big and small.

This expansion of the political also meant that the nature of political messaging and political intent was much harder to decipher. As politics became popularized, the popular element, with its intrinsic transversality, muddied the frontier between cause and effect. That's why a word of caution needs to be issued to the reader who might be expecting a normative disciplinary approach to the study of Spanish populism and its cultural manifestations. Because I look at how the political concept of the people (of populism) is heterogeneously presented through a series of (audio)visual texts that are generally associated with the popular in culture, my central investigative preoccupation does not lie with the sociological category of the people (i.e., the Spanish populace as categorized in terms of class, race, ethnicity, religion, sexual orientation, education, age, linguistic or cultural background). Nor do I focus exclusively on the political construction of the people in the historical moment of what can be called Spain's populist cycle (from 2011 with the irruption of the 15-M until roughly 2019, when the Podemos phenomenon lost a great deal of electoral steam).

My proposition is rather riskier when it comes to a disciplinary commitment. In this sense, I argue for a transdisciplinary approach to how populism represents "the people" in politics in relation to how "the people" are presented in culture. To put it more clearly, the object of my study is populism and its connections to the popular element, whose cultural manifestations are, by definition, as heterogeneous as the people themselves and whatever is considered popular at the time. This means that the cultural artifacts selected in the following pages are analyzed less for their intrinsic cultural value and more in relation to how their popular traits—those characteristics commonly associated with an ethos of "the people"—are able to convey a populist aesthetic. Thus situated, this investigation necessarily stands between the fields of political theory, as it relates to the study of populism as a political style, and cultural studies, regarding how culture articulates the political imaginary of "the people." Admittedly, the project runs the risk of being stranded in between the fields, since the two are not cozy bedfellows (one being focused on high-minded abstractions of the political and the other preoccupied with materialist analyses of the everyday in culture). Yet it's essential to analyze them in tandem, for the reasons I briefly explain in the next paragraphs.

On the one hand, a problem I've encountered when dealing with the main political theorists of populism is their lack of direct engagement with the practice of populism at the level of the everyday (i.e., at the cultural level). This is especially salient when it comes to concrete examples or case studies, which tend to favor macro-approaches that are external to populist praxis (i.e., a theory that understands populism structurally at the level of institutions and party leaderships, generally obviating a populist practice that relates to the way the concept of the people "behaves" or presents itself on television screens, films, the internet, and so on). On the other hand, when the field of cultural studies and the closely related fields of visual, film, or television studies have dealt with populism, the focus is often on the granular analysis of the micro, concerned with what cultural artifacts have to say about the social manifestation of a populist moment (e.g., the so-called crisis cinema in Spain deals with how film represented Spain's crisis and the country's populist upheaval). My arguments, then, stand in the middle of the two analytical efforts to offer a much-needed academic dialogue between two disciplines that should be much closer to each other than they are at present. In this sense, I offer an intellectual bridge to those academics who study populism as political theory and those who study the cultural production that results as part of a populist moment. In such liminal space is where this investigation begins to thread the needle to connect "the people" of populism with the popular in the study of cultural production.

A Transdisciplinary Origin Story

At the most basic level, the politics of populism inaugurated by the 15-M movement popularized a vision—on television screens, in the front page of newspapers, in films, on the internet—that became common place; it was the visualization of ordinary people doing politics (in the broadest sense) as part their everyday lives. This was ultimately the logical extension of one of the first slogans of the 15-M: *No nos representan* (They, the politicians, do not represent us, the people). The lack of representation was bridged horizontally as more and more people saw politics as less of an extraordinary event and more as something that was part of the ordinary, of "the people." And more profoundly, that's how the 15-M begins to inform the conceptualization of populism in Spain's popular culture. The 15-M supposed the irruption of the popular to be populist. At least temporarily, it moved the center of the political from the realm of the extraordinary to the everyday. Amid parliaments, financial institutions, and media conglomerates, access to political meaning-making processes is always restricted, but in public spaces, symbolic representation is taken to be unrestricted, producing political meaning for everyone beyond a concrete political culture as part and parcel of a new popular culture when successful. The 15-M forced this change in the name of the people—and its different synonyms in Spanish, *el pueblo*, *la gente*, or *las personas*—against those traditional custodians of political, economic, and cultural power: politicians, bankers, and experts but also gatekeepers in the mainstream media, in intellectual circles, and in the film industry. As such, the 15-M also began a conceptual shift that (con)fused the boundaries between governmental and activist politics, between high and low culture, between preconceived notions separating the political and the cultural, between the popular and the populist. The change, however, wouldn't be permanent.

A decade later, the center of the political had gone back to its established place in institutional politics, definitely pushing the populist bid that began in the 15-M—in relation to the currency gained by a transversal politics of the "people" without a clear-cut ideology—outside political convention. Proof of that was seen in how the movement was remembered in mainstream media on the commemoration of its tenth anniversary. The great majority of accounts framed the 15-M as an event whose long-lasting legacy was above all cultural and (implicitly) almost void of political substance. That is, the 15-M was not viewed as part of real politics. In a long piece commemorating the movement's founding, the newspaper *La Vanguardia* concluded that if there was a general agreement among all those interviewed for the occasion, it was that they all described the 15-M as a moment of "cultural change."[15] *El País*, arguably the most important newspaper in Spain, also reminisced over the movement's evolution in the previous decade in an editorial opinion column tellingly titled "15-M: Frustrated Hope."[16] There, at the same time that the author regards the movement's politics as an ineffective failure, the movement is considered a cultural force for its ability to popularize key political issues that are still relevant today.

On the one hand, those journalistic accounts point at how the hierarchy of politics over culture is still very much unproblematically assumed in mainstream political commentary. On the other, the coverage of the 15-M's tenth anniversary was particularly salient in treating the movement in an almost ethereal way, as if its substance were acquired only by the amount of change that institutions would later allow.[17] In that way, the 15-M was generally understood as a surprisingly refreshing, novel, and spontaneous political contingency, without tangible political achievements.[18] The consequence is that mainstream opinion on the movement—of which *El País*'s editorial is characteristic—tends to make a cynical distinction between political effectiveness and cultural significance. With different degrees of sophistication, a narrative of the movement's unfolding has been created that reinforces that divide and shapes political opinion accordingly. Despite their diverse assessments, political commentary across the ideological spectrum downplays the movement's politics by overstating its cultural impact—reinforcing a division between politics and culture themselves that runs counters to this book's analytical impetus.[19]

In 2021, the Spanish public broadcaster Televisión Española ran a minidocumentary to commemorate the 15-M's founding.[20] On it, the voice-over narrator told a story that followed the spontaneity argument by focusing on the trajectory of different individuals, most of whom talked about how the 15-M had politicized them. Their testimonies, portrayed as personal vignettes, spoke of people who suddenly fell in and out of love with the movement, with its organizations, or with politics altogether. Although never stated explicitly, the viewer was drawn to conclude that the 15-M and its aftermath were in the end subjected to a kind of natural human fallibility that, combined with amateurism, inevitably led to the movement's fragmentation, thus reinforcing the argument of its ineffectiveness and lack of real political impact. Implicit in this line of reasoning is an assumption that the political can be represented only by institutional politics. So political representation may have political actors, like the 15-M protesters, but ultimately the representative force of politics is at the service of those who pull the levers of governmental institutions (along with their partners in the private sector). That's why, for instance, there is a glaring disparity in much of the mainstream media analyses of the 15-M—mostly regarded as a benign, all-too-naïve moment of utopian protest. Its so-called inheritor, the political party Podemos, is often characterized with different degrees of vehemence as a populist wolf in sheep's clothing that appropriated the movement's rhetoric to fool the Spanish electorate.[21] The difference in perception seems driven by categorical distinction: while the 15-M belongs to the realm of popular culture, and so is portrayed as an inane political manifestation of people's outrage, Podemos is considered part of real politics, and so depicted as a threat to the political establishment.

Social movement theorists have for some time argued against that line of thought by, for instance, delving into the genealogical structures of collective action outside governmental power or explaining the logics of social activism in its dealings with the state, which is indeed guided by very specific principles set to achieve very specific policy outcomes.[22] However, while social movement research and data-driven political investigation are invaluable in explaining the sociological reality of the political cycle that started in 2011,

the distance that separates that reality from its various constructed perceptions falls into the more ambiguous realm of the cultural. And although
culture (in particular, popular culture) can be dismissed as not real politics,
it also has the ability to make constructions and even misconstructions of
reality that can pass as reality itself. In the domain of the cultural, materiality is at the service of representation. As such, this investigation is driven by
the many ways the cultural portrayals of the 15-M's life cycle are guided by
issues of (mis)representation: Who and what did the 15-M and the politics
that stemmed from it really represent? But more critically, how did the representations of the movement by members of the movement negotiate a public
image that became bigger than the movement itself as its legacy stepped into
the interrelated domain of the popular (in culture) and the populist (in politics)? Artistic representations and interpretations of the movement became
(or at least purported to be) representations of the movement; those representations evolved as the movement's popular-populist essence was propelled
into the institutional sphere with the advent of the Podemos phenomenon
and its populist interpretation of the 15-M. To begin understanding how all
this happened, the arguments step in and out of the material reality of the
movement and its consequences, addressing different cultural constructions
of whom and what the 15-M's political life cycle "really" represented from
the days of square occupations in 2011 until the consolidation of Podemos
in parliamentary politics at the end of the decade.

Because representation in culture is dependent on myriad subjective processes linked to the heterogeneous experiences of individuals, there is a constant negotiation between reality and what is experienced to be real. The 15-M
began asking for a real democracy (as declared in one of its most famous slogans, *democracia real ya*) at a moment in the history of Spain when democracy
could be said to have achieved its "realest" point, relative to the country's
fraught historical past of civil war and Franco's dictatorship.[23] To reconcile
those two dramatically opposed ways of seeing the same reality, one looks
to the breach of representation that took place between the demos and the
democratic system, which ultimately created a schism between what was said
to be real (as Spain's two-party system was said to represent at large the will
of the Spanish people) and what was seen as real (when millions of citizens
were seen occupying squares across the country demanding the overhaul of
the political and economic system). In this sense, the 15-M kicked off a crisis
of representation that was as discursive as it was visual.

As a way to bridge the hermeneutical gap at the core of that crisis of representation, a series of thematic lines that attend a regime of (in)visibility is

examined: namely, the visualization of a new political subject outside governmental structures, the evolution of that subject from the "streets" to the institutions, and the representational relationship between new political subjects and new political leaders. A series of visual codes form an idea of what is or is not "real" in the negotiation around what and who is represented through popular culture in politics. The distinction between representation *in* popular culture and representation *through* popular culture is important. Representation in culture is essentially passive in that it embeds in a cultural imaginary about people that is external to the people themselves: for example, stereotypical representations of demonstrators as an unruly mob but also the idealized demotic substance of democracy or the nation. Representation *through* culture implies the active participation of people (at different levels) in the production of new cultural imaginaries beyond the traditional brokers of mediation (e.g., the do-it-yourself audiovisual culture of new social media as opposed to old media conglomerates), and it also relates to the visibility that those people and the new imaginaries later acquire in popular culture (e.g., today's rags-to-riches stories of social media entrepreneurs, the 15-M's visualization of people's power).[24]

Rather than investigating the real (e.g., political, sociological) disciplinary meaning of the cycle of protests inaugurated by the 15-M, a transdisciplinary analysis is needed to examine the dialogic intervals between reality and what is seen and performed as real. To be more precise, the "real" representation of the 15-M and its aftermath—of the wave of protests that followed it, of the meteoric rise and fall from grace of Podemos—is approached as a negotiation between what was thought possible (e.g., protest camps to expand the concept of democracy, massive demonstrations to end austerity measures, the effective abolishment of the two-party parliamentary system) and what was seen and performed as possible (e.g., in films, memes, shared images, banners, and demonstrations). The emphasis is not on who and what gets to be represented in politics—that is, which side of the negotiation eventually wins the battle for the construction of a certain political reality in culture (whatever *win* might be). The focus is on how the political negotiates representation through culture. To reiterate, this transdisciplinary approach stresses the relationship between the historical conceptualization of *the people* (the ultimate political representative) and the visual (cultural) presentation of that conceptualization throughout what can be described as Spain's populist cycle, from the days of the 15-M until the establishment of Podemos in parliamentary politics. Underlying that relationship are the mechanisms that allowed the 15-M's popular protest to be transformed into a populist moment defined by "the attempt to unite social majorities in a new way, to *create* a people that recognizes itself as the subject of a possible collective project."[25] And such creative impetus, along with its many aesthetic dimensions, is the main objective of this investigation.

Populism and its construction of the people is thus understood beyond its political substance. Here, the people as conceptualized by populism is analyzed as presented and represented in multiple ways from multiple angles through popular culture. That's why the 15-M and its aftermath as a populist moment beg to be understood from a transdisciplinary angle; one that acknowledges the importance of established disciplines but that also sees the need to transcend them in this particular instance to establish a dialogue between the study of the popular in culture and the study of "the people" of populism in politics. The examination presented herein relies on but refuses to stay within the boundaries of populism theory. To fully understand the complex cultural ramifications of Spain's populist cycle, several disciplines are needed: a theory of populism, to consider it as mostly an aesthetic phenomenon, as a political style; the field of visual semiotics, to unpack how images acquire cultural meaning; filmic analysis, to comprehend how the political in culture is better seen obliquely, as part of a negotiation between what's explicitly shown in the foreground and what's left in the background that implicitly reinforces or contradicts the image at the fore. That's why, as previously stated, instead of exploring how the 15-M conceptualized its populist essence politically, this investigation examines how a number of cultural artifacts (audio)visually present people's heterogeneous demands as a new collective identity that became embedded within a representative picture of Spain's populist moment—and how that identity was later translated by Podemos, the party that made of populism a political and cultural phenomenon.

The goal is to narrate and interpret the story of how concerned average citizens, temporary protesters, and longtime activists alike were visualized as a new "people" for a new time in Spanish politics—or to put it differently, how the popular in culture was seen and performed as populist in politics. In this respect, this book explores how cultural representations of the demos in Spanish liberal democracy were able to acquire the traits of the people of populism. I show the interpretative processes through which a series of competing visualities negotiate different visions of the people that can be ultimately organized into a (perhaps artificial but nonetheless coherent) visual narrative, telling the life story of Spain's populist cycle. Before venturing into the specific analyses of how that narrative takes form, it is important to deal with the ways the visual representations of the people can be best approached methodologically.

A Methodological Approach for the Cultural and Visual Analysis of Populism

Populism and populist ruptures are closely linked to moments of crisis. As Bécquer Seguín has argued in a special issue commemorating a decade since the 15-M, the movement was the way everyday citizens responded to "the causes and effects of what in Spain is simply called *la crisis*"—a term that evokes both Spain's economic meltdown in 2011 and the mobilization campaign against austerity measures instituted afterward. It was a popular response that radically changed the "standard narrative" of such a crisis.[26] It is in that way that *la crisis* sparked a populist rupture through the 15-M movement and its posterior cultural manifestations, realigning the role of "the people" in Spain's liberal democracy; or as Pereira-Zazo and Torres put it, the 15-M "could be described as the discovery of participatory democracy by a significant swath of the Spanish population."[27] This was a realignment that had consequences for how the Spanish citizenry was not only politically represented but also culturally presented. In this sense, the Spanish populace who had been repoliticized, who had discovered the power of participatory democracy, would be found in a series of cultural products that presented them with the traits of the people of populism.

Populism in Spain started as a moment of tension between two confronted visualities of the people: between a vision of the "real" demos severed from the political institutions that should represent it and the vision of the political status quo that naturally clung to its representative entitlements as unquestionable. This confrontation was an essential part of a process of mass symbolic collectivization that was as visual as it was performative. The 15-M was the beginning of a populist moment whereby a collective (in this case, a social movement) gained political agency by negating how the "real" demos was to be visualized and represented according to Spanish democracy. So, as the public squares began to fill with protesters in the spring of 2011, the protesters' demand for "real democracy now" (or *democracia real ya*) took on dimensions beyond the obvious discursive impetus requesting a true democratic system. They also were expressing a desire for the demos to be seen at the center of politics in practice and not just rhetoric—it was a desire to be seen as the most "real," most culturally authentic expression of political reason. And popular culture offered the most fertile ground for the development of an alternative way to see a populist-styled demos that could question Spanish democracy's inability to be *really* representative.

Yet within that approach an obvious first issue arises: Who are "the people" (of populism)? Regardless of the political system of representation—populist, democratic, or otherwise—"nobody knows for sure what the people exactly wants or look like," the political philosopher Wim Weymans argues.[28] Precisely because of its ungraspable nature, the political identity of "the people" is open-ended and constantly subject to change, which advantages new ways of rethinking political representation as well as political agency. "As powerful as it is indeterminate," the people consequently lacks "sociological certainty."[29] If that's the case, how can one "see" the people of populism? A first step would be to think of political representation and political subjects through the lens what Weymans calls poetic representation in politics—closely aligned with cultural representation: "Representation not only means that someone acts or deliberates for someone else while seeking common good . . . but also that someone's particular story or situation is expressed, shown or recognized."[30] The cultural domain is where people's stories are best represented. Poetic or cultural representation recognizes the value of those stories and offers individuals the "literary" means to connect with a larger group in today's highly individualistic atomized societies: "Unlike political party programmes, narratives or movies . . . have the potential to generate empathy for hitherto unfamiliar characters in particular material circumstances" that ultimately create life stories with which the many can connect.[31] Culture thus has the potential to make the invisible individual visible as part of a collective story. And semiotics, as the study of how meaning is culturally constructed, allows one to understand how those stories can be interpreted in their journey toward becoming meaningful.

In an effort to expand the field of language semiotics to the realm of cultural signification, Roland Barthes developed Saussure's and Peirce's linguistic signifying system into the study of how meaning is primarily signified in culture in two planes of signification: the denotative level, called the plane of expression, involving meaning that is literal or explicit, and the connotative level, which operates through the ideological and mythical plane.[32] For Barthes, meaning is always cultural in that it is always culturally negotiated, and thus signification (i.e., how meaning is constructed) is a "practice" that can never be completely closed or definitive but is always open to new (re)interpretations.[33] Barthes then sought to decode how meaning in human communication is constructed through different types of signs (verbal and nonverbal), layers of signification (explicit or denotative and implicit or connotative), and the contextual choices made around the composition of signs.[34]

A semiotic approach to populism implies that the focus of investigation shifts from the broad spectrum of capital-*C* Culture (of established cultures of representation, perceived as unnegotiable by way of this or that ideological enforcement, whether that be a division according to standards of high and low culture, historical tradition, or social custom) to the realm of popular culture. Some of the general traits of Culture may transfer, but popular culture is distinguished by its ability to extricate cultural manifestations from their original particularity to bring cultural expression to the ambiguous (so constantly open to negotiation) realm of the people, the common folk, the everyday average citizen. In this sense, popular culture has the potential to create dichotomies of inclusion (that which is of the people) and exclusion (that which is not popular and thus could easily be made out to be perceived as elitist). Populism latches on to that potentiality to exacerbate the difference between the "us" people and the confronted elitist other. Yet ultimately the question of who is the people (of populism) cannot ever be satisfactorily answered because *the people* is an empty signifier whose meaning depends on a political logic that is constantly negotiated and resignified depending on the particularities of its signification—it is not so much that the meaning of the people of populism is void but rather that its ontology is empty.[35] A more fruitful enterprise, however, is to examine how the cultural characteristics of political signs work within the construction of the people of populism. Thus, semiotics could help in distinguishing how denotative signs of the popular in culture (e.g., the popularization of a slogan such as the 15-M's *democracia real ya* as visualized by films or discussed in television) could be connoted as populist in politics (e.g., Podemos's reconstruction of a "real" demos as frontally opposed to its elitist other *la casta*—the caste—of Spain's political and economic establishment).

Although cultural semiotics aids in deciphering the cultural substance of populism, another methodological obstacle arises around the very question of what populism is. In fact, one of the main problems when studying populism is its conceptual obscurity.[36] In a brief overview of the most important authors who have proposed key definitions of populism, Antonio Gómez López-Quiñones aptly notes:

A good number of authors such as Paul Cammack (2000), Torcuato di Tella (1965), Ernesto Laclau (2005), Christopher Lasch (1991 y 1994) and Peter Worsley (1969), have proposed different definitions of populism with different levels of theoretical depth. Those definitions have two theoretical challenges: On the one hand, if the criterion of their definition is too specific, populism would be ultimately reduced to one or two very concrete cases. . . . However, on the other, if the definition is general in an attempt to obtain structural validity for different geographical political enclosures in different historical times, it runs the risk of constructing a formulaic definition; one that wouldn't be necessarily incorrect but that wouldn't be able to explain concrete historical examples of populism.[37]

One can escape that conundrum by keeping the theoretical scope restricted to locating and identifying the (visual) signs that are used under a populist prism that understands it as a political style, with different articulations according to its different contextual settings. As such, populism can be better comprehended as a way of doing politics that presents itself through the traits of popular culture (the low, the ordinary, the average citizen's common sense) in an attempt to represent "the people." In other words, populism is less a concrete set of political ideas and more a style of politics, a way of articulating the political, that varies depending on the context in which it arises.[38] Rather than a type of (thin) ideology, as Cas Mudde and Cristóbal Rovira Kaltwasser have most famously theorized, populism can be most fruitfully conceptualized as a meaning-making machine whose main force resides in the "intensification of routine political dynamics, which are themselves conducted through more generalized cultural mechanisms that allow social signification to take place, [and] group identities to be forged" in a process of symbolization that has the ability to pair political agency with cultural identity under the commonly shared name of the people.[39] In that way, the people can be *seen* symbolized through culture as part of a political performance, which ultimately constitutes a populist style.

Assuming a stylistic approach changes the focus of interpretation. That's why, methodologically, the focus here is not so much on what causes the populist experience (i.e., an ontology of populism) but on the ways the populist experience unfolds throughout a particular period of time (i.e., an epistemology of the populist moment). Populist identity evolves in different ways to represent visually the name of the people it invokes, so let us appreciate it beyond its discursive composition in politics strictly speaking. Populism's materiality today emerges through visual everyday praxis, one that pops up on television screens, on mobile phones, and in films. For the most part, these are visualizations of a people posed to grant a sense of belonging (an "us") while at the same time (indirectly or directly) demanding raw power from those who do not appear to look like that populist portrayal of the people (a "them" or a confronted other). To be able to visualize such processes of inclusion and exclusion, the concept of populism requires metaphors that bridge its theory with its more mundane applications. Specifically, visual metaphors are needed to delineate the silhouettes of a new vocabulary that would allow for a different type of dialogue when it comes to the ever-present but ever-fleeting images of the people as seen through a populist prism. Rather than being overly concerned with the ontology of the populist experience, the analysis here is developed at an epistemological level, focusing on the ways the people of populism can be seen. In that light, populism is best analyzed as a political moment with a specific style of representing the people.

From that angle of interpretation, populism is not only a political style that culturally visualizes people as "the people" in the hope that they can achieve a new level of representation. Populism is also understood as "the *performative doing* of politics, outside of parties or other formal organizational mandates," where the main analytical preoccupation is not necessarily with "individual identity, but rather with how individuals connect to a collective."[40] Similarly, as argued by the performance scholar Angela Marino, the populist moment is "a process in which a collective body constitutes itself performatively as a naming act as much as an act in the name of a particular group or people."[41] This means that the emphasis falls on the multiple daily manifestations of populist visualities in culture and less on the cause or effect of populist representation at the political level (i.e., trying to answer questions around what populist governmentality stands for). The focus is on the ways representation is *seen* to take place; that is, when attending to the analysis of populist visualities in this book, the focus is on the role of presentation in representation as people perform being the people. In that way, populist identities are rarely static when they negotiate different (self)representations of the people (e.g., the 99 percent, the indignant citizenry, the precarious youth of the 15-M) with those who hold the power to represent them (symbolically and in actuality).

In an effort to bring the discussion on populism down to earth, complementing but moving beyond Ernesto Laclau's widely acquired poststructuralist theorizations on populist discourse, the political scientists Pierre Ostiguy and Benjamin Moffit tackled the relationship between the people and its (re)presentation.[42] Laclau "tends to remain focused on articulation, and thus sometimes overlooks the mediatized nature and aesthetic dimensions of populist performances, as well as the back-and-forth processes of negotiation at play between populist leaders and 'the people' within populism."[43] Because populism, as proposed by Ostiguy and Moffit, is a relational political architecture, its parts are not statically articulated or merely placed in discourse; they move and negotiate their position in the relationship between the leader and the people, and vice versa. This back-and-forth between populist leaders and the people of populism is mediated by the performative in practice or the "performative doing" of politics, as Marino referred to. To be successful, populism depends on erasing in practice (not simply in the impassioned words of populists in rallies or electoral campaigns) the distance between represented and representative, leader and follower. In the closing of that gap, popular empowerment takes place, as the people are put at center stage of the theater of politics: "populism breaks down this theatrical fourth wall, or the imaginary barrier between the audience and the stage, to forge continuity between the production of politics (staged, framed, on view) and the lived experience, desires, and demands in everyday political making, from the minutia to the rallies to the campaign."[44] That's why a textual approach, the study of words written and uttered by populists, falls short when trying to analyze how people see themselves and perform being the people.

With respect to the practice of populism (i.e., the performance of being the people), Moffit's conceptualization in *The Global Rise of Populism: Performance, Political Style, and Representation* is particularly important. His method of analysis takes into account both the visual (naturally more static and dependent to a certain extent on textual signs) and the performative (dynamic by default and embodied in populist visualities): for him, populism can be "thought of as a performative political style by providing a theoretical framework where the leader is seen as the performer, the people as the audience, and crisis and media as the stage on which populism plays out upon."[45] Under such a conceptual framework, Moffitt argues, populism is "a political style that features an appeal to 'the people' versus 'the elite,' 'bad manners' and the performance of crisis, breakdown or threat."[46] Moffit's approach concurs with the importance given here to cultural (re)presentation in populism, which ultimately points to the need to incorporate both a content analysis (in this case, regarding visual meaning) of the artifacts displayed by populists and the people of populism and also a stylistic or formalist understanding of the theater of populism. Along with the images of populism, the focus needs to be on the theatricalization of populism at different interrelated levels: (1) at the level of the performers, regarding the role of both populist leaders and populist movements; (2) in relation to how audiences identify with populist signification within and without populist movements; (3) in terms of how populist stages shape populist messages (i.e., how the different platforms in which populism happens, such as television sets, films, the internet, and so on, affect populist discourse); (4) and in regard to the mise-en-scène of the populist moment as mediated by culture, with special attention to how populist stylistic arrangements vary depending on political context.

Recognizing the bidirectional or relational nature of the performative act in populism, Moffit notes that during a populist moment, when the symbolic agglutination of demands takes place around a populist leader—or what Laclau described in reference to the idea of "Peronism without Perón" as "an empty signifier that becomes entirely empty"—the people exercise a political agency that is not so much discursively signified as it is played out or performed in the very act of staging political representation.[47] The public space becomes a space for the people beyond the presence of the populist leader. Thus, the constitution of the people at the populist moment is not simply direct or unidirectional, from the leader to the people; it is mediated by the performative act and the space in which political representation takes place. The populist leader may be virtually essential in the theater of populism, but that leader neither constructs nor explains the people's varied performances during the populist moment. Admittedly, the problem for the analyst begins precisely with attempting to grasp the (re)presentation of the people at ground level, when people perform different ways of being the people. That is, one can surmise the political intentions behind the (often curated) theatrics of populist leaders with a certain degree of confidence. But when it comes to analyzing collective expressions in the populist moment, the performances are too many, too varied, and, most critically, all equally important in essence to discern a clear political causality. That is, one can see people performing being the people but can't always know why people choose to perform a particular script (a left-wing populism, say) and not another (a right-wing one). On the contrary, it is all much clearer when populists act out their populism. This methodological obstacle explains the different approaches in this book: the visual representations of the people in the 15-M in the first part and Podemos's populist performances in the second half. Thus, the goal is to have an analytical method to see the people of populism in practice (e.g., in the occupied squares during the 15-M) and to study how populism is performed by populist leaders (e.g., Pablo Iglesias's use of memes) through a series of (audio)visual artifacts within the realm of (popular) culture.

A Chronology of the People

For the launch of Daniel Bernabé's book *La distancia del presente*, which takes stock of Spain's many changes in politics since the 15-M, Podemos's leader Pablo Iglesias was invited as guest speaker. As one of the main figures in Bernabé's book, Iglesias was asked to reminisce about the maddening political cycle of the previous decade. Instead of offering a more or less descriptive first-person account, he began theorizing around the Machiavellian impetus of Podemos's quest for power and, especially, the counterpowers he and the party had faced. In this regard, Iglesias put special emphasis on how the battle had been fought in the sphere of the media, because, he argued, today's political power centers above all on one's capacity to garner *poder mediático* (the power to influence politics via mass media) and take advantage of the media's power to craft political discourses.[48] Iglesias's argument—as well as Bernabé's, to a great extent—is predicated on a constructivist theory of leadership that largely credits politicians, television talking heads, and media moguls with constructing the way people think of and about politics.[49] The present volume is an effort to move in the opposite direction.

Without dismissing the great many forces that externally shape people's political thoughts, the most important events of Spain's last decade (2010–2020) are here analyzed from the messy angle of the people themselves, with the precise objective of disentangling such a viewpoint. Where Bernabé's *La distancia del presente* offers a litany of first names as absolute protagonists of the political, this book does not rely on the many ways the powerful influence people's views of politics. Instead, it dwells on how the people view the powerful and can be seen crafting their own politics to amass political influence. This shift in perspective does not mean to idealize or exclusively validate the views of ordinary people and disregard how influential individuals see and shape the course of history. Further, because those two viewpoints (of leaders and of collectives) are perfectly compatible, this book is in no way an attempt to make the reader choose between one or the other, or even to prioritize any view. What the reader will find is the visualization of a fleeting political subject whose silhouette could, for a short period of time in Spanish history, be better seen in the ordinary experiences and representations of everyday people. With that in mind, a pendular chronology of the people is developed in five chapters and an inescapable epilogue.

Taking the occupation of squares (also known as *acampadas*) as the symbolic moment that kicked off the 15-M movement, the first chapter analyzes how a new visual representation of the people was developed from within and in tension with external old ways of seeing popular subjects in Spanish politics. More concretely, in this chapter a series of visualities from inside the movement are selected according to their popular character—their potential to amass visual cultural capital and their degree of political visibility: from grand interventions of commercial billboards in the two major encampments, or the famous handwritten signs and placards of the movement, to viral videos of livestreamed protests. These images are examples of how the 15-M's self-representations (or self-presentations) transformed the popular into the populist. Prioritizing that development, the chapter explores how the public image from inside the movement—a type of visuality from below—clashed with and fought against the imposition of a top-down "official" perspective that looked at the images of people occupying squares filtered through the historical lens that assumed that governance was fundamentally based on managing the intrinsic unruliness of people. Finally, the chapter explores the dispute between visualities from below and from the top through what can be called the 15-M's inescapable inconsistency of its own way of doing and seen politics due to its unquestioning of middle-class ideology. In this sense, middle-class-friendly conceptualizations positively informed the movement's identity when constructing a transversal political platform that could be inclusive of anyone, which in turns helped protesters break from the so-called activist ghetto. At the same time, the extemporaneous yet de facto incorporation of a middle-class identity framework excluded all those who did not fit its mold. But more importantly, the core issue that affected Spanish politics was left intact: a debt-ridden consumerist economy favored by generalized corruption, hidden under the pretext of maintaining the stability of the middle classes, which also in many ways created the very problems the protesters were opposing in the first place.

In the second chapter, the theory of populism is momentarily left on the back burner to dwell in greater detail on the 15-M's visual construction of its political identity. Cinematic representation helps with identifying the key characteristics of that identity vis-à-vis the enactment of the movement's authenticity. And while the theory of populism may have not much to say about the representative mechanisms that helped with the formation of such an audiovisual identity, the perception of political authenticity is nonetheless part and parcel of populism. Many of the extant films on the 15-M have touched on either the construction of a political place or the experiencing of an unprecedented historical time, but their focus tends to rest on the origins and the future of the 15-M, leaving in the background the process of experiencing a new democratic time in history and constructing a new place in the square for politics. Only a few elaborate extensively on those interrelated perspectives, helping imbue the 15-M with a political identity of democratic authenticity. So this chapter focuses on four documentaries that are regarded as the most representative of the different approaches to filmic documentation of the movement in situ: *Banderas falsas* (2012), *La plaza* (2012), *15-M: Excelente. Revulsivo. Importante* (2013), and *Informe general II* (2016). Although these documentary films are for one reason or another highly relevant in and of themselves, their inclusion is based on the extent to which they cover the tropes of time and place. Two of the most important traits of the movement's self-image were the time and place of Spain's real democracy. The films show a people that stubbornly remained in one place, symbolically occupying a square, performing a new democratic time that had no continuity with its immediate past because the past had been discarded. This was ultimately a negotiation informed by the visualization of an authentic place for the Spanish people (symbolically inside the occupied squares) in direct confrontation to the "official" representation of Spain's democratic timeline.

The third chapter focuses on how the visual representation of political conflict evolved from the time when the encampments in the squares were dismantled by the end of 2011 to the moment before Pablo Iglesias and his political party Podemos burst into public sight in 2014. Specifically, this chapter offers an in-depth visual analysis of political anger with the help of imagery that acquired a high degree of visibility thanks to what has been loosely termed as crisis cinema. The emphasis is on how two interrelated representations of populist affective politics, one seen as plebeian retribution and the other as people's "bad manners" against elites, developed in cinema as soon as the 15-M's encampments were out of sight. The analysis shines a light on how the visualization of collective frustration, once centered on the squares (where the time and place of real democracy alluded to could be seen), dispersed into a series of films that progressively favored images akin to disruptive change or a revolution of the system. As the "system" refused to address the demands of the people in the streets, popular demands most prominently coalesced in culture around cinematic impulses that evoked Bastille-like visions (symbolized not only in films but also in viral videos, memes, and new slogans) and represented the victims of the crisis as "the people." This was so much so the case that both independent filmmakers and renowned celebrities of the audiovisual industry began to be culturally guided by representations of symbolic violence, which were in turn informed by the justification of people's "low" impulses against the system. Thus, the films analyzed in this chapter, Isaki Lacuesta's *Murieron por encima de sus posibilidades* (2014) and Paco León's *Carmina o revienta* (2012), and its sequel *Carmina y amén* (2014), were paradigmatic cultural artifacts of a type of populist aesthetic that justified the underdogs' violent tendencies against an elitist "them" as a type of cultural escape valve for widespread popular suffering at the peak of the Spanish government's implementation of austerity measures. It becomes clear that these films laid the ground for the cultural acceptance of a kind of people's vengeance that allowed Podemos—principally through the televised figure of Pablo Iglesias—to enact its populist strategy, which progressively monopolized popular anger as a way to break into institutional politics.

In the fourth chapter, the Podemos phenomenon is subsequently explored from its theoretical inception in 2010 (the so-called *La Tuerka* hypothesis) to the party's successful run-up to the 2014 European elections and the immediate aftermath, before its entry into the national parliament by the end of 2015. Podemos is mainly explained through its political communication strategy. Nevertheless, the main objective of the chapter is to overcome the overdetermining framework through which Podemos's media politics is often analyzed. The party's main communicative tool, the mediatic charisma of Pablo Iglesias, must be framed beyond the symbiotic relationship between the media and populism, or what has been termed *mediatic populism*. His audiovisual leadership is part of the ritualized phenomenon of television and celebrity culture, which helped Podemos reestablish clearly demarcated (and, in this case, confronted) popular identities for its electoral benefit. The use of *mediatic* thus surpasses its adjectival characteristics: it is more than a mere adjectivization of the noun *media*. *Mediatic* refers to the multiple counterhegemonic strategies used by both Iglesias and Podemos to establish a direct link between their politics, their television audiences, and their conceptualization of the people. These strategies are analyzed through multiple (audio)visual products that include television and film. Critically, these cultural devices refer to how Iglesias's mediatic persona was built through the medium of television but with aesthetics of cinema. These are examples that see Iglesias and Podemos establishing a cinematic emotional relationship with their televisual audience beyond their more or less explicit propagandistic efforts at substantiating an electoral base. Ultimately, the correlation between Iglesias, Podemos, and the media strategy of both crystallizes a political impetus of plebeian vindication that, while it precedes by far the foundation of the party or the mediatic prominence of its leader, could not have happened without them. If television was the conduit for a plebeian conceptualization of the people, then the cinematic affectivity of Iglesias and

Podemos was the electricity that shocked Spanish democracy, illuminating the path of the plebs to the center of the electoral mainstream.

The fifth chapter chronicles the journey of Podemos from its establishment in Spanish politics in 2016 until the much-publicized internal battle inside the party's leadership that led to its poor results in the 2019 national elections. Given how much Podemos had absorbed the populist impetus of the 15-M, the evolution—or rather involution—of Iglesias's party is a window onto a populism as it progressively loses its traction. The causes of the increasing dwindling of populist politics are many, and by no means are all attributable to the loss of Podemos's electoral influence. Yet the electoral pilgrimage of Podemos's politics in regard to its conceptualization of the people affords an opportunity to explore why and how the transversal, antihistorical *pueblo* of populism returned to its sectoral, historical place. The main highlight in that political itinerary was prominently marked by the inability-turned-unwillingness of Podemos when it came to expanding cultural subjectivities beyond the leftist imaginary. Even though Iglesias could be seen everywhere still espousing a type of populist discourse, popular culture increasingly put Podemos in the box of the historical Spanish Left.[50] The Podemos phenomenon evolved as part of the internet culture of memes, and this fifth chapter lays out how Iglesias went from being an empty signifier in populist politics to a "memetic" signified in leftism's culture. This pointed to the online development of a populist common sense that began with a proliferation of hashtags during the 15-M that were later agglutinated in the viral exchanges of memes around Iglesias's populist leadership, only to be progressively disaggregated with the much more curated version of Podemos in its quest for institutional power, which eventually restored a leftist-rightist way of seeing and supposed the end of populism in Spanish politics.

The epilogue of this book is inescapable in the sense that the present of Spanish politics does not seem to have transcended the spirits of its traumatic and unresolved past. The irruption of Vox's postfascist ideology—from marginal political actor to the third-most-voted-for party in the Spanish parliament in 2019—is a stark reminder that perhaps the ghost of Francoism was all along sharing the stage with the people of populism. Postfascism, contrary to historical fascism and neofascism, lacks a coherent ideology. As Enzo Traverso—who coined the term—argues, postfascism is a heterogeneous political movement of the extreme Right that is characterized by its continuous evolution, adapting its politics to the different contexts it encounters, and fueled by the return of political uncertainties after the period of great mobilizations against a common enemy: economic austerity.[51] With that in mind, the epilogue is a brief incursion into how the end of populism gave way to the rise of postfascism, whose fascist roots infiltrate the entire history of Spanish democracy. Rather than a phenomenon of right-wing political populism, Vox is presented as a product of Spain's unresolved cultural fascist past, the radicalization of politics during the populist cycle, and the institutional failure to satisfy most political demands during that time. Accordingly, the Far Right politics of Vox turbocharged the binary processes of populist identification, anchoring cultural identity (namely, a very restrictive view of Spanishness) in a Schmittian friend-enemy paradigm that would later be translated into electoral politics. The populist performance of transversal political change was being substituted by the visualization of a very specific Spanish demos, whose main objective in politics was the recuperation of the "true" essence of the nation. Conceptually, the popular had gotten rid of the populist and was returning to a dangerous historical place shaped by postfascist identity politics. If the 15-M opened a utopian window of opportunity, Vox unearthed a dystopian dynamic that, just as Francoism had after the end of the Spanish Civil War, was carving a politics of despair into the popular imaginary and paralyzing any hope for future change by constantly demanding the exchange of the present for the past.

All in all, this book offers a visual journey from the beginning of Spain's populist cycle until its very last days. The pages that follow look beyond the material reality of that cycle and its political consequences through a series of visual scenes within a cultural negotiation to decide Spain's "real" demos. In that negotiation, different deals are struck about whom and what the people "really" represented from the first days of 15-M and the consolidation of Podemos in parliamentary politics until populism came to an end with the advent of Vox's postfascism.

PART I

Seeing the People

Seeing the Real People of
Spanish Real Democracy

The 15-M movement inaugurated a decade that centered on rethinking what people really wanted from their democracy and, in the process, attempted to show what those people "really" looked like. For a few moments in the spring of 2011, the 15-M painted picture of who the "real" demos was supposed to be by symbolically occupying and transforming squares into protest camps where "real" democracy could flourish. That's one of the reasons these protests, despite their demands for systemic change, could not be so easily dismissed with the usual fear-mongering tropes around their dangerous antiestablishment nature. In fact, the trope was turned on its head, and it was the system that was deemed too radical for the well-being of the average citizen. As one famous banner read during the first days of the 15-M, "No somos antisistema, el sistema es antinosotros," or "We are not antisystem, the system is anti-us" (fig. 1.1).

The feeling that the system had turned on its citizens was very much born of the dire situation of Spain's economic reality, which had gone from bad to worse. With regional governments too highly leveraged and unable to make good on their loans, Spain itself faced a fiscal crisis. Despite cutbacks at all levels, the country "became yet another laboratory for the International Monetary Fund . . . and the European Union's . . . austerity drive" that added only more fuel to the fire of people's discontent after the global economy crashed in 2008.[1] But an antiausterity sentiment was not, at the core, what drove the protests that began the 15-M movement. Austerity measures were a symptom

FIGURE 1.1. Sign in a demonstration for 15-M's first anniversary in Barcelona. "Yo no soy antisistema el sistema es antiyo" (I'm not against the system, the system is against me). Photograph taken on May 12, 2012, by user Wiros, https://www.flickr.com/photos/wiros/7285712314

of a much deeper malaise: a general perception that liberal democracy had stopped working for most people in Spain. That widespread impression came through in the demonstration's most visible slogans on May 15, 2011. Along with the well-known "democracia real ya" (real democracy now), a lesser-known slogan qualified that message: "no somos mercancia en manos de políticos y banqueros" (we are not commodities in the hands of politicians and bankers) (fig. 1.2). The implied demand for a real democracy that accompanies the first-person plural in the second slogan is one of the first visual signs that the protesters were speaking in the name of a common "us" that diluted members' distinguishing traits over and against a clearly defined "them," the politicians and bankers who treated ordinary citizens as assets for enriching themselves. Where the government was offering varied, complex, technical political and economic reasoning for its decision to manage the financial crisis via so-called austerity measures, the protest appealed to a common sense that everyone could immediately understand.

Far from being perceived as radical, these demands were appealing to the great majority of the Spanish population—so much so that in June 2011, the Centro de Investigaciones Sociológicas survey, the most important statistical measure in the country, found that more than 70 percent of the Spanish

FIGURE 1.2. One of the posters calling for the first demonstration on May 15, 2011: "No somos mercancia en manos de políticos y banqueros" (We are not commodities in the hands of politicians and bankers). Photograph taken on May 15, 2011, by Juanjo Zanabria Masaveu, https://www.flickr.com/photos/34268121@N07/5723294578.

FIGURE 1.3. Sign in Acampada Sol: "Tu botín, mi crisis!" (Your loot, my crisis!) Photograph taken on May 18, 2011, by Ana Rey, https://www.flickr.com/photos/anarey/6266182718.

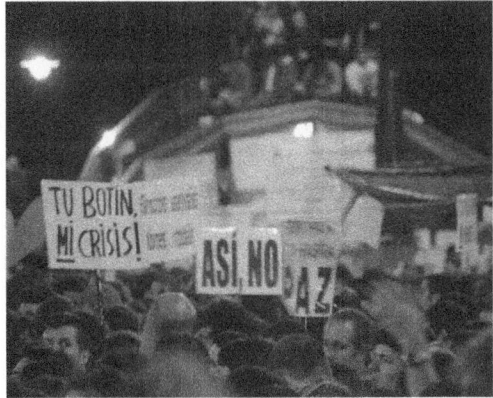

population supported the 15-M movement's calls for a systemic change and that, in fact, nearly 75 percent were unsatisfied with the way democracy was functioning in Spain.[2] The protesters were simply asking for a real democracy that, through a real representative system, could apply some common sense to the government's absurd management of the economic crisis, as could be surmised in another common slogan at the time: "Your loot, my crisis!" (fig. 1.3). There was an increasing understanding that ordinary people's logic was drastically detached from those making decisions in the name of the people at the top. The official channels of political representation were perceived to be so flawed that an unofficial vehicle to represent the people's will—such as squatting for a real democracy on a square like Puerta del Sol—could better symbolize representative democracy. And with the people's occupation of the Puerta del Sol, the 15-M movement started a cycle of popular and populist mobilization that lasted almost a decade.

Taking a cue from that divide between the practice of real democracy in the squares and its opposite other, the ruling institutions like government and banks, this chapter explores the visual presentations of the 15-M's demand for political representation. A series of images from inside the movement is analyzed semiotically to show how different visualizations of protesting during the encampments symbolized the essence of the 15-M's real democracy. Here the theory of populism is of great help in considering how different images of protesters in the 15-M, as well as the many banners they produced, can be visualized as "empty signifiers" that contained the true popular essence of Spanish democracy. All those visualities denoted a process of inclusion, a redefinition of political belonging (of the "us") through the visualization of a public that did not need so much to be heard as to find a public voice. Whether the use of livestreaming technology, the production of self-portraits in the movement's own media channels, or the manufacturing of signs, banners, and posters, a number of widely shared and highly recognizable images of people presenting themselves in the act of acquiring a voice further establish the visual traits of this new collective voice of the 15-M. At the same time, those images—oftentimes implicitly or connotatively—constructed an opposed other through a process of excluding all those perceived as fundamentally counter to the people's newly acquired public voice: parliamentarians, financiers, media owners, cultural elites, what have you. This dichotomized visualization is further complicated by the surreptitious influence of middle-class ideology, as the logic of neoliberalism in the Spanish context necessarily informed the transformation of "us" the protesters into "us" the people.

From Inside the *Acampada*: The Real People of the 15-M's Real Democracy

The demonstrations on May 15 that would later coalesce into the occupation of Puerta del Sol were initially promoted by series of little-known activist organizations under the name Democracia Real Ya (Real Democracy Now). Although these protests were atypical in that they involved a significant number of people without visible partisan affiliations across different cities who were all asking for an overhaul of Spain's democratic system, they were not without historical precedent. Since the autonomous movement at the turn of the twentieth century and its push to work at the grassroots level, there has been a strong sense of continuity between the organizing principles that inspired the 15-M and the previous decades of anti-identitarian, horizontal, consensus-based politics. Referring to the public outburst of protest that kicked off with the occupation of Puerta del Sol in the spring of 2011, neither

the 15-M movement nor its precipitating triggers can be analyzed as spontaneous popular responses, but they were the direct consequence of "the long
march of autonomous social movements over the past 30 years in Spain,
inspired, influenced and often legitimated by outside events and movements
to be sure, but forged on the local and national terrain."[3] Yet while the movement was not new in the tactics and governing principles it deployed, there
was a narrative—partly emanating from inside the movement—that spoke
of the 15-M as a mostly sui generis development that was creating a political
space for ordinary citizens. "Spontaneity (and newness) narratives also make
newcomers feel the movement belongs to them and allow new participants
to develop their own origin myths and distinguish themselves from the past
(e.g., generations; mobilizations; outdated, corrupt and illegitimate political
formations)," so the 15-M could most effectively use its "ordinariness" as its
most defining political essence, very much opposed to all those above the
average citizen who had historically held extraordinary powers.[4] And that
popular political impetus greatly contributed to the 15-M's populist style.

Negotiations of political visibility lie at the core of populist presentation.
The 15-M constructed a series of self-portraits that advanced what have been
here referred to as the transformation of the popular, or the idea of democracy, into the populist, or people's democracy or a "real" democracy. Even
though the present analysis might suffer from a certain "myopia of the visible" by paying excessive attention to the movement's traits with the most
prominent effect on the politics of the time, as argued by Alberto Melucci, the
movement's quest for visibility is crucial to better understanding the logic
behind the movement's self-presentation tactics, which in turn explains how
the popularization of an image becomes a populist visuality.[5] And nowhere
else is that logic better seen than in the 15-M's media and communications
infrastructure—especially within the movement's flagship encampment
Acampada Sol.

The widespread livestreaming from inside the protest camp was an important source for the movement's public-image construction. Live feeds were a
way to circumvent the media political intervention in the movement's messaging, presenting the "real" life story of the movement directly to the people,
"expressing—in content and practices—the populist character of this protest
wave, its appeal to people power and its ambition to capture the support of
the '99 percent' of the population."[6] It stemmed from a strong impulse to
authenticate the political experience from the inside, to take control of the
narrative and (audio)visually record the "real" 15-M in the name of the people.
With that impetus, Audiovisol TV (also known by its now-defunct domain

name Sol.tv) was born in Acampada Sol as a direct source of news on what was taking place in the encampment of Puerta del Sol. Live coverage of the *acampada* was also a way to build and maintain support among all those who did not or simply could not participate directly in the 15-M's actions—those whom Paulo Gerbaudo terms "closet supporters," who could vicariously experience the outrage, indignation, and joy of the movement through the daily livestreaming from the camps.[7]

One of the most watched videos, livestreamed first by Sol.tv but later edited for the 15-M's YouTube channel Spanishrevolutionsol, was titled "#Badcop."[8] The video begins with the ironic caption "Ethics encyclopedia: Instruction manual on how to kick." Along with the first images, the audience sees a police confrontation with protesters who chant a slogan common at the time and in line with the strong nonviolent ethos of the 15-M: "our hands are our only weapons." The shaky camera follows different protesters as they are forcefully dragged and manhandled by police officers, and another caption in bold red letters pops up with the message "No to violence." The focus then momentarily turns to the cameraman recording the confrontation as he is pushed by a police officer who screams, "Get away from here!" Immediately after, a red arrow directs the viewer's attention to the same scene recorded from a different angle: the officer can be seen attempting to trip the cameraman. The video finishes with text taken from a police-conduct manual that speaks to the police obligation to behave in a respectful and proportionate manner toward the citizens whom they have sworn to protect. The video ends with one police officer producing his identification number for a protester without any fuss. Finally, in a calm tone and almost apologetically, an officer in charge implies to one of the protesters that he believes the police action was carried out as correctly as possible and in accordance with what their superiors had mandated.

Compared to other visual documents of police brutality during those days—of which the aggressive evacuation of the protest camp in Barcelona was paradigmatic —as well as the long track record of activists' abuse at the hands of the Spanish riot police, this video seems rather innocuous.[9] The wording of *patada* (kick) in the initial caption appears to be an overstatement when one sees the policeman tripping the cameraman. The officer's identification (a rare occurrence in this type of altercation) makes the police in fact seem to be following protocol.[10] Why would then the 15-M's main media platform livestream and later post the video permanently to its YouTube channel? Couldn't this video be construed as showing the police actually behaving properly—and, by symbolic extension, protesters being treated acceptably by the "system"? Through a populist lens, the main answer to these questions lies in the establishment and interconnection of the three semiotic coordinates that compose populist visualities, which grant a different understanding of the video beyond the mere documentation of bad (or not-so-bad) police bad behavior.

First came the construction of an us-versus-them framework. In this case, the dichotomy came about via the 15-M's strong nonviolent protest culture. By the time the video was shared on June 16, 2011, the 15-M's pacifist political ethos was well established in the popular imaginary—from its international manifesto *How to Cook a Nonviolent Revolution* to numerous media interventions by the movement's spokespeople reassuring their commitment to non-violence.[11] By contrast, police actions were readily seen as disproportionately aggressive, if not outright violent. Livestreaming and video recording via cell phones provided a direct visual testimony to those altercations that represented the protesters as the nonviolent "us" while leaving the police (as representatives of the state) on the violent "them" side of the equation. To that point, one 15-M activist declared: "A very interesting idea was floating around during this summer of protest when so much police brutality was happening: The police wasn't more violent; it was just that cell phone technology had improved and now police violence could be more easily documented. The fact that one could livestream all those confrontations was key to wake up people into thinking more critically about the political reality we all live in."[12]Livestreaming was a means of representing the "real" that the 15-M's activists were pointing out to the rest of the population. At the same time, it was a way to construct a new reality stemming from that vision of what was really "real" that relied on creating spaces for self-representation (tied in this case to a nonviolent "us" set against a violent "them").

Second, given that dichotomized picture, police violence did not necessarily have to be very violent to be inserted into what Laclau has famously referred to as populism's "equivalential chain," which erases all difference in the chain of heterogeneous grievances or demands, making them equal to the "empty signifier"—in this case, the "us" people at the heart of the 15-M's real democracy.[13] That's why a "light" trip by a police officer was in essence no different from the instances of police brutality documented many times before. As part of that chain of equivalences, the video was also constructing a system that was really an antisystem, linked with the 15-M's bigger demand for an alternative, or real, system of democratic representation. Third, that demand was not simply denunciation. Embedded in the final confrontation where the protester requested the police officer's identification was the implied enactment of a new system of representation, this time based on accountability, whereby the stereotype of the brutish Spanish riot police is tamed by the citizens' new politics, by their new real democracy as live-streamed in the 15-M's media platform Sol.tv. These are the three coordinates that semiotically give that video its populist character.

As already hinted, livestreaming was not only a new communication strategy of the 15-M; it was also part of a populist style that favored the voice of the "people" over the "official" representatives of their will in the mainstream media. But it was also found within broader countercultural spaces, as in the encampments' do-it-yourself culture, informed in part by a greater anticonsumerist ethos (fig. 1.4). And although anticonsumerist stances had always been a key identity marker of the Spanish radical Left in general, during the 15-M encampments, a series of spontaneous interventions of commercial billboards occurred that began but quickly went beyond a denunciation of consumerism. These were another example of populist visualities, in this case connected to the visualization of having or acquiring a voice. In the two biggest encampments of the 15-M, Acampada Sol in Madrid and Acampada Barcelona in Plaça Catalunya, a large advertisement that towered over the protesters was visually interfered with and physically modified to symbolically express a type of people's voice.

The L'Oréal billboard that hovered over the square when the occupation of the Puerta del Sol in Madrid began was radically transformed in a matter of days. In a visual push against the neoliberal marketization of life, the Spanish actress Paz Vega, featured in the L'Oréal advertisement, was subjected to a process of popular reappropriation that lasted during the entire *acampada*: "First a banner of the Nazi Heinrich Himmler, with Mickey Mouse ears and a symbol of the Euro in the middle of his forehead, was put next to Paz Vega's face, with the text 'They do not represent us.'"[14] Thereafter, more modifications appeared, broadly expanding the need for "more democracy" and restating other well-known 15-M slogans. The often-playful tone of the defacement was conveying a quite serious message. Beyond the specific iterations of the changing billboard, a new (common) sense was being established, one that held that the public interest needed to rule over private ambitions, especially commercially motivated ones. Paradigmatically, the billboard's transformation preconditioned visually what would be later done, acted, said, and felt as common sense—but also, and more critically, in the name of the people.

Considered side by side, the before-and-after photos of the L'Oréal advertisement (figs. 1.5 and 1.6) surface a characteristic way of visualizing a collective identity. Before May 15, 2011, the symbolism of a billboard occupying the

Figure 1.4. Anticonsumerist street graffiti: "En Navidad consume hasta morir" (At Christmas, consume until you die). Photograph taken on December 31, 2005, by Daniel Lobo, https://www.flickr.com/photos/daquellamanera/85856958.

Figure 1.5. Photo taken on the third day of demonstrations after the first attempt at clearing the *acampada* on May 18, 2011. Photograph taken on May 18, 2011, by El Rojo Mosca (Aranguren), https://www.flickr.com/photos/elrojomosca/5732285018.

Figure 1.6. Photo taken of L'Oréal billboard during the fifth day of the *acampada* on May 20, 2011. Photograph taken on May 20, 2011, by Santiago Ave, https://www.flickr.com/photos/elave16/5845438703.

entire façade of a building at the geographical center of Spain (Puerta del Sol is the so-called *kilómetro cero* of the country) would have passed unnoticed. It would have been just another instance of marketing executives visually screaming at citizen-consumers so that they do not forget that public space is dedicated to the private act of brand consumption. This monotonous presence had been so internalized that onlookers had accepted it as a matter of routine. The visual cacophony went unquestioned: it was the only way the space could be visually absorbed.

Nevertheless, the rapid transition from that anodyne acceptance to the aggressive visually sustained combating of the billboard from the first days of the 15-M until the very end of the *acampada* is quite telling. It directs one's attention to the importance of visual perception. The shift was so aggressive because what had been seen to that point as customary turned out to be a visual act of self-delusion. This sudden revelation made the advertisement unacceptable in the new context of the *acampada*. One of the participants of the encampment told the art historian Julia Ramírez Blanco: "We started to hang things on the scaffolding because there was a hurtful advertising poster which everyone wanted to destroy. We were there, getting stuck in. At first, most of the banners were put on top of that of L'Oréal and the other scaffold was left empty because the important thing was to break that L'Oréal shit."[15] Those words acquire special significance when juxtaposed to the picture of the untouched billboard during the second day of protests (see fig. 1.5). It is hard not to think that all those people gathered under the advertisement collectively saw through the mystifications of brands and neoliberal consumption. The spell was broken in the same way that good impressions can be shattered after just one misencounter. All those people metaphorically proceeded to go further beyond breaking "that L'Oréal shit": they gave the billboard a new purpose. It became the most visible canvas for thousands of *indignados* to communicate their visions. Paradoxically enough, L'Oréal's publicity became a political visuality directed against the rule of marketized ways of life.

Given the physical challenge of modifying an entire building façade, the radical alteration of the L'Oréal billboard was already a key indication of the need to establish an undeniable visual voice. Such kaleidoscopic composition matched the movement's populist essence as a compendium of heterogeneous demands, grievances, or simply self-expression that together indicated that a chain of equivalences was forming and transforming the 15-M from a popular protest into a populist moment. The modified billboard projected a new vision that signified the movement's core values. Individuality, represented by the branded image of Paz Vega, was being replaced with collective agency, with signs being progressively superimposed one over the other on the billboard until the last days of the encampment. The collective appropriated and resignified the individualistic and consumerist traits of a cosmetics campaign to the extent that Paz Vega was "an involuntary muse of the revolution" and "her giant photograph . . . had become a collective mural, a verbal node . . . in the scaffolding" that unmistakably signaled the expression of a new identity marked by popular collaboration.[16] The billboard began to reflect everyone and anyone, a visual mirror of the 15-M's populist bid.

A billboard can be considered print culture, but the encampment's engagements with it rejected most written formalities and were operating under the mores of orality—another way of affirming the movement's nonhierarchical principles. Superimposed on the L'Oréal billboard, statements such as "kereis dejar de jugar con el mundo" (mind if you stop gambling the world away) and "Claro que sí: anti-capitalista, anti-patriarcal, anti-racista, anti-sistema" (Of course we are anticapitalist, antipatriarchy, anti-racist, antisystem) are affirming metaphors. Formally, the first statement stresses both the oral and the informal, and the second frames the message as a spoken rebuttal, as if it were an off-the-cuff declaration of intentions in the middle of an argument. Conceptually, in direct opposition to the L'Oréal commercial, the amateurish form clashes with the depth of the meanings. Behind the façade of what had been traditionally regarded as culturally low (by way of orality), these messages contained the political intellectuality of high culture (the vocabulary of Marxism, social movement theory, and critical race theory). The popular was thereby disassociated from the vulgar and progressively visualized as an authoritative cultural source, at least to the extent that its influence and visibility could not be dismissed in the context of the movement. The culture being created stressed the importance of orality and informality, enhanced by their visuality, because it all was ultimately rooted in conceiving of the popular as populist. The explicit confrontation in the signs demands and connotes an alternative system of representation, marked now by the people's voice.

The billboard was progressively burnished with a vision of a new agency extremely diverse in form, as seen in the collage of slogans, pictures, drawings, and so forth. The democratized perspective enacted there was itself popular and inserted into popular culture. On a closer look, the importance of the popular aspect becomes more obvious. The use of basic humorous codes imprinted on the L'Oréal ad that could be understood by anyone was one of the most apparent links to the popular, a demonstration that playfulness can be seen in the extensive use of puns and plays on words not

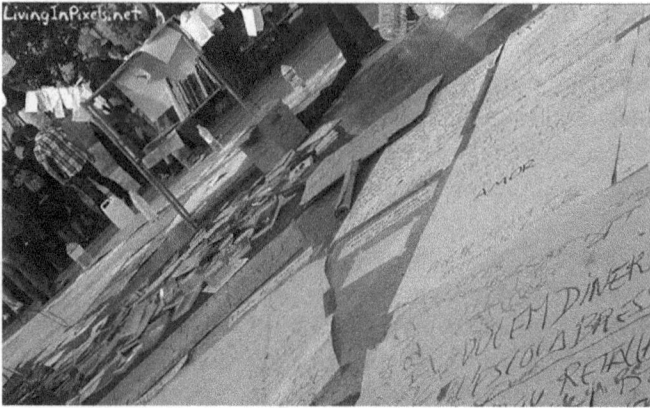

Figure 1.7. Handwritten slogans in Acampada Barcelona. Photograph taken on May 19, 2011, by Pau, https://www.flickr.com/photos/livinginpixels/5738271278.

only in the billboard but also throughout the encampment and the entire movement at large. As a result, double entendres such as "No hay tanto pan para tanto chorizo," or "There's not enough bread for all that chorizo" (in Spanish, *chorizo* can refer to both a pork sausage and, colloquially, a thief), and "Tenemos el Sol ahora queremos la luna," or "We have Sol [referring to the sun and the protest camp in Puerta del Sol], now we ask for the moon," became essential parts of every *acampada* across the country, not just Acampada Sol in Madrid.[17]

The modification of the L'Oréal billboard was an impulse replicated in the second-largest encampment in the country, the *acampada* of Plaça Catalunya in Barcelona. The modification in this case was confined to a simple rewording of a Hyundai slogan in Catalan: from "Encara penses que les bèsties no estimen?" (Do you still think that beasts can't love?) to "Encara penses que els polítics no ens timen?" (Still think that politicians can't swindle you?).[18] "What started out as an attack on an element of advertising," Ramírez Blanco argues, "ended up becoming a *détournement*, a diversion which playfully appropriated the image in the service of a new meaning."[19] And although the extent of the incursion in the revisualization of Hyundai's billboard paled in relation to the progressive transformation that took place in Acampada Sol, both were qualitatively denoting the same type of situationist *détournement*, one that hijacked the ethos of individualized consumerism to express the new collective identity of the 15-M that knew the political game was rigged. The explicit "you" also referred to an implicit "us" outside the encampment, one whose popular essence was being appealed to as populist, as a reminder of

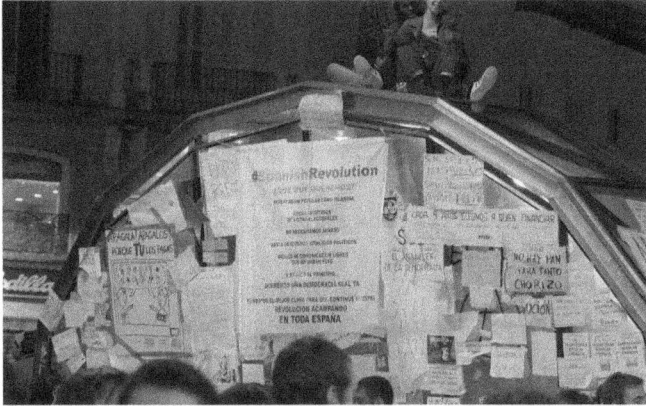

Figure 1.8. Handwritten slogans in Acampada Sol. Photograph taken on May 20, 2011, by El Rojo Mosca (Aranguren), https://www.flickr.com/photos/elrojomosca/5740021776.

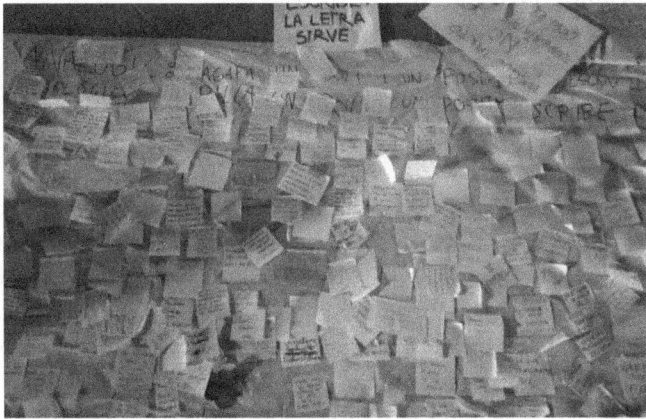

Figure 1.9. Handwritten slogans in Acampada Valencia. Photograph taken on May 22, 2011, by Christian Jiménez, https://www.flickr.com/photos/furlin/5748226075.

the confrontation with an elitist "them"—"the politicians" on the billboard. This time the visualization of an alternative system of representation is, however, much less prominent and connoted much more in the emotional context of the *acampada*. That context is crucial to further comprehending how the need to express a people's voice had a populist impetus prevalent throughout the occupation.

In one of the many live blogs that popped up during the 15-M, a firsthand account of the first days of Acampada Barcelona posted a picture of incursion in the billboard along with a text that stressed the new alignment between the action and the 15-M's new spatial usage of the square: "Nuevos usos de Plaça Catalunya, parte enésima. [. . .] Nos gustó tanto la acción que hemos hasta hemos dejado el patrocinador" (New uses of Plaça Catalunya, for the umpteenth time. We liked the action so much that we even left the sponsor intact).[20] The post finished by sardonically thanking Hyundai for allowing the *indignados* to spread their message. There is an air of empowerment in those words that points to the newfound voice the movement had acquired; at the same time, both the post and the action reveal something more profound albeit only implied: the squares had been filled with an uncontrollable impulse toward public expression that was putting people's actions at the center stage of politics. The tables had been turned, and the people could symbolically look down on old totems of power such as big corporations or the political class. This was a new way of feeling that explains the *acampada*'s emotional context and that was at the heart of the movement's understanding of the "us" people. Tellingly, the day before of the action, the same blog posted a poetic description of that feeling along with a picture of the numerous signs, placards, and banners that were appearing nonstop in Plaça Catalunya (fig. 1.7):

> The square was reclaimed by the people. The noise was also reclaimed by the people. The noise was a physical one of people banging pots in sign of protest. And it was also an ideological noise that accompanied every event and permeated every corner of Plaça Catalunya. It was a deafening noise. The other kind of noise, the ideological one, may sound confusing, but at least we can hear it at last. It is a tsunami of uncontrollable imagination: catchphrases, vignettes, slogans, demands, proposals . . . Everything that anyone can come up with after a long time of being ignored by the political and economic establishment. That's why this picture should be titled: "Move out of the way, swindlers; this is now our time." Lyrics and music: The People.[21]

The account complements the *détournement* action and equates it to the populist impetus behind the incursion in Madrid. The papering and plastering of public spaces with written slogans, banners, placards, and all sorts of signs expressing all sorts of messages became a common occurrence at all protest camps (figs. 1.8 and 1.9). Whether witty catchphrases or more serious rallying cries, they ultimately revealed a feeling of "us" people.

As much as these mechanisms of self-expression and self-representation indicated a new democratic ethos, those signs also created a new pathos. The "voices" stamped all over the encampments also visualized the movement's emotional investments, which engendered the necessary trust and solidarity to form the collective identity in the first place.[22] Populism is here again the link that can connect the (re)presentation of a people's voice with the 15-M's affective turn—and not only because populism is bound by a politics of affect but also because of the stylistic component of populist visualities that connects denotative statements of denunciation (e.g., demands, grievances, written-on commercial billboards, banners) with the connotation of an "empty signifier" that contains and binds together the experience of being seen and feeling like an "us" people. Within the visualization of a collective identity in the shape of all those different signs, a series of emotional investments can be found that refers to the many individual visual expressions of outrage, joy, distrust, frustration—all bound together by the populist moment that the 15-M's *acampadas* encapsulated. As the poetic account of Acampada Barcelona evoked, this was an old feeling of solidarity that was being renewed by all those gathered in the protest camps under the many new portraits of the people's voice.

If there was a single image from inside the movement that best represented the feeling of projecting the people's voice, that was, ironically, the so-called mute scream. This "scream" first came about as a symbolic challenge to the Central Electoral Commission's ruling that prohibited all political demonstrations on the eve of the May 22 municipal and regional elections in 2011. The ruling was based on a technical interpretation of the Spanish electoral law, which states that no political campaigning or political propaganda is allowed the day before any government election.[23] That day is known as a "day of reflection," or *jornada de reflexión*, when voters are expected to weigh their voting choices without the undue influence of political parties. Although the law clearly defines political campaigning, it does not specify very well what can be considered propaganda; it is up to the commission to interpret the rule on a case-by-case basis. Critically, by majority rule, the commission decided that the 15-M movement could unduly influence voters' decisions and that a political demonstration of its nature needed to be restricted to outside the day of reflection.[24] The protest camps were thus declared illegal and so was the movement's most visible and most effective protest action; the one that gave it all its political meaning. The schism between the Spanish demos and Spain's democratic procedures was becoming ever more apparent. The powers that be not only completely misunderstood the movement

Figure 1.10. Protesters gesturing the "mute scream." Significantly, one prominent sign reads "¡No nos callarán!" (We will not be silenced!) Photograph taken on May 18, 2011, by El Rojo Mosca (Aranguren), https://www.flickr.com/photos/elrojomosca/5739985636.

Figure 1.11. Front page of magazine *Madrid 15M*. Photograph taken and kept by the author. The online magazine's domain is no longer active, but the site was archived through the Wayback Machine and is available at https://web.archive.org/web/20120205062658/http://www.madrid15m.org.

Figure 1.12. Poster announcing the national call to march on May 12, 2012, in celebration of the 15-M's anniversary: "Toma la calle" (Take the streets). Photograph taken on May 12, 2011, by Jose Mesa, https://www.flickr.com/photos/liferfe/5717793419.

but, more importantly, effectively told the entire population that democratic expressions, such as demanding a better democratic system, had no place in Spain's democracy and that the demos was secondary in the decision-making process. The ruling was thus synecdochally positioned as yet another sign that Spanish democracy was not "real."

At the minute before midnight on the night of May 20, right before the commission's ruling came into effect, and despite facing prison and steep fines, a sea of people gathered in Puerta del Sol and raised their hands in silence as a grand gesture of civil disobedience. When the "scream" finished, the 15-M was officially declared illegal. However, when the nearby police did not intervene to clear out the camps, the silent political challenge turned into an explosion of collective joy as shown in Acampada Sol's livestream feed.[25] The thunderous noise befitted the historic significance of the action: "It was the biggest act of civil disobedience in the post-Franco history of the country."[26] Ramírez Blanco, following writer Yves Frémion, described it as an "orgasm of history" that resembled the "utopian explosion . . . [that] comes 'after love.'"[27] The emotional impact of this moment had a visual imprint that went beyond the action and its political significance at the time.

A year later, in commemoration of the 15-M's first anniversary, another sea of people gathered in Puerta del Sol to perform again the same symbolic gesture, this time without the looming threat of police intervention. The gesture became a visual symbol that provided direct access to the political emotion of being in the place and time of the 15-M. On the eve of its first birthday, the movement selected various versions of the mute scream to serve as the image encapsulating the 15-M's essence (fig. 1.10). The magazine *Madrid15-M*, an outlet born to represent the many *asambleas*, or working groups, created after the encampments were dismantled, chose an image of people waving their hands in silence in Puerta del Sol for the front page of its May 2012 issue (fig. 1.11). A cutout drawing of the same gesture was also the design choice for the poster announcing the national call to march on May 12, 2012, in celebration of the 15-M's anniversary (fig. 1.12).

Both the initial gesture and its subsequent visual iterations were infused with all the traits that make the popular into populist. That is, they were popularized visual signs of the us-versus-them populist dichotomy, which was specifically condemning the ruling of the Central Electoral Commission while at the same time joining a thick stack of heterogeneous demands, including calls for free speech, the reform of the two-party system, and expressions of the outright illegitimacy of the Spanish democratic system, in an equivalential chain that was ultimately subsumed into the 15-M's real democracy.

Such an adjectivization of democracy was an empty signifier of the voice of the people, whose different visualizations (this time in the form of a mute scream) during and after the movement immediately referred viewers to the emotional essence and affective investment that the people of the 15-M had constructed in the name of the Spanish people from the movement's inception. These populist visualities were a shortcut to the collective feeling of the "us" people that was seen and performed during those days in the spring of 2011. And in such visual presentations a political representation could also been seen, one that became rooted (not without problems) in the term *persons* (*personas*) rather than *people*.

We Are Not *Perroflautas*; or, Why the 15-M Couldn't Escape Middle-Class Ideology

In their sociological study of the movement's collective identity, Perugorría and Tejerina came to the conclusion that most participants avoided using identity markers that could associate them with "the old way of doing politics" and thereby avoided "acronyms and flags, because they divide."[28] Instead, the members of the 15-M whom they interviewed tended to see themselves as individuals belonging to a "community of persons," in the end "united by common sense."[29] Conceptually, the phrase "community of persons" points to the 15-M's self-assessed political essence of radical inclusivity in terms of identity and its avowed transversality regarding ideology. This stemmed from an "an autonomous networking logic" that favored what Flesher Fominaya has termed "the paradox of anti-identitarian collective identity."[30] Riding the longtime ambition of autonomous movements to break free from "the activist ghetto," the 15-M's ambiguous self-identifying mechanisms were designed to foster a "politics of anyone" whose essence was more popular-populist than ideological.[31] As a consequence, different variations of "the people" in Spanish—*personas* but also *gente*, *ciudadanía*, and *pueblo*—were many times used interchangeably during the 15-M. The terminology did not designate a defined political subject so much as it invoked and evoked an abstract, vague popular-populist one. It did not connect the people with a recognizable national imaginary that could be reappropriated for a new reconstitution of the demos—the conceptual lack could be expected, given the muddled history of Spanish nationalism since Francoism.

All that "people" language constructed a self-image that was very soon forced to function in negative terms, as a reaction to everything the people

Figure 1.14. Protest sign seen in Acampada Barcelona in June 2011: "No somos antisistema, el sistema es antinosotros" (We are not anti-system, the system is anti-us). Photograph taken on June 19, 2011, by Núria, https://www.flickr.com/photos/elmsn/5849416371.

Figure 1.13. Ironic protest sign in one of the many demonstrations that took place during the first month after the 15-M in Madrid: "Perroflauta peligroso" (Dangerous *perroflauta*). Photograph taken on June 19, 2011, by Enrique Dans, https://www.flickr.com/photos/edans/5850680102.

of the 15-M were not. From almost the very beginning, the movement sought to dispel from the inside that which was being instilled from the outside: the myth that the people in the encampments were *perroflautas* (a term very loosely associated with the extreme Left in Spain) or simply antisystem radicals.[32] Generally speaking, the term *perroflauta* could be regarded as a historical extension of the 1954 Francoist law of *vagos y maleantes*, which deemed antisocial all those who "in any shape or form disturb or endanger social peace or public tranquility through their behavior."[33] In its most contemporary iteration, the term derogatively refers to "hippy bums" (or even "gutter punks") at the margins of society—people who go against the system because they are antithetical to the system; an "antisystem" that does not fit society's common norms and accepted behaviors. Often with the help of ironic statements or the direct rejection of the ideologized label of "antisystem" in favor of the inclusive, transversal term of citizen (fig. 1.13 and fig. 1.14, respectively), there was an impulse against any attempt to clearly define the movement's collective identity from the outside looking in. Externally, there was an attempt at labeling by "the powers that always operate through *de-limitación*"—a play on word that combines *delimitación* as the act of determining the precise contour of an object and *limitación* as in establishing restrictions or limits—to control the movement's reality by distinguishing between "people who protest and normal people, [implicitly] pointing at the *indignados* as marginal antisystem, violent, or *perroflautas*."[34]

In the context of the economic crisis, the slur *perroflautas* combined the two already-mentioned meanings so that it came to be loaded with a historically acquired cultural stigma and also with a new political utility for blaming the situation of those recently unemployed on their own ineptitude, lack of skills, or simple laziness. Within such a framework, the *perroflautas* were guilty twice over: of disturbing the public order and of doing so for the wrong reasons (which also pointed to their assumed ignorance). In essence, the appellation alluded to their incompetence to represent themselves or speak for themselves. This conceptual domino ultimately reverts to what the historian Pablo Sánchez León has referred to as "the dichotomy of the *pueblo-plebe*, which equates the *pueblo* with the demos and the *plebe* or plebs with a multitude outside the political limits of the demos."[35] In this dichotomy, while the *plebe* aspires to be included in the conception of *pueblo* in any revolutionary context, "these plebs lack the mechanisms of self-representation" because, by definition, the plebs is a category that historically defined all those who did not have any legal standing within the political system and thus "lacked any moral legitimacy to be counted as citizens."[36] So when it came to visually characterizing the *pueblo* of the 15-M, great effort was made from inside the movement to project an image of a people with a voice in the act of representing themselves as a demos radically opposed to images of *perroflautas* or any of their metaphorical extensions.

For instance, in the biggest and most important protest camp, Acampada Sol, multiple signs discouraging and even prohibiting people to drink alcohol while there (figs. 1.15 and 1.16) can be linked with a conscious curation strategy of moving the movement's self-image as far away as possible from the clichéd views of protesters as bon vivant *perroflautas*. Those signs were more than simple examples of the movement's commonsense approach to stopping illicit behavior in the protest camps—that was only their denotative content.[37] Beyond that, the connotation of the message had everything to do with not being associated with the image of the protester at leisure whose radical stance is perceived as temporary, more a pastime than a serious endeavor to effect political change. As the cliché would have it, real political change can come about only from real politicians in real political institutions. The 15-M's distancing strategy was very conscious of the external attempt to label and *de-limitar* the movement. Instead, the people of the 15-M chose to

Figure 1.16. Sign seen in Acampada Sol: "Revolución no es botellón. Democracia real ya" (The Revolution is not a botellón [which in Spain means a social gathering where people drink in the street]. Real democracy now)." Photograph taken on May 20, 2011, by Olga Berrios, https://www.flickr.com/photos/ofernandezberrios/5741793452.

Figure 1.15. Sign seen in Acampada Sol: "Es una acampada, no un botellón" (This is a protest camp, not a drinking camp). Photograph taken on May 20, 2011, by Ana Rey, https://www.flickr.com/photos/anarey/5739949379.

be seen citizens with a just cause, that is, as part of the concept of the *pueblo* (as *ciudadanos indignados*), not the *plebe* (the *perroflautas*).

With the *pueblo* conceptualized over and against some unserious loitering class, "the people" of the 15-M was to be filtered through the prism of the *indignado*. First used by the Spanish media as a way to dismiss the 15-M's power, this new term signaled a successful strategy of political and ideological reappropriation that was to include anyone affected by the crisis. Following Luis Moreno-Caballud's main argument, the 15-M's collective identity was shaped by a "culture of anyone" that primarily valued inclusive processes of identification.[38] Amador Fernández-Savater expands the argument as follows:

> To avoid stereotypes that divide and over-define our reality, the 15-M has proposed "a non-identarian identity." For example, the term *indignados* came up first as a media label. But as the time went by, the people of the 15-M reappropriated the term. Today, the term *Indignados* refers to anyone; anyone who thinks life is intolerable under this capitalist madness; anyone who thinks that it's only through the collective that we can have our dignity back. The term's usage has a subjective component that potentially includes everyone. The *indignados* are not "those on the Left," neither are those that have traditionally identified with radical politics. They are not workers. They are not even the citizenry, because the term *indignados* does not fit into traditional paradigms of political representation such as "unions for workers" and "parties for citizens."[39]

Paradoxically enough, the theoretical inclusivity of the "anyone" excluded all those who did not conform with the 15-M's "nonidentarian identity" because they chose to have a strong political identity or because they had to accept one. That's why terms such as *personas normales* (normal people), *la gente común y corriente* (common, ordinary folks), *el pueblo* (the people), and *la ciudadanía* (the citizenry) were used interchangeably, to privilege political ambiguity over the specificity of ideology and traditional class-based struggles.[40] Already in the manifesto written by the 15-M organizers Democracia Real Ya, there is a very similar terminology used to encapsulate the movement's identity:

> We are common, ordinary "persons." We are just like you: People who get up early in the morning to study, to work or to go looking for work. We are people just like you: who has family and friends outside this protest. Some of us consider ourselves progressives, but others here define themselves as conservatives. Some of us are religious, but some others in this protest aren't. Some

of us have well-defined ideologies, and others in this movement define themselves as apolitical . . . Be that as it may, every one of us is worried and outraged
at the political, economic, and social situation that we all can see around us.[41]

Identity was thus extricated from the materiality of history, unburdened
by realities forged in the past. This nonidentitarian identity brought to the
encampments a discourse oblivious to the acquired privilege of not having to
have an identity, or even the benefit of having the time to reflect and be conscious of one's identity. It overlooked that identities are not so much chosen
as they are imposed: they have a history, and when ridden of it, the process
of identity formation can be obfuscated.

Yet the progressive erasure of class-based conflict was a very effective political strategy during the occupation of squares in the 15-M, as it allowed the
acampadas to bypass the realm of politics as usual (i.e., electoral politics).
The squares served as a fluid stage platform from which people could express
all sorts of ideas—even mutually exclusive ones—ideas that were both and
at the same time incredibly specific (e.g., economic demands to alleviate the
crisis) and absolutely vague (e.g., the demand to change the current neoliberal model or the fight for a true free society as proposed by the November
13 manifesto of Acampada Sol).[42] Under such a fluid conceptualization, the
15-M opened the door to what Sánchez León referred to as a moment of plebeian "inscription" into the *pueblo*: "The dichotomy *pueblo-plebe* has to do
with the inclusion or exclusion in a community based on the principle of
self-governance. . . . The tandem *pueblo-plebe*, by definition, pits against each
other members within the same political community. But, at the same time, it
allows the individuals labeled as *plebe*, even though they are excluded within
that community, to be able to subjectively identify with the label *pueblo*, to
be inscribed into the *pueblo*. Thus, the plebs are to be always motivated to
fight for such political recognition [that is, for their "inscription" into the
pueblo]."[43] With respect to the possibilities of "inscription" that the 15-M had
granted, Sánchez León's conceptualization points to the rare opportunity that
the plebs, the *perroflautas*, are given in times of popular upheaval. Otherwise,
they are made politically invisible or simply deemed irrelevant by virtue of
their animalistic, unhuman, reactions to those in power, whom they charac-
terize as overly rational. But in moments of crisis, the plebs can be demargin-
alized and re-delineated into an institutional "us" (i.e., a *pueblo*). The push
against the labeling from outside the movement is evidence of that conceptual trajectory in which all attempts to identify the 15-M within the domain

of the plebs were counteracted by the historical impetus that "inscribes" the *plebe* into seeing themselves as part of the *pueblo*. The people of 15-M could not but reject internally the external pressures for its plebeianization.

From a broader perspective, the conception of the 15-M within the historical parameters of the *pueblo*—in this case as a community of *personas*, *gente*, *ciudadanos*, and so on, that was clearly separated from the *plebe*, "persons" who were not *perroflautas*, antisystems, radicals, et cetera—was also tied to the conceptualization of the middle class. The version of the *pueblo* internally conceived that successfully repelled its external (de)limitation held fluid potentialities. But the conceptual essence of the term couldn't escape the aspirational tentacles of middle-class identity construction that, in theory, didn't belong in the 15-M. The fact is that many of the young activists who formed the organizational core of the movement were poster children of Spain's (failed) middle class: "urban university students or graduates who had been widely trained in the use of the new information technologies, a generation of digital natives that were educated in the culture of mass consumerism."[44] And as the 15-M necessarily moved away from the Left-Right framework and started thinking in terms of those at bottom versus those at the top (even the 99 percent versus the 1 percent), the structures built around the middle class remained, inevitably, unseen. Built in a crisis of representative democracy, the shift of perception that the 15-M promoted also permitted a way of being perceived, the promotion of a self-image, that could be very well accommodated by the middle-class ideology at the root of the crisis itself.[45]

An idea progressively internalized by a vast majority of Spaniards eventually turned into national dogma: "When the idea of social class comes up, this is really a reference to the middle class, because [in the Spanish context] it is taken for granted that we are all middle class; . . . under that idea there is another one subsumed: . . . social class is only a question of income and purchasing power, and one moves up the ladder of social class through . . . one's effort and talent."[46] This historically and politically concocted belief became a way of life that called on citizens to see themselves as middle-class subjects positioned at the hegemonic center of Europe. Fundamentally, as the cultural theorist Jim McGuigan has contended, along with the ideation of the middle class, "a neoliberal structure of feelings" was created that regimented the lives of citizens as a series of individualized self-betterment procedures.[47] The neoliberal subjectivity in Spain (and essentially across the globe) had propped up a fallacious model in which the individual is an autonomous, self-regulated, and self-sufficient subject whose ideal existence is to be optimized in order to satisfy mostly individual desires. Because this structure was quite nebulous, in that it was designed to be felt rather than logically explained, McGuigan argues that it was able to incorporate into the neoliberal capitalist logic the political disaffection of the middle classes that never saw their material aspirations fully granted. The renewed ideology of "cool capitalism" individualized rebellion by glorifying the disaffected nonconformist with an intuitive distrust of the "system" and a patrimonial sense of political change.[48] Beneath the outraged citizens who denounced the unviability of the Spanish democratic system in their many individual handwritten signs and slogans all over protest camps, who would take turns speaking in the camps' general assemblies about which policies and politics they personally favored, who avoided being compared to the low-life *perroflauta*, there was an invisible conflict between the individualist system of "cool capitalism," the failed promises made to the Spanish middle class after the economic crisis, and the 15-M's autonomous structures of political identity. As much as the 15-M's self-image allowed for very effective political inclusivity, it was also blindsided by the invisibility of its ingrained exclusivity, which (as is showcased next) privileged individual abled voices that could bank on their "cultural capital" (gained through the perks of belonging to the urban middle classes) to present themselves as informed, up-to-date, indignant citizens speaking in the name of the many other outraged citizens just like them. That's how these privileged individuals dissociated themselves and effectively excluded from the movement those who couldn't, wouldn't, or simply didn't have anything to say.

One of the few films that extensively and minutely focus on the development of the 15-M's ideas from inside the movement is Alfonso Amador's *50 días de mayo (Ensayo para una revolución)*, from 2012.[49] As opposed to other films on the movement, this one does not stop for a moment to contextualize what is filmed. All the scenes revolved around (mostly) unedited long debates that took place during one of the most common tools in the decision-making processes of the protest camps: the general assemblies. Although one cannot pretend that Amador's film is a raw anthropological document, it is the closest that outsiders can get to an ethnographic account of the main political debates that shaped the movement's self-identity. The 15-M was moving away from the image that insiders' perspectives (to a lesser or a greater degree) tried to convey in order to combat the external views imposed by mainstream media at the time. The film is set in Valencia, away from the epicenter of the movement in Puerta del Sol, and it consciously documents the entire duration of the encampment (fifty days) to situate what took place in Valencia as paradigmatic of the 15-M in the rest of Spain. To that end, the film uses the assembly as a collective character constructed of a diverse array of personalities. The filmic content does not really advance a clear plotline so much as it intends to represent the movement's many hopes and disappointments through the eyes of its personalities. Admittedly, Amador's main objective from the beginning was to document how "la gente rompió a hablar de pronto" (people suddenly broke into speaking).[50]

Most notably, the film obviated the context around the encampment in Valencia (where, for instance, the corruption of the Popular Party was already well known and could have undoubtedly influenced the film's storyline) to represent the act of *tomando la palabra* (roughly translated as "gaining a voice") as the original political act that birthed the movement. As the political commentator Noelia Adánez confirmed in a roundtable with the director, the film was "about the process of gaining a public voice, about how regular people are able to speak up in order to occupy a space they were not used to inhabit; . . . and that's why the space of the assembly in the film is paradigmatic . . . because it replicates what was happening in many other places."[51] In the same roundtable, the historian Pablo Sánchez León connected the assembly seen in the film and the *toma de palabra* with the basis of democracy. Sánchez León linked it to the Greek concept of *isegoria*, or "the irrespective capacity of any citizen to publicly express their thoughts; the capacity to create a place where there is still not an institutional mechanism that hierarchizes . . . one's opinions."[52] The film is said to visualize archetypes representing different roles within the democratic enablement of the *isegoria*—as the new moral institution of the 15-M—that the assembly presupposed. By that interpretation, the people in *50 días de mayo* were portrayed in a continuous act of *toma de palabra*. The multiple tensions and drastic differences of opinions that eventually stemmed from such an act were in the end the visualization of a community of "persons" with a diverse voice and immersed in the politics of self-representation. Per Sánchez León's argument on the dichotomy *pueblo-plebe*, the film exhibits a collection of self-represented outraged citizens who refused to become the *plebe*. In the film, speaker after speaker reject any external impositions that could marginalize their voices or circumscribe them through lens of the *perroflautas*. They were instead *indignados*.

Amador's *50 días de mayo* was illustrative of different angles beyond the mere act of democratic inclusion that made the identity process from *perroflautas* to *indignados*. At one point in the middle of the film, a young man speaks of how some committees were apparently slacking off, not working hard enough to make more of a visible impact. He wonders whether the movement would actually be better off without those less productive groups.

He then claims that such thing seemed to be a widespread attitude in the movement: "I read today on Twitter that 'Acampada Coruña [a region in the northwest of Spain] does not represent me,' and I have to say the same about this *acampada*."[53] On one level, this is just one of the many tensions typical of all assemblies. In the wider political context of the neoliberal logic of "cool capitalism" and the middle class, that type of indignation also represents a general attitude in the movement to identify the *indignados* as productive people in a system that proved itself to be unproductive. The *acampadas* could not let themselves be pigeonholed by the external stereotype of the equally unproductive *perroflauta*; they had to set an example from the inside that, as the same participant says, "we are here doing serious business."[54] Underneath this refusal to be stereotyped was an identitarian impulse that conformed with the ideology of efficiency, productivity, the ethics of hard work, and individual meritocracy that spoke of citizen's indignations in the 15-M with the vocabulary of the aspirational middle class in the neoliberal era of capitalism.

Right after this young man's last words in the film, a middle-aged woman takes the stage to speak about different ways to actually improve organization in the camp. She then goes on to say that after people in the *acampadas* enjoyed a *revolución cutánea* (a revolution based on close emotional and physical connection but also superficial), the movement needed to start going deeper to achieve the set of goals laid out during the first days of the encampment. But when she is about leave the stage, she seems to express an unspoken internal conflict and is compelled to add the following admonition: "I just want to add one more thing. Others have remarked several times that we shouldn't be a bunch of anarchists. . . . This hurts me personally because here [in the encampment], yes, there actually are anarchists, and communists, and those who like smoking a joint, and *perroflautas*, and a bunch of hippies. Do you truly want us all to get up and leave? All the anarchists, all the trade unionists, the *perroflautas*, the hippies, and those of us who like smoking joints? Really?"[55] On the face of it, the reproach is a request for a broader inclusion and tolerance of others. However, in the context of her previous statement on the necessity of becoming more effective, the reprimand appears to be also directed at reconciling the sphere of work and productivity with the realm of individual identity, aesthetic expression, and lifestyle. The association of anarchists, communists, and unionists with *perroflautas*, hippies, and "those who like smoking a joint" does not speak to the influence of working-class politics so much as it reflects the progressive ideological emptying of the working class. Her inclusive impetus was not class based, or even ideological. It was instead a politics of indignation that referred to the

movement's practice of radical inclusivity "in order to jump over the sociological and ideological walls that divide us on an everyday basis . . . and to
avoid becoming another of those small 'radical' groups isolated from mainstream politics, unable to take a real swing at changing reality."[56] This inclusive impetus acquired a transversal nature that also demanded an aesthetic
neutrality, in the sense of what Fernández-Savater had argued when referring
to how the 15-M practiced "the art of staying in the blur . . . the technique of
the sfumato as the positive appropriation of uncertainty and ambiguity."[57]
And this indefinition was key to the 15-M's radically inclusive nature. So if
political ambiguity was a trait to be cherished by the movement, excess—of
the banks, of the politicians, of the system in general—was explicitly rejected.
However, in the same conceptual tandem, underneath the surface of ideological uncertainty and radical inclusivity, there was also a blanket rejection
of excess that danced around and inadvertently hid deeper issues of class
and marginalization.

The movement avoided internally "those ideologized factions that wanted
the movement to have a more explicit identity (to be a social movement,
a leftist or a revolutionary movement)."[58] It thrived in the undefinition of
its political borders but was also blind to forces from above that privileged
ambiguity over the specificity of ideology and traditional class-based struggles. The 15-M favored a frame of reference marked by cultural norms that
could promote a symbolic and aesthetic rebellion against the upper classes
in accordance with the leeway offered by the logic of "cool capitalism" in the
neoliberal era. As much as it shunned the excessive image of those at the
top (and thus did not include them in their way of seeing the "real" people
in Spain's "real" democracy), it was also uneasy about the lower classes and
their excesses (which was indirectly assimilated as a sign of being the *plebe*).
As seen in Amador's film, much of the movement's discourse around the centrality of *tomando la palabra* presupposed a privilege that only a sector of the
Spanish citizenry (mostly urban, middle class, university educated, socialized
in democracy, generationally young) was accustomed to exercising. Then,
though mostly an unspoken norm, the ability to include and convince others
in a public forum such as the assembly was implicitly framed as the antidote
to the violent and excessive urges of those in the lower strata of society who
were also the hardest hit by the crisis.

Because in Spain "we were all middle class," class struggle, with its inherent potential for violence, was dismissed even as a category. Class was a
means of sociological identification that unproblematically and indirectly
invited those at the bottom to join the citizenry of the precarious Spanish

Figure 1.17. Members of Juventud sin Futuro in one of the protests of the 15-M holding a banner: "Sin casa, sin curro, sin pensión, sin miedo" (No job, no house, no pension, no fear). Photograph taken on June 15, 2011, by Neil Vega Murrieta, https://www.flickr.com/photos/neilvm/5859139641.

middle-class youth in their struggle against the elites in power for a better future, a future that in the early stages of the movement overrepresented a young generation of university students. They saw themselves literally and symbolically as part of Juventud sin Futuro (JSF, or "youth without future"), the name of both a student platform responsible for the first 15-M demonstration and a popular banner seen around protest camps. One of the key visual features of the JSF's identity revolved around a yellow and black banner usually accompanied by the refrain "sin casa, sin curro, sin pension, sin miedo" (no house, no job, no retirement pension, no fear) (fig. 1.17). The banner denoted an incontrovertible fact about the 15-M youth: their economic future was bleak. But it also implied a (very understandable) desire to recover times when the young could aspire to own a house, have a stable job, and expect a dignified retirement. And thus their fearless political persona, reflected by the last bit of the refrain (no fear), also connoted a fight for a future that was embedded in a rather conservative middle-class imaginary.

The aspirational model of the middle class was very much left intact. The model was an invitation by JSF "to all those who couldn't gain social mobility to pursue it and desire it" as part of a future fundamentally based on a psychology of the middle class.[59] This is not to claim that the middle-class political framework was unquestionably internalized, as both the members of JSF and the young participants in the 15-M were in truth "advocating for a politics that is proactive not reactive, based on collective self-empowerment not service provision, framing political demands around dignity, labor, and social justice, and breaking from ideology-based politics to praxis-based politics by politicizing the everyday reality of precarious people," as shown by Flesher Fominaya's ethnographic work on the organization and its offshoot Oficina Precaria.[60] Rather, JSF's visual banner was a synecdoche of the invisible and arguably inevitable gridlock between the pervasive logic of middle-class politics and the successful articulation of the 15-M's political strategy beyond any ghettoizing calls for a working-class revolution (which would have truly opposed the idea of the middle class as much as it would have set itself up for a much-expected political failure). The 15-M's forging of its own political identity allowed for the ideation of a transversal political subject, one whose representation was placed "between 'the people of the social movements' and 'the people of television' . . . between a radical protest that did not want to be Leftist and a fatigued population that thought itself to be on the Right."[61] That was an unspoken and mostly unseen tension formed between the political aspirations during the 15-M and the economic and ideological reality of "the crisis of the post-Francoist middle class, which was upheld as the hegemonic, collective referent . . . for a majority of young people . . . who were indeed socialized in Spain's middle-class culture."[62]

The 15-M's political identity showed a preference for a specific vision based on "the exclusion of certain groups in respect to the middle class, whose identity was also supported by another structural as well as determining feature: one's cultural level."[63] That mechanism of exclusion inevitably viewed Spain in relation to the legacy and restrictive authority of what Guillem Martínez termed *la CT*, or the culture of the *transición*: Spain's transition to democracy in the late 1970s and early 1980s.[64] Although at its core that legacy was frontally opposed by the 15-M—because *la CT* mainly aimed to depoliticize culture—one must admit the ideological parameters of the middle class that climaxed in the *transición* were never questioned beyond a contingent sense of outrage—or, as the libertarian activist and renowned author Carlos Taibo put it: "One of the collateral effects of 15-M has been the development of . . . a really vivid criticism of the current political system. . . . [C]ertainly there are complaints about corruption, criticisms of the bipartisan system, and even about the monarchy, but the debate is about the regime and not really a critique of the system that upholds it."[65] In other words, although it was true that the 15-M shattered the foundations of "a hierarchical consensus culture, a culture self-perceived as unproblematic, a depoliticizing culture, which *la CT* secured for three decades via the monopoly of words, topics of discussion, and democratic memory," the culture of consensus and horizontality stemming from the autonomous tradition in the movement was also blindsided by three decades of middle-class ideology, part and parcel of *la CT*.[66] That being the case, precisely because the movement wanted to have the largest possible reach, most popular indignation channeled through the *acampadas* became largely directed at how the economic and political ideation of the middle class had stopped working for the majority of Spaniards and less at how that model was essentially flawed.[67] Consequently, although one of the 15-M's primary goals revolved around achieving real democracy, the idea of an alternative economic system progressively lost traction until finally disappearing with the emergence of the new political party Podemos in 2014 (which understandably corralled the rationalization of conflict around the politics of what was institutionally possible).[68]

Conclusion

From the first images of the occupied Puerta del Sol to the livestreaming of the general assemblies or the heterogeneous audiovisual reproductions of people's indignation, this chapter has examined how the 15-M's political bid for representation was culturally presented in a series of populist visualities: explicitly, the 15-M visualized a public political voice for democratic change; implicitly, it created a populist dichotomy between "us" citizens and "them" elites. These were populist visualities that gave access to the collective feeling of an "us-people" inside the movement and, at the same time, visualized a new political subject in need of representation at the institutional level. In this sense, the 15-M's (re)presentations aimed at constituting a collective vision of who the "real" people were in and around this climate of social upheaval. That visualization ultimately expanded the political imaginary of what was possible and inserted the popular as populist in a new cultural framework of Spanish politics, with varied consequences. The first ramification was the successful renegotiation of the essence of the people and their political reality. The second was, however, complicated by the intrusion of middle-class ideology, which understood class as an ambiguous political subjectivity based on a self-identifying process of material aspiration. In this sense, on the one hand, the 15-M's ideological ambiguity fostered a type of radical inclusivity that allowed for a very powerful transversality, breaking a great many political actors from the activist "ghetto." On the other, the movement was intolerant (more unconsciously than otherwise) of the most socially marginalized, the ones hit the hardest by the economic crisis. The 15-M's inclusive impetus was also shaped by the established hierarchy of the middle class. Not unproblematically, such a middle-class framework was a culturally transversal springboard key to redefining Spanish politics. When the people of the 15-M were asking for a real democracy, what was stake was the redefinition of whose reality really mattered—all reduced to a simple question and a simpler choice: Who were the authentic representative of the Spanish populace? The "real" people in the squares or the ersatz elitist other and the falsified realities coming from those at top? As the government's austerity measures ravaged Spain's social fabric, the answer to those questions became clearer, and as a consequence, the 15-M successfully self-authenticated itself as the public image of the Spanish demos's indignation.

2

Documenting Negotiations around the Place and the Time of Real Democracy

The fall of the Egyptian military dictator Hosni Mubarak on February 11, 2011, not only supposed the climax of the Arab Spring but also produced the most iconic image of that time: the aerial view of the occupied Tahrir Square in Cairo (fig. 2.1). The image helped to redefine long-held assumptions about what it meant to be Egyptian, Arab, and—by assumed extension—Muslim, around the world. It revealed that a new way of seeing and knowing the Arab world was possible beyond the clichéd view of it as fundamentally undemocratic. If only for a few moments, an image of a specific place in Cairo, Tahrir Square, was proof that radical democratic change could be achieved against all odds. Three months later, inspired by the image of Tahrir, hundreds of Spaniards in the Puerta del Sol in Madrid staged a very similar visual composition (fig. 2.2).[1] This was the beginning of what would later be known as the 15-M movement, or the Indignados. Correspondingly, the aerial image of the occupied Puerta del Sol became an icon that could bridge the disconnect between what was seeable (i.e., thousands of people demanding radical change from the bottom up) and what was knowable (i.e., that real change happens from the top down) in Spanish politics. The image would be seen as evidence that a fundamental rethinking of democracy in Spain could also be possible.

Building on the conceptualization of the 15-M's identity established in the previous chapter, here we explore the extent to which the stereotypes imposed from the outside could be a window to further understanding the construction of an authentic inside. In this sense, the many filmed documentations

Figure 2.1. Image of Tahrir Square during the Egyptian Revolution. Photograph taken on February 8, 2011, by Mona, https://www.flickr.com/photos/89031137@N00/5427680747.

Figure 2.2. Image of the occupied Puerta del Sol during the first days of the 15-M. Photograph taken on May 18, 2011, by Carlos Daniel Gomero Correa, https://www.flickr.com/photos/cdgc/8393930673.

of the time (i.e., May 15) and the space (i.e., the square) of the movement supposed a key battleground on which the 15-M's political essence was to be settled. As such, on the one hand, the image of the Puerta del Sol was the visual "origin story" of the 15-M; the multiple angles of the same view denoted a moment of political awakening, encapsulated by the well-known slogan "dormíamos, despertamos" (we were asleep, but we just woke up). It was a sudden rousing, directly linked to the cover-up of the economic crisis, that in turn uncovered a deep crisis of political representation.[2] As the 15-M unraveled and the image of the Puerta del Sol gained visual specificity, the images of protesters—the *indignados*—with signs that demanded a real democracy acquired more prominence.[3] Probably the most celebrated slogan of the 15-M, this demand for real democracy had been historically sustained by the more or less stereotypical assumption that Spain's transition to democracy from the Francoist dictatorship was not fully genuine.[4] Both the demand and the assumption underlying it were part of Spain's political façade. That is, they were not deep-seated statements but were the frontispiece of Spanish politics, as they resonated with a large number of Spaniards at a superficial level. Outside specialized circles, these were thought of as clichéd views of the Spanish democratic system, ones without much political traction and certainly regarded as anathema in electoral politics.[5]

However, the image of Puerta del Sol reveals that such stereotypical views cannot simply be dismissed as superficial or inauthentic (i.e., not true to Spain's real democratic substance as rooted in the Transición). They instead point to the common divide between politics from the top, with its established ways of seeing and knowing, and their counterpart at the bottom, whose vision and knowledge of politics at different times in history have the power to disrupt the most authorized political truths. In the case of the 15-M, the well-received demand for a real democracy broke with all established assumptions about Spanish politics. This demand for an authentic democracy was not so much opposed to a past time characterized by a thin democratic veneer as it was a case of unearthing—at least momentarily—a new way of seeing and performing a newly emerging democratic reality, a new way of understanding Spanish democracy beyond the old centrist or moderate rationales that put the people occupying squares, protesting in the streets, at the center stage of politics. In other words, the iconic image of the Puerta del Sol represented not a moment of political truth (i.e., the unmasking of Spain's true demos) but a moment of political performance that demanded a new political identity—one marked by the construction of a real democracy whose democratic realness stemmed from its popular-populist politics.

It was, then, the theatricalization of a moment when a significant number of Spanish people attempted to create a new political constitution by popular demand.

When the masks of economic prosperity and political stability were figuratively falling away, the 15-M's *indignados* put on a series of dialectically opposed masks that effectively acted out the rupture with the version of democracy instated following the Transición. In this sense, the iconic occupation of the Puerta del Sol could be seen as a people's masquerade that projected a new political self-perception of what it meant to be a new Spanish *pueblo*, a new demos visibly separated from the one seen during the democratic transition. The forging of that novel self-image was to Spanish democracy what the images of Tahrir had been to the stereotypical assumptions of governance in the Arab world. The self-image theatricalized a collective will in the act of performing what a "real" or authentic democracy looked like.[6] Thus, the 15-M's most salient political demand was above all a performance of authenticity. Interestingly, although the 15-M's authentic essence derived from being unmediated by external actors (e.g., politicians, union leaders, journalists) who were outside people's experience in situ (in the 15-M's main stage, the occupation of the Puerta del Sol), the movement's political identity was ultimately constructed by means of being (audio)visually mediated, particularly by film. The many documentary films about the movement became windows through which one could see, behind the scenes, how the 15-M's collective protagonist "really" worked. These documentary films provide another opportunity to see how the movement's political identity was not only visualized (as explained in Chapter 1) but also negotiated between its claims to realness and those of its institutional other—the Spanish state—beyond a specific historical contingency and concrete political agendas.

With that in mind, as an analytical springboard, this chapter draws inspiration from Ann Davies's argumentation of how Spanish cinema had negotiated a conceptualization of national identity that "acts as a sort of masquerade, a 'pretense' of Spanishness[,] that in many ways becomes indistinguishable from whatever the real thing might be."[7] In her study, which draws on the ideas of Susan Hayward—who conceptualized national identities as a type of collective masking—Davies explores the ways in which the cinematic trope of the femme fatale and the understanding of femininity as a form of masquerade confuse the relationship between what can be seen and what can be known as real when constructing group identities—that is, the relation between what appears to be from an outside viewpoint (outside the group's identity) and what emanates from self-perception (from inside the group) and hence is thought as well as projected as real.[8] When it comes to thinking about Spanish identity concretely, Davis argues that what differentiates the insider's authentic portrayal of Spanishness from the outsider's artifice is purposefully indiscernible as envisaged by some of the best-known cinematic symbols—namely, Spain's femme fatale par excellence, Carmen.[9]

Similarly, the 15-M and the images it produced can be considered a process of negotiation between views from inside the movement's demotic authenticity (regarding the movement's projections of what constitutes real democracy and true popular will) and outside of it (in relation to institutional representations of democratic will as mostly informed by electoral politics). As such, the filmic representations of the movement highlighted several moments of negotiation both from outside—in that those in power did not understand who all the people in the Puerta del Sol really were, and from inside—as the people of the 15-M did not see themselves as represented by those in power (who insisted that they were the only ones who could represent them).

The cinematic images of the 15-M gave those moments a multivocal meaning that is very similar to the way national identity works as expressed by Davies: "Spanish clichés of the flouncy dress, comb and veil, the bullfight, the flamenco song and dance, act as masks of the exotic, orientalist and thus—feminine—other, but they do so to the extent that we can draw no clear dividing line between authentic and ersatz. This orientalist identity has to some extent been forced on Spain from outside. . . . But this imposition does not necessarily prevent Spanish culture, or women, making use of the masquerade for its or their own purposes."[10] In this sense, the 15-M was both a disguise or masquerade of popular authenticity (regarding how the protesters' holistic claims could very well mask a political contingency that was not representative of the entire Spanish demos) and, at the same time, a revelation of a new "us" with real symbolic value and practical consequences with respect to the cultural value produced by the portrayals of the 15-M's *indignados* as the will of the people that would later be capitalized on by a party like Podemos. Thus, an image taken during one of the first days of the protests in the Puerta del Sol could be presented simultaneously as the proof that Spain needed "democracia real ya" or as confirmation that those asking for a real democracy were in reality asking for the suppression of the country's true democratic will as represented by the electorate. Mariano Rajoy's absolute majority in the November 2011 elections, after the 15-M had retreated from the squares, reaffirmed the schism in that dichotomy.

Such a dichotomic view was negotiated cinematically and in situ from the very first days of the *acampadas*. Filming became a way of controlling the movement's own hopes and dreams, the sweeping impulse toward control relating to *des-intermediar*. The concept of *des-intermediar* (or "disintermediate") speaks to "the attempt at reducing the likelihood that information and/ or news about the movement were created based upon the logic of collectives external to the movement."[11] That is, while an outside gaze was perceived as trying to impose a view of what the people of the 15-M were (radicals, *perroflautas*, or simply not Spain's "real" demos), filmmakers inside the movement were making use of those outsider preconceptions as a way of showing who the people of the 15-M actually were. The idea of *des-intermediando* revealed the need to *mediar* (mediate). Documentary films were thought of as truth-telling intermediaries that would help to uncover Spain's authentic democratic reality, contrasting it with the version of that reality imposed from above. They were a way to mediate between being and seeming. In this sense, these films went well beyond the documentation of the 15-M and its many demands and denunciations. They treated the movement as a popular outburst that in many ways had disrupted the timeline of Spanish democracy's assumed natural progression by stubbornly remaining in one place, symbolically occupying a square, producing a parallel democratic moment (which was thought to be sufficient to bring about a new democratic time).

These films mainly negotiated two visual coordinates: the visualization of place (i.e., the positioning of those outside the square versus those inside the *acampadas*) and the representation of time (i.e., the cinematic relation between past, present, and future in the 15-M as a whole). Accordingly, the analysis that follows shows how some of those films were mediated by those coordinates when recording the diverse performances of 15-M's moment of populist formation. Four documentaries warrant attention. The first two films, *Banderas falsas* (2012), directed by Carlos Serrano Azcona, and *La plaza: La gestación del movimiento 15-M* (2012), by Adriano Morán Conesa, visualize the movement in situ as an experience around popular (in)authenticity, which demands to be visually located (e.g., regarding how Serrano Azcona visualizes antagonism or political conflict as the essence of politics and, accordingly, as the place where the people, as a political subject, always reside) and spatially viewed (e.g., in terms of how Morán Conesa's film makes the square the source of the 15-M's popular essence via its politics of democratic participation). The last two films, Pere Portabella's *Informe General II: El nuevo rapto de Europa* (2016) and Stephane Grueso's *15-M: Excelente. Revulsivo. Importante* (2013), situate the movement as part of a narration of a time dislocated in history, a rupture in the historical continuum of Spanish democracy as understood since the Transición. Although these two very different filmmakers approach the same subject from two equally different cinematic angles—Portabella uses filmic self-referentiality and metacommentary as his main political tool, whereas Grueso inserts himself in the film as both subject and object of his politics—they both reach essentially the same conclusion: the 15-M inaugurated a new mythological time for a new *pueblo* in what seemed to be a new historical moment. Taken together, these films offer the chance to observe how an extremely vague political construct such as the *pueblo* can be cinematically created.

Being in Place: Locating the People in *Banderas falsas* and *La plaza*

Serrano Azcona's *Banderas falsas* (2012) was one of the first filmic accounts that tried to explain in images and with few words the spatial genesis of the people of the 15-M. It is the first part of an experimental documentary film project that stressed the power of the image in the making of a people by juxtaposing (oftentimes counterintuitively) scenes of the cycle of protests in Spain since 2011 to moments of popular fervor (from political demonstrations to religious gatherings to sports celebrations).[12] The film focuses above all on how the 15-M believed there to be a crisis of political representation that was in turn a crisis of visual representation, which blurred how one can relate to images as a vehicle for seeing and knowing reality. *Banderas falsas* emphasizes those blurred lines in between representations to locate where popular power resides. However, the precise location of popular power in this film is continually negotiated between polar opposites. The director finds that power can be visualized and, hence, filmed only in moments of conflict. In this sense, *Banderas falsas* explicitly captures the paradoxes of popular fervor by situating the visual action between images of the celebration of the World Cup, which was won by Spain's national football team in 2010, and the first days after the encampment in Puerta del Sol on May 15, 2011. The filmic juxtaposition of those two moments of public ecstasy conveys the contradictory nature of "the people." Further, its political essence is visually located in the actions of subjects in conflict. As such, in the film, the chants of football-infused nationalistic passion—"yo soy español, español, español" (I am Spanish)—are parallel to those of the 15-M's "qué no, qué no nos representan" (they do not represent us). At first, the filmed representation of such a dichotomized view of the Spanish people could be considered facile. But beyond the apparent politicized clash of these contingents—the sports fans and the activists—the film visualizes the rupture, divide, or antagonism that is inherent to any moment of *pueblo* formation. It places the people of the 15-M alongside the people at the World Cup celebration and, by extension, in proximity to any other people who could be thought of as ideological opposites to the transversal popular base of the 15-M.

Serrano Azcona intersperses images of a Semana Santa procession and scenes of the crowds that turned out for the Pope Benedict XVI's visit to Madrid in 2011 with iconic scenes of the many popular assemblies that took place during 15-M, establishing "a divide between the visible and its representation, as an equivalence of the political crisis that was at the root of the 15-M movement."[13] Born of the movement's understanding of Spain's political crisis (which considered that Spanish democracy's fatal flaw was at the top, with the elites, exonerating everyone below), and visualized in the juxtaposition of these scenes, the representation of such antagonism holds an implicit warning for the viewer. That is, the popular masses that started a revolution "with a radical inclusive character . . . that invited anyone and everyone to belong" are inseparable from the exclusionary conceptualization of the Spanish *pueblo* that tied together football and nationalism.[14] In the film, this juxtaposition is meant to put the popular outburst and the hostility it creates at the center of the action. Serrano Azcona rejoices in the representation of symbolic conflict and even leads the way by placing himself at heart of it: in the first moments of the film, a close-up frame of the director pops up, unannounced, as a female voice asks, "¿Carlitos, estás feliz porque ganó España?" (Carlitos, are you happy that Spain won the match?).[15] The question is answered immediately with a silent, ecstatic celebration on the part of Serrano Azcona. Expressions of national devotion like these create something of a cognitive dissonance for the film's Spanish audience. In the context of a documentary whose main plotline revolves around the 15-M, the director's expressed fervor not only opposes the 15-M's system of values (antisymbolic, inclusionary, and transversal); it becomes undeniably connected to past Francoist obsessions with an imperial unified Spain and to the country's symbolic placement under one Spanish flag—waved under the pretext of cheering for the national football team.

Although, on first viewing, the scene of the chanting crowd could again be thought of as merely polemical, it points toward the visualization of a dichotomic antagonism intrinsic to popular subjects, of an "us" versus "them" that is seen as inextricably related to the ideation of the *pueblo* as a political construct.[16] As such, the entire documentary is riddled with permanent visual conflict that strings together sequences directly opposed to each other at different symbolic levels. The film opens with the celebration of Spain's victory in the 2010 FIFA World Cup, then rapidly cuts to the first protests in the spring of 2011 and the encampment in the Puerta del Sol. Next shown are unidentified protesters singing and demonstrating in Mexico City's Zócalo against the privatization of national oil; at this point, the film fades to images of police violence during some of the 15-M protests and then cuts to images of a religious procession in Madrid, where several *legionarios*—army soldiers from the still active Francoist Spanish Legion—are singing the old fascist tune "Soy el novio de la muerte." These scenes finally connect with a series of sequences on the gathering of the Christian youth commemorating the pope's visit to Madrid in June 2011, which took place simultaneously and in tension with the Puerta del Sol encampment.

The director's lack of explicit critical commentary as those images are displayed is not intended to create a heterogeneous conceptualization of the Spanish *pueblo*, which could lead to understanding the film as an implicit call to the Habermasian rationalization of conflict.[17] On the contrary, the film represents and exhibits the fallacy of popular consensus. If anything, the almost ontological division between the people in *Banderas falsas* calls for management of political conflict by means other than the consensus that the 15-M's many assemblies famously advocated. Instead, the film asks its viewers: How do you integrate nonhierarchically all those people who insist on being placed in a hierarchy? How can one reconcile the values of ecstasy that Serrano Azcona films in the religious procession or in the military formation of the *legionarios* with the ecstasy of Acampada Sol? No consensus could be reached between those people, and it is difficult to imagine any overlap between them. Nevertheless, *Banderas falsas*' own answer to those questions is inconclusive, as it refuses to give the exact location of where one could draw the line that would differentiate one *pueblo* from another.

At most, the contradictions in Serrano Azcona's film highlight the legacies of inequality and violence inherent in the construction of the *pueblo* beyond the 15-M's horizontal politics of consensus. Similarly, Alberto Medina argues that "popular horizontality as an essential, inalienable principle to construct a political common good runs the risk of fetishization . . . and is dangerously close to making invisible the implicit violence inherent to the vital trajectories of all those people that form the horizontal commons in the first place."[18] A politics of consensus dominated by a horizontal conceptualization of the people and its inherent radical inclusivity erases a politics historically built on dissensus (according to Rancière's definition).[19] Serrano Azcona's film opens the door to historical antagonisms and allows for the exploration of the problematic angles of the consensus in the 15-M that inadvertently "erases exclusion and inequality."[20] *Banderas falsas'* own ambiguous message suggests a role for the people away from the abstraction of consensual horizontality and located in practice (where people are physically side by side) within the inherently conflictual place of the *pueblo*. However, the *pueblo* suggested in the film is not—and may be never—visualized in situ, because its location depends on the materialization of political certainty. Both this film and the object of its representation are built on the ambiguous relationship between Spain's "real" demos and its ersatz other.

On the contrary, Adriano Morán Conesa's *La plaza* is the visual manifestation of how political uncertainties can be masked through the construction of spatial certainties. With a linear narration of events that took place from the first day of the occupation of Puerta del Sol until its dismantling on June 12, 2011, interrupted only by commentary from within (i.e., analysis given only by those with firsthand knowledge), *La plaza* visualizes the location of popular power as unambiguously in place. Morán Conesa draws a line that divides the outside from the inside of the *pueblo* via the representation of the public square, which serves to separate a visible, popular will in the *acampada* from an invisibilized but institutionally represented demos. *La plaza* negotiates the meaning of the *pueblo* by means of a process of visual (de) selection, which is destined to unproblematically affirm a genuinely democratic popular inside as radically distinct from an institutionalized outside that is in crisis because of its lack of democratic authenticity. In this sense, the film frames the occupied square as a people's space, inside of which its participants are offered a true democratic experience, nowhere to be found in the crisis-ridden institutions outside the encampment.

The square cinematically embodies what Henri Lefebvre described as a lived space: "the space of the everyday activities of users [in opposition to] the abstract space of the experts (architects, urbanists, planners)."[21] *La plaza* represents space as radically public (i.e., nonhierarchical), livable (as in Lefebvre's idea), and truly popular. To remind viewers of the space's "popularity," where experts of the past and their authority have no place, the film stages a new type of popular expertise based on an understanding of the political as rooted in a people's common sense.[22] The square is synecdochally represented as a type of popular knowledge that ultimately not only is the source of a popular common sense but also constitutes it politically. This popular common sense visualizes the square as something beyond a mere physical support for the 15-M. It is a visual representation of the square that follows the 15-M's conceptualization of political performance, which was "dependent on the occupation of public space: on the existence of camps that, even if only a small minority would stay overnight, provided the setting for the counter-society that materialized the dreams of real democracy."[23] The square is the stage on which a new polity is constituted that in turn constitutes the basis of real democratic representation. This experience is lived (according to Lefebvre) as long as it is performed. In this way, the performance of a real democracy in the square serves to mask the practical impossibility of enacting the 15-M's participatory processes outside the encampments, in an external reality of democratic lack—in the way Spanish democracy is experienced through its institutions.

Further, *La plaza* reconfigures (in)authentic popular constitution by visually negating the traditional spaces of governance—even though the main character in the film, the Puerta del Sol, hosts the imposing building of the Madrid regional government. The symbols of top-down politics that appear in the film are resignified both by their positioning relative to the overwhelming presence of the encampment in the square and by their contextualization in the cinematic sequence. The statue of King Carlos III's imperial figure dominates the center of the Puerta del Sol, and from the beginning of the film, its blurry image is left in the background as organizers and participants in the encampment are interviewed. These scenes are shot from an angle that magnifies the interviewees in relation to a dwarfing image of Carlos III on his horse, which, by this point is surrounded by handwritten placards and 15-M slogans. By the end of the film, the statue appears by itself for the first and only time. It is a low-angle shot of the king on his horse surrounded by the strings that hold together the tarps of the makeshift tents in the encampment. In parallel, the ambient sound captures the noise of the many people in Acampada Sol along with the voice of an interviewee speaking on the importance of consensus in the 15-M. In the next frame, the monument of the first Spanish emperor vanishes from sight. The film then goes on to show a still image of the iconic hands up in the air, a commonly used gesture of consensus in the assemblies. Visually overwhelming the symbolic top-down power the monument represents with representations of the bottom-up politics that constantly accompany it, this cinematic sequence resignifies the grandiosity the figure of Carlos III has accumulated. From a filmic standpoint, the obvious, imposing presence of the encampment aimed at occupying all symbols of traditional power, from statues and government buildings to the famous resymbolization of the L'Oréal billboard (analyzed in Chapter 1). When seen in this way, these images represent a new popular common sense, one that visually reordered the historical locus of power embedded in grandiose monuments and staggering buildings and reinserted it in the square, which can be seen beyond its public function as a people's space. That is, a real democratic place opposed to the manufactured grandiosity where institutional democracy resides, whose politics are visually located as foreign to the genuinely democratic experiences in the square. Democratic institutions are thus "otherized" and placed outside the encampment's enactment of real democracy.

This kind of democratic realness is primarily characterized by the performance of democratic participation. So much so that the performative impetus progressively substitutes for the political content of what is performed. This is most obvious in the film's emphasis on what have come to be recognizable instances of popular participation in the 15-M, such as the assemblies' establishment of a new, gestural political language. The most iconic gesturing observed in the encampments and throughout *La plaza* came to be known as the *grito mudo*, or the mute scream. Memorably, a sea of people waved their hands in the air in unison at midnight on May 20, 2011, as a sign of protest against the encampment being declared unlawful by the Central Election commission (*Junta Electoral Central*) and a self-affirmation of collective agency and empowerment. In the film the mute scream is more than a symbolic contingency: it is seen as integral to the 15-M movement's assembly-based character and the documentary's representation thereof. All assemblies filmed feature the establishment of gestures as a permanent way of conveying agreement and disagreement, and a host of scenes emphasize gestures that minimize dialectical confrontation and maximize channels favoring assembly-based consensus. Nevertheless, the content of the represented consensus does not carry as much political weight as the cinematic representation of its format. As such, the film prioritizes performance over substance.

The square is shown throughout the film as the ideal platform for performing a fundamental rethinking of democratic participation while de-emphasizing the political contents of the participatory process. As a result, for instance, the film's reconceptualization of precarity is achieved via the performance of a real democratic participation. *La plaza* visualizes the square as full of citizens living in precarious situations both physically, as the *indignados* in Puerta del Sol are taking shelter in a makeshift tent city, and financially, given that many of the recorded testimonies speak of systemic economic uncertainty and structural unemployment. However, the content of their testimonies is never specifically addressed. Apart from their declarations, there is not any other background information. The film does not spend time giving voice to experts that could speak to the root causes of these citizens' precarious lives, because what is important is that these anonymous voices can be heard and seen speaking of an authentic firsthand experience. The square favors a space for anyone that parallels "the opinion of 'just anyone'— of someone who does not belong to the group of 'those in the know.'"[24] Their participation in the democratic life of the square is cinematically accentuated over their actual precarity outside of it. The square—as seen in the film— compels its dwellers to a performance of the common good, which substitutes material precarity with real democratic access to an alternative system of values that prioritizes, above all, collective well-being via multiple avenues of popular participation, of the *toma de palabra* (speaking up in public), without dwelling on the specificity of those words or *palabras*.

The horizontal structure of the Acampada Sol encouraged the broad participation of "just anyone" and was reinforced by a spirit of collaboration portrayed in the film as not having visible fissures.[25] Accordingly, the documentary recounts how a new collaborative culture sprang from the encampment—a new *cultura del esfuerzo* (a culture based on hard work) opposed to the one fabricated during Francoism and transposed into the idea of the middle class in the democratic years. Clear examples of this resignified *cultura del esfuerzo* in *La plaza* lie in the testimonies of several participants who speak with joy of their long hours of non-stop work in the encampment. A young man in a hat declares: "I've been here since the second day [of the occupation]. I first worked twenty-seven hours straight. I thought that was my personal record, but then I managed to work forty-nine hours without a break; and they still have the nerve to call us *perroflautas*."[26] This type of work was another way to enact a new popular identity, one that unquestionably served the common good and was far removed from the individualistic efforts of self-betterment typical of the dominant neoliberal persona. It was a type of collaboration that generated an identity whose representative mechanisms were based on the projection of all-encompassing values, none of which could be externalized to the institutional space. This was a new experience of the common good that performed the radical opposition between the popular and the institutional spaces as inserted in the demand for real democracy. Accordingly, the means (i.e., the square and the participatory processes it implemented) became an end (i.e., real democracy) in the filmed performance of those values. In this sense, *La plaza* disregards the actualization of political demands and privileges the actualization of political space. *La plaza* acts as a representation of not only the struggle of the people *"in* space but also as a struggle *for* and *with* space, a struggle for the (re)appropriation of the skills, capacities and social capitals to organize it."[27] The mere act of establishing the encampment in the Puerta del Sol is an act of people's occupation that inherently visualizes an act of popular agency.

This is a performance that simultaneously unmasks the widespread popular demand for more democratic participation and masks the reality of the claim. The realness of the demand (a real democracy) resides in the act of demanding its realness, via the performance of a real democratic process, and not so much in the concreteness of what is demanded. Consequently, the square as a people's institution par excellence is emptied of the political specificity of democratic institutions outside the encampment because what matters is the lived experience shown in *La plaza*; the performance of real democratic participation overrides the realness of institutional participation. The implication is that only the 15-M's representation of the demos in the act of performing its own demotic essence (i.e., occupying and participating in a real democratic place) can be thought as genuinely democratic (i.e., one rid of the Francoist baggage that the Transición passed on to Spain's democratic system). In this sense, *La plaza* re-creates a people's place, where a popular performance (a people's masquerade) is staged, in which the medium (democratic participation) constitutes the end (the representation, the acting out, of a real demos). *La plaza* represents the performance of a demos authenticated in place, in the square, and "otherized" in the time spent outside of that democratic experience.

A New Time of Popular Reconstitution: The Filmic Dialogues of Portabella and Grueso

Pere Portabella's documentary filmmaking has been engaged in decoding the Spanish demos even before Spain had a democratically elected government. His film *Informe General II: El nuevo rapto de Europa* was produced between the 2011 emergence of the 15-M and the climax of the Catalan independence movement in the regional elections of 2015, which were thought to be tantamount to a popular referendum on the region's self-determination. A cinematic *retablo*, *Informe General II* shows how Spain's latest systemic crises—of its politics, economic model, and national representation as a (dis)united body—reflect a *pueblo* that is always awaiting its time at the center of history. Placing itself in historical dialogue with its own past, Portabella's *Informe General II* is a sequel of sorts to his 1976 *Informe General sobre algunas cuestiones de interés para una proyección pública* that explored the different political trajectories for the country in the wake of the long-awaited transition to democracy after Franco's death. Four decades later, *Informe General II* looked at the cycle of political mobilizations triggered by the 15-M movement as the opportunity to launch a new democratic trajectory, which "stages the *making-of* emerging political parties and citizen platforms" at the center of what could be a new democratic time.[28] To such an end, the film weaves together a series of "cuentas pendientes" (or "unfinished business," a coded expression referring to Spain's democratic transition as viewed from more radical or purist leftist circles) around how dissent has been unrepresented in Spanish history and, as such, opens the door to repoliticize and rerepresent the historical present (marked by the previously-alluded-to systemic crises).[29] The Catalan director bridges the time of the Transición with a new time of democratic transition inaugurated by the 15-M to visualize the principle of popular sovereignty, which has been readily forgotten by the political elites throughout the course of Spain's young democracy.

Allegorically, Portabella's film is the construction of a new mythical time for a new demos born in the 15-M that awaits a new moment of popular constitution. Political time masks historical time and gives way to a new mythology of the people, which would eventually substantiate the movement's claims to democratic realness. Thus, *Informe General II* begins by building on the mythical reference expressed in the subtitle: "el rapto de Europa," that is, the myth of the abduction of Europa by Zeus in the form of a white bull. Their forced mythological union is cinematically developed as a series of visual metaphors that foresee the remaking of a Spanish *pueblo*. Besides the topical connection between Spain and the image of the bull, Portabella's use of this myth points at the portrayal of a *pueblo* in the making (as Europa would later birth the Minotaur), after being *raptado* by Zeus-like elites in Spain as well as in Europe at large.[30] Conceptually, the film's subheading signifies beyond the symbolism of the myth itself. In Spanish, the polysemic word *rapto* can mean the act of seizing someone or something by force (as in kidnapping or abduction) as well as the experiencing of a mystical sense of unity, a rapture. Portabella's cinematic account incorporates both meanings, intertwining the two types of *raptos* in conceptual blocks, which are then woven together as one single structure. Accordingly, the film is divided in four sections: the first one on the 15-M, the second one on the irruption of Podemos, the third on the Catalan referendum of independence, and the last on the climate crisis. The four constitute an allegory of an expected moment of popular reconstitution, mediated by the visualization of *raptos*. Of all those *raptos*, the first one—the *rapto* of the people of the 15-M that takes place in the first part of the film—is here the most significant, as it visualizes the disruption that the 15-M supposed when it comes to representing a new *pueblo*. More concretely, the first part of the film is a negotiation of Portabella with his own cinematic time regarding the representation of popular authenticity. Portabella grapples with the filmic documentation of the 15-M as a historical moment vis-à-vis the antirepresentational nature of the movement and its construction of an ahistorical people (i.e., a demos consciously disjoined in history, which rejects the past and accepts its present only in relation to the future). The contention ultimately points to how to represent from the outside this radically new time of the 15-M that claims representation can occur only in the inside. Portabella starts dealing with the issue through the idea of representation as appropriation.

Informe General II begins its dramatic action in the Museo Nacional Centro de Arte Reina Sofía in Madrid. The museum embodies the act of seizure, which the film then treats as a type of vampiric repossession, already an important trope in Portabella's cinema.[31] The film opens with a wide shot of the museum. It is then that two consecutive superimposed labels appear at the bottom of the building: "Museo Nacional Centro de Arte Reina Sofía. Madrid" and "Edificio Sabatini (S.VIII)." The camera moves to the left, revealing the best-known building of the Museo Reina Sofía, and another label pops up, reading "Edificio Nouvel (S.XX)." In these first images, a new time is already proposed for the film's archetypal protagonist, the museum. In this new time, the past is conflated into the immediacy of the present and directly linked to a future of (vampiric) repossession. After a few moments, the viewer is presented with a paradigmatic example of this new time, represented by the symbolic vampirization and repossession of the Reina Sofía's board of trustees' room. The names of the board members slowly appear in speech balloons coming out of the switched-off microphones next to each of their empty seats. The viewer reads the trustees' names—from the honorary presidencies of the king and queen of Spain to the politicians, art professors, and renowned businesspeople, including César Alierta, owner of Telefónica; Ana Patricia Botín, chair of Santander Bank, and Isidro Fainé, chair of CaixaBank. At a discursive level, the litany of trustees becomes a clear commentary on well-known "matters related to the neoliberal co-optation of state-managed institutions, [as well as] the entrenched corruption amongst the political class."[32] At another, regarding Portabella's visualization of the new time inaugurated by the 15-M, the names are a reference to the past that will be discarded and reappropriated to make room for a future of unknown possibilities.

It is an allusion to a new time, in which grandiose icons and their political stories have no representative significance. The anonymity of the collective is represented instead. The representation of the collective requires a kaleidoscopic cinematic gaze that is inevitably reflective of its making-of essence.[33] Crucially, these characteristics in Portabella's film point to a political project that is in constant *mise en abyme*, as two cameras reflect on each other eternally. For instance, in the documentary's final minutes, the camera pans in and out on the manufacturing of transparent ballot boxes. This moment intentionally takes the viewer back to the beginning of the film, to the multirectangular composition of scenes after the opening credits. The closing and opening scenes of the film visually recall Manuel Castells's reference to the 15-M movement as a "network of networks" and to the vision of an ever-recurring cycle of a people's politics. The transparent ballot boxes then appear again (as in the beginning) fused with the film's own images of (by this point) past sequences in a way that directly references the editing process, whose cinematic nature is also anonymous (much like the voting process the ballot boxes allude to). The self-referential aspects of these images are connected with the constitution of a collective whose history is essentially anonymous and its time unknown.

Having that in mind, Portabella's film erects a new type of museum that quickly uses and forgets the past—like a vampire's discarded victim—to seize the present, marked by the force of the 15-M's collectivized anonymous identity, that would open the door to the collective ownership of the future. And directly linked to that metaphor of the museum's foundation, the first *rapto* takes place in the form of an exceptional moment of cinematic reappropriation. This *rapto* consciously diverts from Portabella's visual system of self-referencing, because what is to be revealed is a truly singular event of political authenticity; the raw material that makes the new mythical time Portabella's film is seizing on. When it is time in the first part of the film to show explicitly the events that took place during the 15-M, the Catalan auteur's cinematic gaze is turned off (at least, to the extent that the lens of his camera is literally switched off for this part of the film). Portabella's cinematic viewpoint is masked by the filmic representation of the people of the 15-M. That is when an extract of Stephane Grueso's documentary *15-M: Excelente. Revulsivo. Importante* is inserted. This is a first-person testimony by Grueso (a relatively unknown and much younger filmmaker) that makes all-encompassing historical sense of the 15-M, which directly opposes Portabella's overall style.

That sweeping, contextualizing testimony conceptualizes a *rapto* that is simultaneously a rapture and an abduction. The Catalan auteur appears to have discarded his own cinematic soul as an act of political admiration. Portabella temporarily mutes his gaze—and self-identifies as an outsider—to infuse representative life into an account of real democratic history as viewed from inside the movement. Grueso's account in Portabella's film presents a homodiegetic character (Grueso himself) whose main objective is to make the viewer understand his own life experience in and around what came before, during and after the 15-M. Grueso's story becomes the 15-M's history. In this sense, the 15-M is seen as inaugurating a new filmic time (which is at the heart of the 15-M's crafting of its own mythical time), informed by a logic of diegetic narration that favors the collectivization of stories and a more didactic exploration of political events. That logic is decisively counter to Portabella's cinematic production, confronting the Catalan director's preference for "antinarrative design of his cinema" (i.e., one that subsumes the coherent narration of filmic events under the display of suggestive imagery) and the subversion of "the institutional, diegetic temporal-spatial framework."[34] Contrary to those principles, in the represented-as-irrefutable testimony of the people of the 15-M during Grueso's account, the logic of narration takes exceptional precedence over the cinematic experience that could otherwise be re-created around the movement. Portabella's gaze has nothing to subvert when it comes to the movement's collectivizing logic and the simplified political discourse of the new emerging *pueblo* versus a past ruled by corrupt elites.

Suggestively, Grueso's filmed account of the 15-M movement is preceded by an image of a museum worker bringing out a stored painting: *Madrid desde Capitán Haya* (1987–1996), by the realist Spanish artist Antonio López. The iconic painting shows a view of the Spanish capital from above, filled with sunlight and crowded with buildings but devoid of people. Symbolically, the street from which the painter and viewer observe the city is named after the infamous air pilot Carlos de Haya, who fought and died in Franco's army during the Spanish Civil War. The camera slowly closes on the painting. The painted image of Madrid progressively fuses with its video-recorded counterpart. The scene then cross-fades to a panoramic view of the Puerta del Sol at dusk. The sound in this scene follows a similar path; the mechanical noise of the storage shelf that holds López's painting in the Reina Sofía fades into a strong, constant wind, as if the viewer were atop the building on Capitán Haya Street that oversees Madrid. As a siren sounds in the distance; the noises fuse with a roar of rhythmic clapping and repeated chants of "qué no, qué no nos representan" (they do not represent us). At this point, Portabella's *Informe*

General II converges with Grueso's *15-M: Excelente. Revulsivo. Importante* and the *rapto* as abduction is resignified as rapture in the form of admiration for the people in Grueso's film.

Stepping into Portabella's interpretation of Grueso's documentary, the former's representative machine is called into question and substituted by the latter's representation of the movement's antirepresentational stance. As such, the filmic transition from Portabella to Grueso is marked by the 15-M's chants: "¡Qué no, qué no nos representan!" The cinematic authority that Portabella himself represents has been vampirized. From the viewpoint of the prestigious auteur, the cinematic authority is transferred to the 15-M's "us" that Grueso is about to enact. Portabella's film does not attempt the act of representation and uses Grueso's filmed account, as he seems to consider Grueso an integral part of a new collective vision that shapes the new "us" birthed by the 15-M.[35] The introductory scene finishes emphasizing this interpretation as the narrator, Grueso himself, states: "[Acampada Sol era] toda una ciudad *autosuficiente*" (The Sol encampment became a *self-sustaining* city; my emphasis). Grueso's final words in Portabella's film constitute a new intergenerational dialogue typical of the 15-M. It is conversation about the chance of a lifetime to build a new time of political authenticity, characterized by a new "us" evoked in the earlier films—one that cannot be captured from above and outside, that needs to be observed from below and within. It is a self-sufficient "us" that does not need external representation because it is seeking self-representation. Accordingly, outside the fragments used by Portabella, by the end of *15-M: Excelente. Revulsivo. Importante*, the homodiegetic narration of Grueso evolves to the appropriation of the present and the shaping of the future, anticipated by Portabella's expected path of popular reconstitution.

Over its duration, Grueso's film progresses from an initial, somewhat neutral characterization of the encampments as "la gente del 15-M" (the people of 15-M) or "la gente corriente" (the common folk) to the more explicitly confrontational idea of the 99 percent versus the 1 percent. The *percent* terminology is here important because it was never really popularized in the Spanish political context. Its usage is more reflective of the intensified antagonistic characteristics with which Spanish politics were imbued after the 15-M. In this sense, Grueso is returning to Serrano Azcona's view of the *pueblo* as conflictual in essence. The difference here is that Grueso characterizes conflict as a matter of time or, more precisely, as the inauguration of a new time. Accordingly, a looming on-screen question finishes the film: "¿Y ahora qué hacemos?" (And now what shall we do?).[36] As a preliminary answer, a rapid succession of images directs the viewer's attention to the disastrous effects of the economic crisis on the average Spaniard (e.g., foreclosures, rampant unemployment, child malnourishment). The screen fades to black, and a statement pops up: "Hay un país donde ya estamos parando deshaucios, perdiendo el miedo, creando la República del 99%" (We are creating a new country where we are stopping foreclosures and losing our fear: the Republic of the 99%).[37] A new sequence of images, now of protesters, appears. Epic music fuses with progressively louder chants of "estas son nuestras armas" (which refers to the slogan "our hands are our only weapons"), and several other images of confrontations with the police are shown.[38] The scene ends with a defiant declaration: "Hemos declarado al gobierno irrelevante. El mundo está cambiando y lo estás cambiando tú" (We have declared the government irrelevant. The world is changing, and you are driving the change).[39] Perhaps jarringly, a final statement appears indicating that the last few minutes of the documentary are in fact a cinematic "occupation" unrelated to the film producers' intentions.

Beyond the ironic pose that such takeover could elicit, a distinctive element in this last part separates it from the spirit of all the previously documented events of the 15-M in the film. Occupation, direct action, and the inevitable violence carried with them are at center stage. They are the precursor of a new time that has substituted *la gente*, *el pueblo*, or *la ciudadanía indignada* for the people of the 99 percent. If only symbolically, these people are occupying public spaces, creating a republic; they have "weapons" and are proscribing the government. In a context still dominated by the murderous history of Francoism, the film's final declaration undoubtedly engages the collective imagination of Spaniards with visions of a ghostly past. That is, any call to confront the government and establish a republic (never mind a people's republic) in one way or another can surely bring memories of Spain's seemingly everlasting wounds from the Civil War. Nonetheless, Grueso's proposed visualization of the 99 percent at the end of its film uncovers an impending desire to forget Spain's past, as if to disjoin the 15-M from history. The conflictual essence of this visuality acts like a mask that can be used to perform a new *pueblo* that requires a new temporality, one that favors the abstraction of conflict separate from both practice and history, continuously deferred into to the future (i.e., into the realm of political hope). In an attempt to fast-forward a democratic tabula rasa, Spain's past of violence is necessarily forgotten in the creation of a new mythical time, a new origin story, mediated by film.

Conclusion

Beyond showing how the 15-M constructed its collective essence through populist visualities of an "us" people against a "them" elites, this chapter has shown that the 15-M needs to be also understood as the performance of that essence, as a masquerade of popular authenticity. That is, the *indignados* theatricalized a collective character that was speaking for the great majority of Spaniards while, at the same time, as indicated by the landslide electoral win of Mariano Rajoy's right-wing Popular Party (which frontally opposed the movement), a significant portion of the Spanish people could be said to oppose the very premise that performance was based on. Documentary filmmaking was best positioned to visualize that tension between Spain's real politics of the government and the 15M's demands for "real" democratic representation within the "real" political system of the people.

The films analyzed in this chapter showed the clash between those two different realities. Concretely, they were witness to how the 15-M constructed a place of radical democratic inclusion for the advent of a new time in Spanish democracy that opposed any political truth coming from the outside (i.e., coming from outside the people themselves, whatever "the people" may be). Ultimately, these films were cultural mediators between the visualization of the movement's political performance of democracy as the most democratically authentic and the outside pressure of institutional politics claiming to be the sole democratic representative of the Spanish demos. More importantly, they hinted at how those confronted views of Spain's democratic reality anticipated the acceleration of the political cycle in the following few years, given that the political establishment kept dismissing the theater of indignation seen throughout the 15-M's occupation of the squares as unsubstantial performances of (unreasonable) protest—which would quickly prove a real threat when people's discontent was growing only larger until the point of no return. Moreover, these films revealed a new confrontation that could be concretely located (in the squares, against specific political and economic institutions), generating a very particular and effective indignation, but one that was historically shortsighted (more influenced by the global framework provided by the crisis and the dystopian immediacy product of neoliberal capitalism). The 15-M could be understood in that way as a (filmed) rehearsal of what "we" can be in the future in spite of Spain's historical ominous baggage. A cinematic practice through which the *indignados* were Spanish democracy's new protagonists, performing the strategical substitution of Spanish history and its ever-haunting Francoist past as the source of all political and economic malaises for the transversal but ahistorical fight of the 99 percent.

In the end, the identitarian masks in this people's theatricalization of democracy were not makers of democratic realness. They were devices of performance that represented whatever real democracy may be—regardless of its actual democratic essence. Yet their performative essence did not preclude the enactment of real democracy to be any less politically relevant than so-called real politics (i.e., institutional or party politics). These performances were conduits of a collective political anger that, after the *acampadas* were dismantled, would forcefully push Spanish democracy to see its democratic shortcomings. What is more, as the next chapter develops, the sustained visualization of that anger was so effective that it created an audiovisual national culture of the people that, for a few moments, threatened the status quo with the materialization of popular outrage into populist rebellion. The threat was credible enough that it triggered arguably the biggest upset in the entire history of Spanish democracy when, in a matter of months, a completely new party like Podemos kicked the door open for the increasingly enraged "spirit" of the 15-M to enter the tight-sealed halls of Spain's parliamentary politics.

3

People's Bad Manners

Seeing Populist Antagonism in Cinema after the 15-M

After the 15-M retreated from the squares, the people in those squares did not simply disappear from public life: "nos mudamos a tu conciencia" (we are moving to your consciousness), as the slogan went. But that also meant that the movement's most visible demand of overhauling the Spanish democratic system lost its most immediate point of reference. As the people and their anger were seen dispersed across multiple nodal points, that demand for a "real democracy now," as an empty signifier, was left visually anchorless. The number of demonstrations and protest actions grew exponentially from 2012 to 2014, but the presentation of political conflict was compartmentalized according to specific goals within specific battles in different spaces (material and symbolic). This was an aesthetic break in the presentation of the 15-M's populism, which did not mean the force of the populist bid had somehow receded. Far from it: people's outrage had considerably expanded.[1] Discontent was being channeled by different organizations with more concrete goals, such as the antieviction group Plataforma de Afectados por la Hipoteca and antiausterity activists of the *mareas*, all with the same diagnostic: the democratic system not only was not working but also seemed to be actively working against the demos.

Populism's stylistic features would morph away from the images of the *acampadas*, which had been characterized by a constructive democratic ethos (e.g., regarding the construction of a new demos in the act of *tomando la palabra*, in the act of acquiring a political voice in the square, along with a cultural one in its visual manifestations and filmic documentation). The visual representations of the demos would be soon informed by an increasingly antagonistic pathos characteristic of populist affectivity.[2] The change of style did not reflect a change of political substance, whereby political rationality could have been clouded by strong feelings of popular animosity. What really changed was the intensification of the populist cycle as well as a shift in the 15-M's affective politics' visual center. The analogical correspondence between the material expression of the people (in the 15-M's protest camps) and its visualization (in slogans, documentaries, and iconic images) changed to a symbolic relationship, best encapsulated visually by a new cinematic impulse to represent the crisis and its victims as "the people." Politically, antagonism was at that stage the most visible strategy of populist identification, building an "emotional habitus" that would "authorize specific feelings and actions as fitting or necessary in response to shared challenges."[3] It was an antagonistic logic: "us," victims of the crisis, versus "them," the elite responsible for the crisis. And this logic was not only at the political forefront determining "affective registers of populist discourse"; it would also be at the cultural audiovisual center.[4]

With that in mind, this chapter looks for images of populist antagonism and "bad manners" in three films that reached much popular success relative to their very limited budgets: Isaki Lacuesta's *Murieron por encima de sus posibilidades* (2014) and Paco León's *Carmina o revienta* (2012), as well as its sequel *Carmina y amén* (2014). These films enjoyed popularity in terms of both number of viewers and the very familiar faces that appeared in them. They also further expanded on and dug more deeply into a thematic thread typical of many other films of the time: different expressions of violence, from verbal abuse to explicit torture, could be seen as constituting the people's populist "bad manners" against the system. The films are analyzed through two interrelated ways of presenting violence. Visual signs of systemic violence are considered proof that the "system" had turned against the people, and in contrast, those signs are examined vis-à-vis visualizations of people inflicting or threatening the infliction of symbolic violence on agents of that "system." The selected films also were made within the two years immediately after the dismantling of the 15-M encampments. The choice of this temporal restriction is equally important because those two years signal the climax of a populist sentiment that was decentralized, somewhat unguided, and visually unrestrained, without a clear established referent. This is an opportunity to dwell on (re)presentations of the people "uncontaminated" by curated strategies of populist leaderships, such as the one enacted by Pablo Iglesias and Podemos after 2014 (see Chapter 4).

A Note on Populist Antagonism and Bad Manners in Crisis Cinema after the 15-M

At the height of the crisis, precarity went hand in hand with antagonism. And the two were exacerbated with the election of Mariano Rajoy soon after the 15-M occupied squares across Spain. In impromptu televised appearances and in staged parliamentary speeches, Rajoy's Popular Party not only discursively minimized the extent and depth of precarity suffered by many Spaniards; his government also incremented the material pain of the Spanish citizenry by doubling down on the unpopular austerity-led recovery out of the crisis. The dire suffering of those hit hardest by the crisis couldn't be decoupled from a general sentiment of anger against a system and its representatives that, to add insult to injury, were shamelessly telling the population that "Spaniards had lived above their means"—as the minister of employment and social security, Fátima Báñez, put it during the first months of Rajoy's government in 2012.[5] By that time, the flames of popular outrage ignited during the 15-M were being recklessly fanned by a new government that seemed to have lost touch with ordinary reality. In retrospect, it looked as if those in power had built a fictional reality that blocked them from seeing civil society's most visible demand at the time: the need for a *real* democracy.

When the minister of education, José Ignacio Wert, implemented a series of radical cuts to state investment in the arts and sharply increased the value-added tax on tickets to cultural events, the cultural industry was almost deliberately incited by the government to match civil society's political anger. And so the cultural responses to the crisis became inevitably tied to popular reality. People's political outrage appeared as representationally unavoidable not only in a strictly political sense but also in culture, when making a new film, writing a novel, or thinking of a new television product.[6] As Nuria Triana-Toribio argues, "the crisis became unavoidable" as popular frustration permeated everything and "changed cultural agendas gradually" and, intentionally or not, forced mainstream culture to deal with the increasing anger and crisis-induced pain of the population.[7] The response of the Spanish film industry was in that respect one of the most visible examples of the explicit coalescence of political and cultural sensibilities. Spanish cinema thus entered into a "crisis mode" that had become very much attuned to its viewers' crisis on the other side of the screen.[8] In line with that change of perspective, myriad (specially) independent films started to portray the "victims of the crisis directly" and, more importantly, to devise a visual narrative that had those victims gaining "some kind of revenge even in their misery."[9]

That was a cultural animus of people's vengeance most clearly visualized by what Dean Albritton had called "Spanish crisis cinema."[10] These were a series of films by both new and established directors who turned their camera lenses to representations of lives in crisis. This cinematic enterprise "need not necessarily focus directly on the crisis or its effects, but often touches them tangentially or metaphorically, imbued with the temporalities, subjectivities, and relational networks instantiated by the crisis mode. This emerging cinematic field is striking for its unifying emphasis on different kinds of suffering."[11] Accordingly, the crisis cinema this chapter focuses on has to do with the filmic representation of victims of the crisis who attempt to liberate themselves from their own victimhood through acts of vengeance.[12] These are films that implemented a cinematic language of plebeian retribution directly connecting with people's excess of frustration. In the context of the crisis, they tended to speak about people's precarity away from condescending discourses of victimhood, through explicit representations of popular anger and with a conscious lack of decorum. On the screen, collective grievances were given free rein through the visualization of (violent) revenge by underdogs with nothing to lose, which allowed for a type of emotional catharsis focused on the symbolic suffering of the elite. What could have simply passed as a moment of cultural representation typical of the years after political conflict and square occupations was instead evidence of a populist impetus; cinema ostensibly aligned the visualization of political violence with the context of political dissatisfaction and, generally speaking, framed it within tropes of the people's justice.

Many of the characters in film would be signified by a type of populist antagonism that was not simply violent. Their violence would be more subtly informed by a lack of desire to appear "good" or anything resembling model citizens. Critically, these characters above all else appeared as "normal" people, who in the context of the crisis could be anything but well mannered. In politics, such an impulse had been most famously conceptualized by Benjamin Moffit and Simon Tormey as a populist style of bad manners.[13] Part of their argument centered on how populists—apart from speaking in the name of the people and simplifying the political battlefield between "us" and "them"—would style themselves as bad-mannered, tell-it-like-it-is ordinary individuals with a "disregard for 'appropriate' ways of acting in the political realm."[14] Fictional characters on the screen would make all type of audiences identify with those at the bottom, creating a symbolic alliance with stereotypical representations of the culturally "low" by means of "use of slang, swearing, political incorrectness and being overly demonstrative and 'colorful,' as opposed to the 'high' behaviors of rigidness, rationality, composure and technocratic language."[15]

To analyze populism's discourse of bad manners, the applied linguist Argyro Kantara has drawn on the idea of conversational violence, which can be defined as discursive strategy based on personal attacks that otherize and diminish the overall integrity of the other side, the "them" in the equation of populism.[16] This type of verbal aggression stems from populism's antagonistic principles and reinforces whatever frontiers are established in populist discourse—for example, the authentic people of Spain's real democracy versus the cunning elites of the Spanish undemocratic system. Accordingly, traditional cinematic representations of the popular as vulgar acquired a new, effectively populist dimension through bad-mannered characters fighting the system or their systemic state of crisis. What is more, bad manners in culture opened the door to reconceptualize violence in politics. In terms of visualizing systemic invisible violence, the cultural was acknowledging publicly what the institutionally political refused to even admit as real; at the same time, the schism between the politics of culture and political institutions in the recognition and visualization of the many types of sufferings caused by the crisis subsequently provoked the need to at minimum see the political system suffer at the symbolic hand of the people.

Films representing lives in crisis connected with wider audiences through genres associated with popular culture: melodrama, slasher horror, slapstick comedy. And that was another symptom of their popular-populist cinematic ambition (i.e., as a cinema of "the people"). They were cultural artifacts without clear auteuristic impetus, the effect of which somehow muddled the clarity of the film's message. They otherwise dealt head-on with people's violent tendencies as an expected, even natural way of responding to the moment of crisis. The importance of this change in (re)presentation cannot be overstated: to that point, cultural products that aspired to stay within the boundaries of acceptability had seriously limited the legitimacy of political violence on-screen. Terrorism had left scars when it came to dealing with representations of violence in Spanish contemporary politics.[17] At the peak of the crisis, those boundaries had significantly expanded to include films in which characters representing the rich and powerful were harmed without remorse and even tortured as part of their symbolic punishment in a collective act of cathartic popular vengeance.

Conceptually speaking, popular vengeance, whether symbolic or material, is at the root of how political antagonism can foster social change. When stripped of discursive layers (of narration and ultimately of official history), the constitution of the popular resides in the ability to forcefully visualize, to impose the sight of potential violence as a form of secular power. The origins of modern sovereignty, intrinsic to the idea of popular constitution, are found "in the *internal* constitution of sovereign power within states through the exercise of violence over bodies and populations."[18] In the context of Spain, the legitimacy of the repression coming from the state against the body politic was not merely questioned (as it was by the 15-M) but also visualized as possibly shifting in its course—shifting from the people against the state rulers, from YouTube videos and alternative film to mainstream cinema. The political cycle inevitably accelerated. Visual metaphors threatening plebeian retribution on the screen culturally guided institutionalized political change in (attempting) the reconception of popular sovereignty.

Those metaphorical visions in fact have a long tradition in Spanish history. They go back as far as the *pueblo* imagined in Lope de Vega's *Fuenteovejuna*. This early seventeenth-century play narrated the killing of the royal *comendador* in the small Andalusian town of Fuenteovejuna. After being repeatedly tortured by the authorities in search of a culprit, the townspeople famously maintained that "Fuenteovejuna lo hizo" ([The people of] Fuenteovejuna did it). With its depiction of collective refusal to blame a particular individual, the play became a well-known allegory of popular power. Not surprisingly, as Matthew Feinberg recounts, several performances of the play were prominent in the days after 15-M, and the staging of its violence "remains consistent across interpretations and adaptations."[19] Fueled by the unremitting pernicious effects of the financial crisis, as well as the ever-growing sense of impunity among those pulling the levers of Spanish capitalism, the calls for wider political representation (which often implied a structural overhaul of democracy) as well as the representation of those popular calls gradually acquired a more bellicose tone. The many films that evoked people's vengeance amount to a cultural signal of the acceleration of the political cycle. These films were a development of what was previously referred to as "Spanish crisis cinema," which confronted the distressing reality of the crisis but fundamentally were films that "attempt[ed] to organize the individual experience of precarity and vulnerability into a communal one."[20] And in the case of the films analyzed in the next sections, violence and vengeance provided that communal experience for their viewership, which in turn laid the cultural ground for an imminent political change with the advent of the Podemos phenomenon.

Austerity Kills (Them): Systemic Violence and *Esperpento* in Isaki Lacuesta's *Murieron por encima de sus posibilidades*

Visually, from satirical magazines such as *El Jueves*, as in the issues of January and March 2012, Mariano Rajoy is depicted bleeding while he asks for "más recortes" (more cuts) or holding a chainsaw along with the headline "40 billiones de euros de recortes" (40 billion euros of austerity cuts) to signs directly denouncing that "austerity kills" repeatedly seen in myriad protests (fig. 3.1), the representation of systemic violence took many forms during those years after the 15-M's encampments vanished from public sight.[21] There were mainstream films such as *La chispa de la vida* (2012), directed by Álex de la Iglesia, in which a recently unemployed advertising executive resorts to monetizing his own accidental impalement to secure his wife's and children's future; this made him into a martyr of the crisis and eventually a popular hero. Although less mainstream than De la Iglesia's filmography, Max Lemcke's *5 metros cuadrados* (2012) also reflected the violence of the "system" on people's dreams of dignified life: the two protagonists (celebrity actors Fernando Tejero and Malena Alterio) enter a spiral of violence when fighting a corrupt developer who refuses to compensate them after knowingly selling the couple a defective, half-finished apartment unit. The similar cinematic production of Ignacio Estaregui's *Justi y Cía* (2014) combined a low budget with very recognizable talent in front of the camera: the late Álex Angulo and the more recent star of the Netflix blockbuster series *La casa de papel*, Hovik Keuchkerian. The film narrates the plan of two unemployed miners to find and kill a corrupt businessman in the industry; it ends with the two leads acclaimed by multitudes in a secret journey of popular retribution against all corrupt elites across Spain.

Promoting analogous themes in the domain of "alternative" or independent cinema, new independent production companies appeared. Mundo Ficción created the hugely successful film *El mundo es nuestro* (2012), in which a couple of downtrodden, lumpen-like petty criminals devise a bank robbery and adopt a telling motto—"Ante el terrorismo financiero, expropiación

Figure 3.1. Sign seen in a Seville demonstration in commemoration of the 15-M's first anniversary: "Los recortes matan" (Austerity cuts kill). A version of this slogan, "Austerity kills," was the catchphrase announced in the poster for the demonstration against austerity across Europe on June 1, 2013. Photograph taken on May 12, 2012, by Ana Rey, https://www.flickr.com/photos/anarey/7187465820.

bancaria" (In the face of financial terrorism, bank expropriation [is the solution])—only to find out that a small business owner, cheated by the bank they are about to rob, has entered the bank ready to immolate himself unless the economic situation (in general) was solved. In the online sphere, the combative but short-lived company Insolentes Bastardos managed to get more than twenty thousand views with its first short film, titled *Bastille: La r-evolución ha comenzado* (Bastille: The e-revolution has begun; 2012), which depicted a violent mob of outraged citizens about take over the secluded location where the symbolic representation of country's elites went into hiding.

Despite following a rather despairing thematic blueprint, all these audiovisual products were reasonably popular. In a context informed by the violent consequences of the economic crisis, physical violence not only was represented as inevitable but, at a more literal level of interpretation, also was offered as the only solution to deal with the crisis—and not so much as a way out of it. Whether the violence was exerted on the people or was coming from the people, if one stayed within the analogical boundaries of their cinematic plots, the prospect presented was altogether bleak, as none of the films proposed an explicit "revolutionary" path against the elites and out of the crisis—contrary, for instance, to trends in the 1960s and 1970s within the neorealist Nuevo Cine Español, or New Spanish Cinema, linked to Carlos Saura, Basilio Martín Patino, Mario Camus, Manuel Summers, and the like.[22] With that in mind, how could one surmise from the so-called crisis cinema after the 15-M that any type of popular revenge or popular retribution implied the acquisition of political agency?

The answer lies in the reinterpretation of violence beyond its analogical referencing to materializations off the screen. To such end, the tradition of the *esperpento* epitomized by Ramón del Valle-Inclán at the turn of the twentieth century offers an interpretative framework through which one can reread the symbolic violence of the crisis. The first impulse is to see obvious despairs in the situation and regard those lives in crisis from a nihilistic angle, as people passively destroyed by their dire circumstances or actively participating in their own destruction as a symbolic last resort to a terroristic solution of sorts. To the contrary, the *esperpento* was "characterized by the grotesque distortion of reality, with an intent of a critique of society."[23] In that way, the depiction of violent realities in crisis is a mirror that laughs at the political absurdity of that violence. The critique then is conveyed by a conscious break in the referentiality between the symbolic, as represented in fiction, and the real, in its allusion to some political background (in the broadest of senses).

Concretely, given the break of referentiality that the aesthetic force of the *esperpento* granted, the act of killing or being killed, hurting or being hurt on-screen, would be poised to generate a message unburdened by the weight of Spanish history (from the Spanish Civil War and Francoism to terrorism in the democratic era and the so-called austericide after 2008). The *esperpento* shown in this set of films allowed for new type of political representation to be imagined.[24] Recalling Valle-Inclán's metaphor of the concave and convex mirrors in "el callejón de Gato," the blind protagonist of *Luces de Bohemia*—Max Estrella—can see "el sentido trágico de la vida española" (the tragic sense of Spanish life). Filmic representation aligned with Max Estrella's conception of the *esperpento*: "Spain is a grotesque deformity of European civilization. In a concave mirror, the most beautiful image looks absurd. Let's then express such a deformed absurdity by looking in the same mirror that deforms our faces and reflects the deformity of the misery that is Spain.)"[25] On the cinema screen, reality was equally being deformed by the crisis. "Esperpentically," the allusion to violence in films pointed at a deformed reality, whose features *esperpénticos* revealed the paradoxical nature of Spanish democracy after the 15-M. Because, despite the total absurdity of invoking change through political violence in the context of Spanish politics, given the country's bloodstained history, the only demands that were taken absurdly seriously—to an absurd degree—were those that entertained the idea of violence.

More than a hundred years after Valle-Inclán, Isaki Lacuesta momentarily abandoned his cinematic status as auteur to create a consciously popular dark comedy in *Murieron por encima de sus posibilidades* (2014), which addresses head-on the need to entertain violence in the face of the violent behavior of the "system." *Murieron* is of special importance because it shows how the politics of the time spoke to the need for a change of cultural sensibility. In that film, auteurs such as Lacuesta felt compelled to take a chance on appealing to mainstream audiences with the objective of, at least, expanding the political dialogue. *Murieron* was the Spanish filmmaker's fully fledged attempt to engage in dialogue with the mainstream "in the tradition of 1950s Spanish comedy associated with filmmakers such as Luis García Berlanga and Marco Ferreri."[26] That's why it was taken as paradigmatic of the inescapable cultural impetus to deal with explicitly political representations of the crisis. Lacuesta's film was particularly significant because those representations were not metaphorically oblique, left to different possible interpretations more typical of the filmmaker's experimental "collage approach" to cinema.[27] Far from it. Lacuesta's representation of political violence in *Murieron* is as explicit and direct as it could get. *Murieron* is was one of the best representative films of how grotesque or esperpentic systemic violence at the time proposed a type of populist antagonism to empower Spain's crisis-ridden audiences, if only culturally.

The film tells the surreal unfolding of the vengeful scheme to kidnap and torture the chairman of the central bank, who stereotypically held the most power in a Spain at the peak of the crisis. The plot is ideated by five men interned in a mental asylum for their violent psychotic tendencies, which are explained and openly justified as a direct consequence of the crisis. Following Max Estrella's idea of the *esperpento* at its most literal sense, the characters in the film proceed to physically deform all those in charge of Spain's deformed reality. The most visibly sadistic scenes result from the encounter with fictional members of the Spanish government in the last part of the film. By staying within the tradition of the *esperpento*, *Murieron* encapsulates its notion of political change through an intense dark humor that arguably escapes nihilistic despair. The film is a further exploration of the connection between the economic crisis and the illogical cycle of violence it provoked. It proposes a response to the crisis as violent as it is absurd. Political representation is taken to its most farcical limits, the implication being that a twisted regime can be represented only by physically mangled representatives. Whereas from an analogical reading the film can be said to alienate politically its potential audience through the hyperbolic use of violence tout court, from the angle of the *esperpento*, it can be argued that viewers are in reality pushed to see themselves mirrored in the deformed images of comic relief that very same violence produced. What follows is an analysis of the most important scenes in which deformity is esperpentically represented as a way to reinterpret systemic violence.

By the end of *Murieron*, after breaking from the mental institution where they are held, the five men find the hideaway where Spanish elites regularly meet to enjoy long nights of debauchery in secret. These closing scenes are reminiscent of Luis Buñuel's *El ángel exterminador* (1962), and although a sustained comparison of both films would not hold water, correlating certain scenes can be telling in terms of class representation (which was essential to Lacuesta's conceptualization of violence). Buñuel's film was inspired by Géricault's painting *The Raft of Medusa*, depicting the moments of crazed starvation and cannibalism after the historical wreck of the frigate *Méduse*. Fittingly, the final moments of *Murieron* are set underneath a fishing boat, where guests can hide their overindulgence literally underwater, as in a metaphorical shipwreck. The exclusive patrons are depicted as morally starved and even practice a sort of class cannibalism, as they are seen feasting on food placed on the naked bodies of men and women lying down as human decor. Evoking Buñuel's main plot in *El ángel*, the guests are oblivious to the dangers above. Even when the five men dressed in panda costumes and armed to the teeth crash into their submarine party, everyone remains unmoved. Nonetheless, a social (ship)wreck is in the making that will mirror the collapse of Spanish society already on the surface. Those in the underwater celebration are about to experience the breakdown of their privileged society's rules at the hands of the least privileged.

Unlike Buñuel's film, *Murieron* is purposefully explicit in the visualization of the invisible, never-explained disruption of the upper classes and their class-based disdain. However, there is specially one scene in *El ángel*—when during the first gathering at Nobile's mansion a group of women exchange impressions about the derailment of the Niza express—that is highly suggestive when compared to Lacuesta's archetypal representations. In that scene in *El ángel*, two women refer to the passengers of the third-class wagons who died in the Niza train wreck in this way:

> Ana: I must be insensitive because I wasn't moved by those poor people's pain.
> Rita: I think *the people*, the lower classes, is less sensitive to pain. Have you ever seen a wounded bull? Impassive![28]

The five men in Lacuesta's film are the cinematic reverse of that conversation. They are the reflection of Rita's bull analogy on the convex and concave mirrors of *Luces de Bohemia*: they are the mirror image of an *esperpento* that, instead of the pitiful sight of the wounded bull, reflects five men suited in the artificial animal skin of their ridiculous panda costumes, with deadly assault rifles in place of horns, about to disrupt the world enjoyed by the likes of Rita and Ana.

Murieron esperpentically reflects the cruel words of the women in *El ángel* when, in another scene, Albert (Albert Pla's character) delivers a rambling tirade at the start of the group's eventual plot to break into the party boat where Spanish elites are being secretively regaled. Albert's monologue is worth quoting at length:

> I want to enter a bank, and I want to steal all the money, and I want that the bank employees try to stop me so I can kill them all. And I want the clients in the bank to say to me: "Very well done, kid! We should have done the same thing a long time ago." And before I make my big escape, I'd go to the Congress or the Senate or Parliament House, whatever the fuck, I don't care. I'd come in guns blazing, scaring the shit out of their cunt faces, like a true bad boy; politician that moves . . . *Pop! Pop! Pop! Pop!* And people would shout: Bravo! Bravo! Bravo! I know everyone would be ecstatic. I'd be their hero. Finally . . . oh, what do we have here? It is the Justice Hall. Let's kill a couple of judges. But for these ones, I'm not using a gun. I'm using my fists to beat them to death. That's what I call divine justice. And by then everybody would be elated, screaming: "There goes our avenger! Keep up the good work!" And as I pass by the offices of four transnational corporations, you can guess which ones . . . Hey! Unlike them, I won't speculate! I'll kill everyone in there. Then I'll kidnap the hotshot president of a hotshot bank. And I'll make him suffer. I'll torture him. And at that moment everyone will say: "He is mad, but he's been so nice to us. We love him after all."[29]

Despite the natural temptation to interpret the vindictive harangue within the tropes of (working-)class revenge, the wider role of the character points to a different meaning. In fact, the character's last words already signal an interpretation that links political solidarity and death with the absurd and the grotesque.

Albert is the only character who ended up in the asylum for a reason other than an act of vengeance. Instead, his origin story is rooted in love, care, and solidarity, though tainted with darkness. The story begins when his ex-girlfriend Ana (Emma Suárez) was diagnosed with an undisclosed fatal disease but, due to the cuts in health care after the crisis, cannot receive proper treatment. Despite Albert's readiness to go above and beyond for her, she is medically discarded. As they learn there was no cure, he resorts to constantly caring for her even though Ana's pain is unremitting. Their breaking point comes in her last days when, to add insult to injury, Ana tells Albert that a doctor with a group of his students came to visit her and molested her while practicing a rectal examination, which was, on top of it all, unrelated to her convalescence. At this point, Albert can't stop crying. Unexpectedly, after hearing her story, he says: "Estás como una cabra. ¿Estas son las cosas que te da por imaginar?" (You must be as nutty as fruitcake. This is the type of stuff you like to imagine?)."[30] More shockingly, Ana replies with amusement, "Que no es imaginada; le pasó a una señora el otro día que estaba en el quiró-fano" (It is not imagined; it happened to a lady the other day when I was in the operating room).[31] As they kiss, Ana stops abruptly to remind Albert of the promise he made to terminate her life.

Immediately in the next scene, while Ana peacefully sleeps, Albert throws her out of the hospital window. The somber absurdity of the scene connects to her death but is also noticeably tied to a solidarity impulse in both Ana and Albert. The link is metaphorically exemplified, on the one hand, by Ana's made-up story of sexual abuse—which, under the parameters of the *esperpento*, unites reality and absurdity with striking darkness to denounce a vulnerable situation that many other women recognize. On the other hand, the scene is esperpentically closed by Albert's choice to sacrifice his life of relative material comfort to express his love for Ana in public by fulfilling his fatal promise inside the publicly owned space of the hospital.

The publicness of the assisted suicide is quite relevant, as one can easily imagine how Ana's life might have been terminated in a more private setting, in a less flamboyant manner, in an attempt to avoid attention as well as legal repercussions. As a public sacrifice, Ana's death emphasizes the importance of the hospital as a public good that has also been sacrificed in the realignment of priorities after the crisis. It is, then, no coincidence that the hospital where the scene unfolds is papered with signs and slogans against austerity measures in health care. At one point, a sign comes into view, reading "los recortes matan" (austerity kills), which foreshadows and informs Ana's death. Ingrained in the couple's love-death relationship is a general protest against the cuts in the Spanish universal health-care system that is grotesquely visualized as the scene advances. In the end, these characters' lives are both sacrificed as part of a cinematic political ritual that reveals to the viewer how their private lives are closely ruled by malformed public governance. In the context of the Spanish crisis, the two—Ana and Albert, private and public— are thus esperpentically connected, as in a concave heterotopia of mirrors.

Lacuesta's *esperpento* in this film can be compared (albeit obliquely) to the once-common Marxist analysis of *El ángel exterminador*, now mostly abandoned within Buñuel criticism, which almost imposes an act of working-class contrition when viewing the latter's film.[32] In that way, Buñuel's stated disavowal of *El ángel* as a manifesto against the upper classes echoes Albert's rambling words and actions against the system in that both similarly resist a clear class-based interpretation (especially when considering the key role that madness and surrealism play in the films). Following Marc Ripley's reading of *El ángel*, Albert's diatribes in *Murieron* are better understood as the starting point of a quest for self-representation that, in an evocative parallel to Buñuel's proposal in *El ángel*, is "grounded in the negative mode, actively seeking discomfort, disorientation and disillusion both on and off-screen."[33] To that end, the most discomfort, disorientation, and disillusion peak and all take place together during the torture of the three government ministers at the end of Lacuesta's film.

The three politicians are first seen on the screen mindlessly counting money while the president of the Central Bank is relaxing in a spa in an adjacent fortified room. That tableau makes the hierarchy of power apparent, although the three representatives do not know how to handle their impending doom when the armed "pandas" barge into the scene. Unable to find a solution, they constantly resort to political jargon and inherently flawed reasoning. In the role of one the ministers, the actor Imanol Arias presents his unilateral resignation as way out of his kidnapping: "Mira joven yo puedo marcharme ya porque acabo de dimitir" (Look, young man, I can leave now because I just resigned).[34] In another instance, the character played by Luis Tosar phones someone in the cabinet of ministers and starts an illustrative one-sided conversation: "No, mira tienes que solucionarme esto ya. No, ya es ya. No hace falta reunir a nadie. [. . .] ¡Qué! ¡Qué estáis votando! ¡Qué coño estáis votando cretinos! [. . .] Fernando no te despidas de mí. Fernando no tolero que te estés despidiendo de mí" (Look, you have to help me with this issue now. Immediately. There's no need for a meeting. What! That you are voting! Voting on what? You bunch of idiots!).[35] As no solution can be found, the three representatives are given the impossible choice of "recortar o ser recortados" (a play on words on austerity cuts: "to cut or to be cut").[36] Mirroring the hopeless future procured by the government's austerity measures, the three have to choose which parts of their bodies to dismember until they reach the (neoliberal) "optimal" percentage of mutilation that will secure their release. They are also given the option of foisting the burden of mutilation onto just one of them—that is, literally *recortar* or be *recortado*. Following the archetypal representation of the unscrupulous politician, two of the ministers rapidly conspire against the third and proceed to maim him on-screen. The scene is brutally gory.

The three ministers are played by some of the best-known faces in the Spanish film industry. However, these are not main characters or protagonist roles. They are introduced only for a few minutes at the end of the film, as stunt-casting cameos. When the viewers see the gratuitous torture of Imanol Arias at the hands of Carmen Machi and Luis Tosar, they are not seeing their dramatis personae. For a viewer, their off-screen celebrity status, confronted with the sudden violence of their actions on-screen, produces laughter. A process of identification takes place that imbues sadism with comic relief. The close-up shots of their blood-soaked faces along with the clownish background music contribute to the viewers' suspension of disbelief, the division between the on- and off-screen spheres temporally eliminated as one laughs more at the actual actors' absurd situation than at the characters' dramatic action. In this scene, Lacuesta orchestrates an *esperpento* that takes aim at the process of representation at multiple levels. At one level, the chain of fictional representation is broken. For a moment, the actors represent themselves instead of their assigned roles. On another level, they are playing government representatives who are literally and metaphorically incapable of representing anyone (i.e., they are already corrupt politicians out of step with their constituents who have now taken their corrupt nature to the extreme by dismembering a colleague, which unmasks their inability to serve the public beyond their own private twisted interests). At the level of the *esperpento*, the scene represents three (morally and physically) deformed Spanish representatives of a deformed Spanish society. Finally, at a political level, this moment of on-screen *recortes* esperpentically mirrors the off-screen cuts to social spending that many viewers were possibly suffering at the peak of the crisis, when the film was released.

In a looping feedback of identification from the real to the fictional and vice versa, Lacuesta stated in an interview that he purposefully cast actors who were in his mind the truest representatives of Spanish society:

> I was really interested in getting a cast with the most recognizable faces in Spanish cinema, because I wanted to create a portrait of Spain (so to speak). And . . . who would be better suited to draw that portrait than those actors

that have put a face to the name of this country in the past few years on our screens? I also liked the mix of generations within the film. That is a dialogue between worlds that many may think are on opposite ends. But I like it that way because the film could be then said to be a "metaespañolada."[37]

With the inclusion of other famous cameos, Lacuesta had pushed for the grotesque representation to occur at both sides of the screen. That is, the very familiar faces of the cast were set to lure the viewers into making them accomplices of the violent desires promulgated by the film beyond mere dramatic identification. In that way, violence was not only cathartic; it was a mechanism of representation that could acquire populist characteristics. Within Lacuesta's cinematic framework in *Murieron*, the representation of violence on the screen also represents the possibility that the legitimacy of violence might be exchanging hands from the few to the many off-screen. That is, as the idea of the *metaespañolada* suggests, the film opened the interpretive possibility of populist antagonism as symbolic violence was "mainstreamed" from below; a violence with which *un cualquiera* could identify—in Spanish, an "anyone." In its dual meaning, referring to either a transversal popular identification or to someone without social status, the *cualquiera* qualities of Lacuesta's *metaespañolada* opens the door to a transversal politics of popular vengeance against Spanish elites rooted in populist antagonism.

The concept of *metaespañolada* in *Murieron* gives the characters archetypal features (i.e., as *españolada*) and simplifies the identification of political tropes in the film (i.e., as cinematic metacommentary). As in the genre of *españoladas*, these archetypes go beyond their humorous characteristics. Their comic traits signal what Mercedes Camino suggests are their "contradictory embodiments of a type of populism" that are best represented by Ortega y Gasset's views of class and the historical role of the aristocracy in Spain.[38] The Spanish philosopher argues that since the eighteenth century, with the advent of the Bourbon dynasty, the Spanish aristocracy have differed from their northern European fellow aristocrats in that they "openly displayed their admiration for and even imitated the mores of the lower classes."[39] Historically, as the Spanish aristocracy of the late nineteenth century lost influence, the perception among the elites increasingly was that Spain needed a new ruling class that would avoid vulgarity and the tendency to imitate the *vulgo*. As Sánchez León has argued, "in nineteenth-century Spain, the aristocracy was [etymologically and socially speaking] vulgar . . . and thus plebeian identification also applied to the elites, because they were historically related to the 'vulgo' [or populus] in their vulgarity. That is, Spanish aristocracy was defined by their bad manners."[40] Their bad manners signal the tendency of

Spanish aristocracy to acquire and accept populist attitudes in the form of admiring and imitating the lower classes, as Ortega y Gasset first reasoned. And here lies the root of elites' fear as well as the implicit power the mere suggestion of popular violence may invoke—a dread rooted in their mimetic attitude and supposed secret admiration that can lead a significant part of elites to betray their own class without much hesitation when confronted with the people's ire, as Lacuesta's film shows.

In the aftermath of the 2008–2011 economic crisis, fingers were increasingly pointed at European centers of power, like the so-called Troika, the decision group formed by the International Monetary Fund, the European Commission, and the European Central Bank. There was a mounting anxiety that Spain would not follow suit, that Spanish rulers wouldn't be "European enough" and maybe "a little too Spanish," just like Greece and its leftist party Syriza. The division between rational governance and emotional populists that was established was reminiscent of what Sánchez León had argued about the nineteenth-century Spanish aristocracy: "Those elites who lower themselves and see eye to eye with the 'vulgo' [just like the Spanish aristocracy] and satisfy their most vulgar, lowest passions . . . were labeled as demagogues or populists. Nevertheless, the 'true' political representative was supposed to be one who would elevate the people morally, intellectually. . . . And in that way the latter would be offering the people the politics they 'really' need."[41] In the twenty-first century, that division would be informed by the fear that Spanish elites could succumb to the irrational demands of the people and their push against austerity.

With that phobia of the *populus* in mind, the influential Confederation of Employers and Industries of Spain (CEOE) authored an extensive report in 2013 focused on restoring European institutions' confidence and thus counteracting the distrust produced by the seemingly unappeasable popular discontent after the 15-M. Among other things, the CEOE proposed deepening social cuts (i.e., *recortes*) or, as they call it, measures that "racionalicen el gasto del Estado del Bienestar" (rationalize social spending of the welfare state).[42] These measures were to appeal to a new European "aristocracy" that became omnipresent in the following years. Their presence dominated Spanish life on many fronts. At a popular level, they were represented in the triad that united the Troika, the influence of German banks, and—especially after the multiple clashes with the Greek government of SYRIZA—the unremitting power of Chancellor Angela Merkel in the European Union. They were perceived as a twenty-first-century European neoliberal aristocracy whose mandate was to be unquestionably followed by Spanish rulers against their citizens' will. In this sense, the Troika and Germany became antithetical to

Spanish democracy in the popular imaginary. Within that frame of mind, Spanish representatives were to choose between real democracy (i.e., the populist choice as it was repeatedly and pejoratively designated at the time) and aristocratic rule (i.e., the "rational" choice proposed by the CEOE and the Troika). The anxiety lay precisely in the possibility of choosing the first option, as the election of Podemos would soon exacerbate the angst.

Lacuesta made an illuminating use of those political anxieties in *Murieron*'s final scene. As the blood-drenched faces of Carmen Machi and Luis Tosar finish the mutilation of Imanol Arias, two black-suited characters appear on the screen. Resembling what in Spain at the time was commonly referred as the Troika's *hombres de negro* (men in black), they apparently take on the duties of ruthless debt collectors. The character of Spanish-German actor Àlex Brendemühl then begins addressing everyone in the room in German. As shown in the Spanish subtitles, he starts to admonish: "Otra vez la habéis cagado, ¿no? Gente, gente, gente . . . Típico español" (You fucked it up again, right? People, people, people . . . Typical Spanish).[43] Then Sigrid, the other character in black, depicted by Bárbara Lennie, an actor of Argentinean descent, continues the rebuke in thickly accented (German) Spanish: "Lo tenían todo a favor, caballeros. Toda la opinión pública estaba con ustedes. Pero la situación se les ha ido de las manos. ¿Por qué? Por falta de profesionalidad, señores; porque son ustedes unos aficionados. [. . .] Por culpa de ustedes han matado a doce empleados de cajas [bancarias], a doces trabajadores. ¿Qué pensaban? Ahora los banqueros están escondidos en sus mansiones y sus imitadores están matando a pobres trabajadores como ustedes. Han conseguido lo contrario de lo que pretendían. Han perdido el apoyo popular. Y han convertido en un mártir al presidente de las libertades civiles" (You had everything going for you, gentlemen. Public opinion was on your side. But you have lost control of the situation. Why? Because you are not professionals, you are amateurs. Because of your amateurism, twelve bank employees were killed. Twelve workers. What were you thinking? Now all those hotshot bankers are hiding in their mansions and your copycats are killing poor bank employees, mere workers just like you. You got the opposite of what you set out to achieve. You've lost popular support. The only thing you've achieved is helping the president to become a martyr of civil liberties).[44] As if Lacuesta's analogy were not already clear, Albert then asks Sigrid, "Perfecto señora *führer*, pero ¿cuál es la oferta de la Troika?" (OK, lady *führer*, but . . . What's the Troika's offer?); Sigrid responds by shooting all the politicians in the room, gorily splashing blood throughout the scene.[45] A voice-over then begins speaking of imitators popping up throughout the world.

The scene finally culminates with the camera cutting back to a close-up of a visibly distressed news commentator who affirms: "Con el paso de las horas el fenómeno está adquirendo relevancia mundial. [. . .] El pánico y el caos han invadido las redes sociales. Los Panda son ya trending topic mundial" (In a matter of hours, the phenomenon has gone global. Panic and chaos have taken over social media. The Pandas are already the world's trending topic]).[46] The absurd gap between the pain inflicted and what is achieved (i.e., the takeover of social media) falls again within the parameters of the *esperpento*.

These final moments were also the director's reminder of the chasm between the great suffering triggered by the Troika's austerity measures and Spanish civil society's insufficient political response in allusion to the 15-M's supposedly lack of "real" revolutionary influence. Nevertheless, the filmmaker's veiled (unfair) criticism of the 15-M in reality points to the chasm between political desire and reality. As a result, representation took place in a gridlock between the images of political desire in fiction (e.g., targeted violence, popular justice) and words of reason in reality (e.g., strategic activism, pragmatic demands). In the face of the generalized vulnerability and structural precarity still prevalent in Spain after the 15-M, the imagined destruction of the "real" enemies of the Spanish people (mainly bankers and politicians) was one of the few ways to break this gridlock, if only at a cultural level. It supposed a cultural victory of sorts. And it was more than cathartic. The representation of violence against traditional figures of power was being made culturally legitimate (even though, paradoxically enough, it would soon be legally forbidden with the passing of the so-called *ley mordaza*). Accordingly, in *Murieron*, violence is a Benjaminian attempt to invoke a "Copernican revolution" of the past to "strike us" into a future of political agency that "shatters the illusion of continuity and progress on which . . . dominant views of history are based."[47] The film's idea of violence is a mechanism of representation to revolutionize or "strike" a present typified by unrepresentation into the promise of a future of representation—a not-so-distant future that will be shaped by the irruption of populist leadership.

Carminism, Bad Manners, and the Melodramatization of Populist Affection

Paco León's debut film *Carmina o revienta* (2012) and its second part, *Carmina y amén* (2014), center on the ordeals the main character, Carmina (Carmina

Barrios), has to go through to surmount the less visible violence of the "system" and its intrinsic disregard for people's well-being. Carmina is not only the sole driver of the action in both films but also their political anchor. León has constructed a character that embodies politics. Carmina's words, actions, and decisions incarnated and circumscribed the political itself—or, as the director has put it: "For us, to believe in Carmina means to believe in another way of doing things; to connect with who you are (for better or worst) and evolve, to believe in your freedom and in your power to change things around. Carminism preaches tolerance, hedonism, commitment to your people and the faith in your convictions, whatever they may be."[48] Through "Carminism," León's films go beyond Spain's cinematic reality of the *esperpento* and propose a new symbolic referent anchored in a strong popular-populist leadership. Thus, Carmina's Carminism is imbued with an "affective investment" through which the film's politics acquire their force, and cause the characters around her (and the viewers, by symbolic extension) "to rise up, . . . to determine the necessary and sufficient conditions for the foundation of a new order of things."[49] Her politics run parallel to populism's affective drive by which an idea (real democracy now, the 99 percent, or Carminism) or a person (a populist leader or Carmina herself) is articulated as an empty signifier that emotionally binds together all sorts of different political demands. In cinema, those demands take on symbolic counterparts represented on-screen—(in)direct allusions to lives in crisis that demand popular-populist accountability.

Carmina's cinematic persona can be interpreted through the lens of populism not because she represents on the screen the "pure" people versus the "corrupt" elites or is simply visualized as on the side of the people. Apart from the importance of the political context of her films (set during two of the most intense years in Spain's populist cycle), Carmina embodies "the performative staging of a wrong"—in this case, in relation to how the crisis had wronged the ordinary people of Spain.[50] Her character makes "us"— both "us" the audience as Carmina's populist creation and "us" as the receptors of León's films in the context of the crisis—emotionally invested in her fight against and out of the crisis. Carmina's affective investment resembles populism in that it is formed "through 'low' cultural appeals that have the capacity to resonate and receive positive reception within particular sectors of society for socio-cultural reasons (linked to an antagonistic understanding of socio-cultural differences)."[51] Carmina's performative repertoire is very similar to the way populist leaders stylistically present their politics. Carmina promoted an affective relationship among her, the rest of the characters, and the audience through "low appeals" or "bad manners" while at the same time "antagonizing" through verbal (even physical) abuse the representatives of the elites.[52]

Significantly, her character has a strong Andalusian accent that is never masked in any shape or form; in the context of Spain, her inability or unwillingness to code switch into the Castilian standard readily associates her with the lower strata of society.[53] And as the Andalusian dialect has been historically stigmatized, considered "bad" Spanish, linked with a low level of education, and often ridiculed and otherized in popular culture, so too Carmina be marked. Besides her "improper" speech, her character displays a total lack of decorum: constant swearing accompanied by multiple scatological performances. Despite all that, Carmina in the films is not represented as a marginal character. On the contrary, she uses her "bad manners" as the basis of her politics' affective investment—not dissimilar in essence from Pablo Iglesias's unmannerliness in his meteoric rise to political fame that will later inform Podemos's populist politics, as explored in Chapter 4.

In concrete terms, the first film, *Carmina o revienta* (Carmina or Blow Up, 2012), is set in the aftermath of the economic crisis. Facing bankruptcy due to the many debts of her family business (a *venta*, or restaurant and bar for truck drivers and for family weekend gatherings at the outskirts of Seville), Carmina devises a plan to cheat the insurance company when it refuses to pay for the stolen lot of *jamones* (high-quality cured ham traditionally bought for special celebrations) she had bought to sell during Christmas. The sequel, *Carmina y amén* (Carmina and amen, 2014), expands on that theme by substituting the object around which Carmina schemed her cheating: instead of stolen goods needed for the family's survival, the sudden death of Carmina's husband, Antonio (Paco Casaus), might prevent the family from getting his monthly pension that they need to cover basic daily costs. To avoid that, Carmina again has to cheat the "system," pretending Antonio died on the first day of the month—two days later than he actually did—so his government money will be deposited. Stylistically, both films use the technique of the false documentary, consciously blurring the lines between fiction and reality, between melodrama and the real-life dramas of the crisis. And through that conscious blurring, León transforms Spanish film's typical picaresque character—poorly educated, bad mouthed, street savvy, commonly associated with urban marginality or the poorest regions of Spain such as Andalusia, whence hail both the director and the main characters—into a representation of political rebellion against the crisis, a metaphor of plebeian retribution against the systemic forces that brought about the crisis, and ultimately a symbolic representation of populism's bad manners.

The two main actors, who in both films play the characters of Carmina and her daughter María (María León), are the director's mother and sister, respectively. In the films they are exaggerated versions of themselves, infusing their on-camera relationship with an affective bond so strong that the viewer is prevented from distinguishing staged acting from genuine reacting that goes along with familial ties. In this respect, the first layer of the films' political message can be located in the overlapping of the "real." In the same way that the characters' fiction and reality can't be easily distinguished, viewers can't prise apart the substance of the tragedies presented on-screen and the tragic lives touched by the crisis. This blurring entanglement forces the viewer to accept Carmina's reality as "real," or, more simply put, Carmina's gospel becomes the audience's truth. In both films, what can be regarded as patent, obvious lies are instead simply political mechanisms to deal with either the characters' lives in crisis or with the imminent violence of the crisis. That's why when one of Carmina's friends, an older and respectable-looking gray-haired lady, talks about her close friendship with Sofía (the former queen of Spain), nobody questions her. Everyone accepts her story, because her fabrication is not a way of aggrandizing herself and belittling Carmina and the rest of her friends. Instead, it is a mechanism of imbuing with status the place they all inhabit. As such, their run-down building, their neighborhood, and ultimately the materiality of all their lives is marked as the place where Sofía came to "take a break" from her daily "struggles" as a monarch. The fact that the story is never believable doesn't matter, because, besides of course supplying comic relief, the purpose of the story is to establish a mechanism of political reclassification by way of "creating" new realities that in turn were the product of a "new way of doing things" or what León has termed *Carminism*.

Both of León's films purposefully (con)fuse tragedy and comedy when it comes to structuring their political ethos. When watching Carmina's intense laughing in the middle of profoundly tragic moments (e.g., total bankruptcy, lack of money for food, the sudden death of the family's sole provider), the viewer can't possibly pity her as another victim of the crisis. In fact, one can only laugh at Carmina's Carminism. Thus, León defies the tradition of political cinema delivering a message through the clear-cut relationship between a fictional representation of characters' tragedies and the real tragic lives alluded to off-screen "to create a mobilization effect in the spectator so the film is not merely a tool for entertainment but an instrument for social intervention."[54] On the contrary, the character of Carmina avoids the rational impetus of such representative relationship. She mobilizes audiences emotionally and counterintuitively through her contagious laughter, which confuses and mixes her infectious vitality with the profound misery of her life situation on the screen and the crisis outside it. Provoked by Carmina, the viewer is apt to laugh at the brutality of the system instead of feeling sorry for her. Such laughter is a second layer in the films' political toolbox. In this respect, her laughter is neither cathartic nor limited to the laughing sounds her character emits. Under a more expansive definition, one linked not simply to moments designed to make the audience laugh, Carmina's laughter or, more generally, comedy is an instrument of antagonism that follows the steps of the *esperpento* tradition previously analyzed in Lacuesta's film (i.e., a renovated tradition that laughed at the absurdity of the violence generated by the crisis as a way to critique it) and, in the case of Carmina, further weaponizes laughter as part of a populist response to such a violent reality. In both of León's films, the most intense comedic moments go hand in hand with the representation of antagonism as embodied in Carmina's verbal abuses (i.e., her bad manners) against her victimizers (i.e., the representative of the system). To further exemplify Carmina's populism, a series of key moments that portrayed her as a bad-mannered (populist) avenger are briefly discussed.

The first illustrative moment takes place in *Carmina o revienta*: after the audience knows of Carmina's economic distress, Carmina and María can be seen doing a series of chores. As the couple walks back from the supermarket to where their very old car is parked, they realize the car has been stolen. From the start in this scene, the car is positioned as one of the many symbols that conceptualize Carmina's politics through her conscious nondivision between fiction and fact. She states: "Yo no quiero ni pensar que se hayan llevado el coche del abuelo. Este coche es muy goloso y últimamente le están dando por él" (I can't even begin to think that grandpa's car is stolen. This is a very appealing car and lately is getting eyed by thieves).[55] Yet the car is an old Citroen 2CV wagon from the 1960s, affording a moment of comedy while illustrating Carmina's construction of (ir)reality. As mother and daughter board a taxi to report the theft to the police, their car suddenly appears in front of them, driven by two junkies. In a campy version of the traditional car-chase scene in action films, Carmina tries to get off the taxi but is impeded by her daughter, who tries to reason with her mother: they should call the police. Carmina vehemently refuses, insulting her daughter and the taxi driver. However, Carmina's bad manners mean very different things when directed to those at the bottom, toward symbolic victims of the crisis as opposed to those representatives at the top, the symbolic victimizers of the former. Carmina finally exclaims: "¡Qué no llamo a la policía! ¿la policía pa' qué? [. . .] ¡Qué me dejes! ¡Qué los sigas, coño!" (I'm not calling the police.

The police . . . what for? Fuck it, let me be! Follow them!).[56] Nevertheless, none of her bad manners or curse words convey an affront toward them. They are part of her affective performative repertoire spurring those around her—all those who can be perceived as her equals—into action. Carmina's bad manners here are part of the solution, whether that be to hurry other characters into doing something, or a method of emotional catharsis, or a way of bonding with those closest to her such as her daughter, who is constantly referred to as *hija de puta* (roughly translated as "whore") and *cabrona* (bastard).

When the stolen car finally stops, as Carmina keeps bossing María and the taxi driver around, she rushes toward the vehicle, where she meets the two junkies who stole it. Rocking the car back and forth, she forcefully gets the two criminals out of the car while María insults them from a distance (the scene foretells María's path to Carminism that is completed by the end of the second film, when she transforms into a version of her mother). As the thieves run away in fear of her, Carmina calmly walks back to the taxi, quietly cursing to herself. As omniscient voice-over, she then takes control of the action and begins narrating what happens next: mainly, how Carmina quickly resolves the situation and delivers them from trouble. At this point in the film, the scene proves Carmina's unstoppable determination, linking her with the film's title, "Carmina or bust." León's film title is a play on words on Vicente Aranda's *El Lute: Camina o revienta* (1987; literally translated as "El Lute: Walk or bust," although the official English title was *El Lute: Run for Your Life*). The film by Aranda was based on the memoirs of El Lute, the iconic thief and fugitive of the 1960s. Not coincidentally, Carmina's stolen car in the previous scene was a model built during the time El Lute, a criminal most famous for stealing cars, was active. Despite the fact that one stole cars for a living and the other was recovering her stolen car to be able to survive, their actions do mirror each other in that their respective marginality and bad manners are symbolically repositioned as culturally valuable. But the symbolism here can be also connected with the "real," as their fiction and their reality became (con)fused: in the case of El Lute, by literally packaging his pauperism as a cultural commodity to be consumed in popular culture, and in the case of Carmina by representing low status as cultural capital, which both the actress and her eponymous character use in the construction of Carminism both on-screen and off.[57]

When Carmina faces those representing the Spanish elites, her bad manners turn into an effective weapon of political aggression. In the scene that immediately follows the recovery of their family vehicle, María, who was to finish the errands they were running earlier, phones her mom to tell her she's just had a car accident. Because María does not have a driver's license, Carmina must go to the site of the crash to sort out the situation. As the scene unfolds, the viewer realizes that Carmina's old wagon was crashed into by two men in suits driving a brand-new luxury car the wrong way down a one-way street. Visually, the scene clearly separates the "us" around the bad-mannered Carmina and the "them" in the shape of the good-mannered, rich-looking drivers of the luxury car. The latter then behave as the obvious representation of Spanish elites, ready to exert their power over Carmina and her daughter.

Before Carmina can say anything, one of two men condescendingly explains the incident to her as follows: "Hemos tenido un golpecito. [. . .] Pero el problema no es que yo venga por mal sitio. El problema es que la niña no tiene carné de conducir. Y la niña no puede coger el coche" (We've had a little incident. But the real problem here is not that I may have been driving the wrong way. The problem is that missy does not have a driver's license. And the girl can't drive without a license).[58] Carmina's reply immediately refers to Carminism's politicization in the con(fusion) of fact and fiction: "Te voy a decir una cosa. ¿No te acuerdas que el coche lo llevaba yo? Y la niña venía a mi lado" (Let me tell you something. Don't you remember that I was driving the car?" And that girl, my daughter, was by my side?).[59] In vain, the driver tries to defy Carmina using the common patriarchal tropes of the hysterical woman: "¿Cómo? Señora, usted ha perdido la cabeza" (What? Woman, you have lost your mind).[60] Carmina's reply is paradigmatic of her bad manners: "La cabeza la vas a perder tú de la hostia que te voy a meter. El coche lo traía yo conduciendo y la niña venía al lado. Y es tu palabra contra la mía. Y testigos que tengo" (Your mind will be the one lost when I punch the shit out of you. I was driving the car and my daughter was by my side. It's your word against mine. And I have witnesses).[61] Embodying the stereotype of the *cani* (the chav or hoodlum), two neighborhood teenagers in their scooters suddenly appear and ask Carmina if she needs any help.

Carmina then calmly tells them the situation is under control while addressing the other two men: "No pasa nada. Estos señores venían en contramano y me han metido un topetazo en el coche. Y yo pienso que lo vamos a arreglar. Tú dirás, porque no es ya el topetazo que les ha metido sino el dolor de cuello que tengo. Porque me has dado fuerte con cojones. Y no sé las consecuencias que esto puede tener. ¿Tú piensas que lo vamos a arreglar, verdad, hijo?" (Nothing is the matter. These two gentlemen were driving the wrong way down and hit my car. I think we can fix it. You tell me, because it's not only that you hit the car, which you did, but the *real* problem is that my neck is hurting. Because you really crashed the shit out my car. And I don't know what effects this will have on my body. You think we can fix this, right, son?).[62] Carmina has suddenly turned the tables on the two men in suits. She is the one patronizing them, making her gospel their reality and the truth. Further, her bad manners are used as political tools in the form of antagonism, establishing a frontier between "us" (those on Carmina's side, including the audience) and "them" (representatives of the swindling elites who are, to the audience's delight, being swindled). The scene finishes with a flash-forward, cutting to Carmina's kitchen (from where she omnisciently narrates her story throughout the film), as she tells us how it all ended: "Quinientos euros les saqué. Les podía haber sacado más . . . ¡Qué hambre! Yo con los nervios es que me entra un hambre . . . Los nervios es que son mu' malos" (Five hundred euros I got out of them. I could have gotten more . . . I'm so hungry! Every time I get shook up I get hungry. Stress is the worst).[63] Carmina has thus symbolically avenged "us" through her (con)fusion of fact and fiction with the help of her bad manners. Notice how even in her own accounts of the situation, after acknowledging she swindled the two men without much effort, she consciously and sardonically keeps up the act for the audience, pretending to be shaken up by the whole experience

The ending of *Carmina o revienta* is especially important in that regard, directly connecting with the central thesis in the sequel *Carmina y amén*. By the end of the former, Carmina has successfully managed to cheat the insurance company by staging the theft of a much larger lot of *jamones*, for which the company can't refuse payment this time around. During the last scene, as a flamenco version of Gloria Gaynor's "I Will Survive" tellingly plays in the background, Carmina can be seen filing the claim with the same insurance agent who denied her claim at the beginning of the film. In parallel, a close-up shot of María's astonished expression appears on-screen. The daughter can't believe that her mother has pulled off what seemed at first impossible. Carmina then approaches María and tells her: "No te dije que nos iba a ayudar el Señor. Pa' que veas tú lo de mis santos" (Didn't I tell you the Lord would help us. My saints always help, how about that?).[64] The reference to God and her "saints" mirrors Almodóvar's campy use of religion, but it is also a reference to the power of Carminism—a gospel represented by Carmina's "saints" that change realities into truths and vice versa. The scene finishes with Carmina winking at camera and a fade-to-black shot in which a famous Tom Clancy quote appears in Spanish: "¿La diferencia entre realidad y ficción? La ficción tiene mayor sentido" (The difference between reality and fiction? Fiction makes more sense).[65] However, the novelist's original quote was not "fiction makes more sense" but "fiction has to make sense," stressing the idea of life's chaotic nature as opposed to the control writers and readers may feel when immersed in fiction. León's mistranslation or manipulation is still appropriate, in that it aligns once again with Carminism, emphasizing how Carmina's "reality" ruled over the film's message.

In *Carmina y amén*, that message is even more explicitly conveyed, as Carmina again faces the obstacles of the system and confronts her own death; by the end of the second film, it is revealed that Carmina had lung cancer as result of her compulsive smoking. The relationship between her and María evolves from the first film to play an even more central role in the second film, because the daughter is represented in the sequel as the natural inheritor of Carminism. Their relationship in *Carmina y amén* encapsulates the entire spectrum of Carmina's cinematic politics (i.e., the representation in film of a new way of doing things when dealing with a life in crisis product of *the* crisis), especially when it comes to dealing with their changing reality. Apart from bad manners (the most salient and more visible aspect of Carmina's "politics"), in the sequel, the construction of a new "real" to successfully deal with reality is further emphasized, revealing this time the most explicitly emotional side of Carminism. Importantly, emotions here have to do with what had been previously referred to as the mechanism of (populist) affective investment. In that way, in her bond with María, Carmina represents cinematically how affectivity can change not only the way one perceives what is real but also reality itself. And what could be more political than the successful attempt to change reality?

The scene that best condenses the politics of Carminism takes place toward the end of *Carmina y amén*, right after Carmina's plan of cheating both the insurance company and the government regarding the date of her husband's death, when María (along with the audience) realizes that her mother actually killed her father, Antonio, by accident. After forensics talks to Carmina in front of her, María learns that Antonio was taking a higher dose of his epilepsy medicine than recommended; combined with his alcoholism, it proved fatal. What the doctors don't know, but María does, is that Carmina was in charge of administering the dosage. That's why when everyone leaves, having already succeeded in establishing that Antonio died the very day he received his pension, instead of a scene of joy, the viewer witnesses the most emotionally charged scene of the film. With tears in her eyes, María immediately confronts her mother: "¿Por qué me mientes? ¿Qué? ¿que tenía yo razón, eh? ¿Que le has dao las pastillas malamente y te lo has cargao? ¿Qué ha sio sin querer pero te lo has cargao? ¡Mírame a la cara y dímelo! ¿Por qué me mientes a mí, mamá? ¡Mamá, mírame a la cara! ¿A mí por qué coño me mientes?" (Why are you lying to me? Why? I was right, huh? You gave him the wrong stuff and killed him? That you didn't mean it, but you killed him? Look me in the eye and tell me? Why are you lying? Why are you lying to *me*, mom? Mom! Tell it to my face! To *me*, why the fuck are you lying to me?).[66] Carmina then slowly rises from the table displaying the signed paperwork, a symbol of their success in cheating the system and of a better life ahead of them. With her back still turned to her daughter, a weeping and enraged María keeps asking her why she lied to her. At one point, Carmina turns, faces her daughter, looks her in the eye, and defiantly but calmly gives her an answer that no one could expect: "Mira, María, yo no miento nunca. Yo cuando digo una cosa se convierte en verdad. Y amén" (Listen up, María. I never lie. When I say something, that something becomes true. And amen to that).[67] Carmina's amen is the ultimate symbolic proof that her words do indeed create a new reality, to which everyone (including her disciple and daughter) must fold. That's why María eventually accepts Carmina's reality and, thus, still weeping, can only say back to her: "Júrame que ha sido sin querer" (Swear it was an accident). Carmina quickly replies, "Te lo juro que me muera" (I swear it on my life).[68] And when by the end of the film it is revealed that Carmina will in fact die, her words do not lose any potency, nor are they symbolically invalidated to convey a new message to the audience. On the contrary, her words immediately connect with her daughter's visual transformation into Carmina, which happens in the following scene.

After the neighbors, family, and friends leave their apartment, where Antonio's wake has taken place, María curses them out in typical Carminist fashion: "¡A tomar por culo! ¡Qué pesaos! Se lo han comío y se lo han bebío to'" (Fuck them all! What a pain! They ate and drank to the last bit).[69] The camera then follows María instead of Carmina, who remains seated in the background by the kitchen table, the place where María used to be when they were both in the kitchen, quintessentially Carmina's place. The kitchen was the "place" Carmina was assigned by patriarchy as well as the place she radically appropriated and transformed into an instrument of change; it was in the kitchen that Carmina devised all her schemes, and that is what María symbolically inherits in this scene. María is the one standing up, in front of her mother, ruling over the kitchen, with a cigarette in hand, shown in profile, surrounded by the same smoke that had accompanied Carmina since the beginning of the first film. The smoke kills Carmina, but the smoke also symbolizes Carmina's agency and empowerment and, by extension, her daughter's. Because none of the symbolic representations of the system could rule over Carmina's life—not the economic powers symbolized by the insurance company, not the political powers symbolized by the government agent in charge of deciding whether she could get her dead husband's last pension payment, not her own husband acting as the symbol of patriarchy. In the end, it was her decision to smoke what killed her, on her own terms.

Older women in cinema are commonly represented as respectable, abnegated mother figures, fragile but resilient, powerless but dignified, subdued but righteous, victims of their own empowerment. In symbolic defiance of those norms, Carmina's bad manners not only break with cinematic conventions but also create an alternative to her given reality of crisis. Her déclassé conduct symbolically offers a new future, in this case, for her daughter to live on. In that way, conceptually, Carmina's representation on the screen is a new way of doing things much as the 15-M advocated a new way of doing politics when a real democracy was performed across the protest camps in the spring and summer of 2011. But even more importantly, after having "received the full endorsement of the mainstream hegemonic film culture through Goya awards," the symbolic representation of Carmina was one of the cultural symptoms that the populist cycle was accelerating; getting Carmina's audience closer to seeing the actual performance (not simply its symbolic counterpart) of a new populist leadership.[70] Ultimately, Carminism is a personalized, cinematic response to a plebeian vision that invokes a political desire to destroy from below entire systems of power installed at the top.

Conclusion

In sum, the three films analyzed in this chapter are responses to a populist aesthetic that emphasized the underdogs' legitimate resort to violent means against an elitist "them," as both a cultural escape valve for widespread popular frustrations and as a symbolic precursor of the new political phase that began with the irruption of Podemos. These cinematic representations of the crisis were synecdoches of the new populist style that would bring Podemos and its leader, Pablo Iglesias, to the center stage of Spanish politics. But the filmed images of these vengeful underdogs run the risk of imprinting a quasi-nihilistic image for the people in the public consciousness. Once the 15-M's visual reference as the constructive place for a new time of real democracy was out of sight and because "the people" seen during and after the 15-M were given no political place, culture was the only space where the popular (in films but also in many other types of cultural artifacts, such as novels, debates in television, and memes on Twitter) could find breathing room as populist (i.e., representations of the people where political agency was seen constructed by and for the people). Nevertheless, despite the powerful images portraying people's cathartic revenge on Spanish elites, culture alone was by no mean sufficient to endure the increasingly suffocating political climate.

So, as the distance between the people in culture and the institutional in politics grew wider, frustration, and also cynicism, became deeper.[71] This widening gap was breached only when Podemos walked into the picture. With the appearance of this political party, the "plebeianization" of the people of the 15-M and their bad-mannered representations—despite being at the center of Spain's popular culture—began a journey from the margins of politics into the electoral mainstream. Podemos and the figure of Pablo Iglesias, as a ready-made allegory of the Spanish *pueblo*, channeled the plebeian desires into the political institutions and so into a new hopeful visualization of a legitimatized new demos. Pablo Iglesias became the most visible personification of the popular-populist hero that was called to finally reset the system from within the system. He was the personification of the chance to reconstitute the increasingly violent reality of the people in crisis into a vision of a future with, at minimum, an empty signifier in which people's suffering and demands could be contained. The stylistic evolution of such vision is continued in the next chapter. These plebeian representations of the people, widespread but displaced from the political mainstream, transformed into the televised, culturally mainstream images of Iglesias as the populist leader of Podemos at the center stage of Spanish politics.

PART II

Performing Populism

4

What Did the People See?

Beyond Mediatic Populism

In tracking the political cycle that accelerated after the 15-M, it is difficult not to be absorbed by the magnetic irruption of Pablo Iglesias and Podemos. Iglesias's media persona was audiovisually conceived in 2010 by the so-called *La Tuerka* hypothesis, which sought to translate the media communication strategies of the "pink tide" in Latin America to the Spanish context.[1] Accordingly, Iglesias began to be constructed as an archetype of political common sense who offered alternative views to the increasingly unpopular ideas professed by the government and talking heads in the mainstream media. Consequently, once the figure of Iglesias had acquired enough mainstream capital, the party could launch (in January 2014 in preparation for the European elections of that year).[2] Podemos's unprecedented results (five seats in the European Parliament and over one million votes in an election that was and still is given little to no coverage) marked a period of media obsession with Iglesias, Podemos, and everything around it. The camera lenses turned from the increasing anger of people in the streets to the television sets and their *tertulias*, where Iglesias and other well-known members of Podemos channeled popular discontent into sound bites. "If the revolutionaries of the past went up the mountain to fight," stated the party's prominent founding member Juan Carlos Monedero, "now they fight from television studios."[3] As a result, both Podemos and Iglesias were often accused of resorting to mediatic populism.[4]

Even though its major critics have acknowledged the complete success of the party's (populist) communication strategy, the media's labeling of Podemos as "populist" was never meant to be a description of the phenomenon. It certainly appeared closer to a communicative counterstrategy (used by the major political parties and their accolades on the media) that was directed at dismissing any ideas coming from any member or perceived sympathizer of Podemos with the label "populist." Moreover, even though many in Podemos had extensively theorized about the political possibilities of populism, the label "populist" did not so much refer to Podemos's theorization of the people but mostly, in media circles, became interchangeable with negative characterizations of Pablo Iglesias's television appearances. But the criticisms were not always unjustified. As Jorge Sola and César Rendueles have pointed out, Podemos's communication strategy had a major inconsistency. While the party presented itself "as a project of democratic depuration" that would deepen citizen participation across governmental institutions, Podemos was, on the other hand, "perfectly comfortable in a hypertrophied version of 'audience democracy' in which charismatic personality takes precedence over party, performance over program, and authenticity over competence."[5] More specifically, that political contradiction crops up in the interrelated visualities further explored here, such as Iglesias's mediatic personality, Podemos's cinematic style, and the performative attempt to represent authentically the Spanish *pueblo* (whatever "authentic" may be).

To overcome the overdetermining framework through which Podemos's communication strategy is commonly analyzed, one must consider Podemos beyond its famous media politics that, following the discourse produced during the 15-M, aimed to reframe political conflict outside the limits of the Left-Right spectrum and around the construction of Iglesias's leadership on the screen. Iglesias's charisma was certainly, and self-consciously, mediatic in nature. Beyond the party's symbiotic understanding of the media and populism (which alludes to the previously mentioned mediatic populism), the audiovisual shape of Iglesias, first, and the Podemos phenomenon, later, was based on implementing a mediatic practice of politics that, as Oliver Marchart states, "'ritualized' forms by which protest identity is established."[6] In this context, the term *mediatic* is not only a mere adjectivization of the noun media. It also refers to the politico-mediatic dispositive used by both Iglesias and Podemos to allow for "a counter-hegemonic formation [that] might be organized on the terrain of [visual] culture" (following the Gramscian understanding of the inseparability of culture and politics).[7] As such, *mediatic* encompasses a wide array of (audio)visual products that go from television and film to YouTube videos and internet memes. And when used in reference to Iglesias and Podemos, it designates a Gramscian impetus to give the phenomenon an "organic" cultural force through their media appearances that mediated between the people (as television audiences, internet users, newspaper readers, and so on) and institutional politics. In that way, "every mediatic practice" has the potential to create "a moment of antagonism, that is, a moment of *the political*."[8] In this respect, beyond media analysis of the party and its leader, *mediatic* here refers to that potentiality as guided by an audiovisual momentum to make populist politics popular in culture.

If the previous chapters dwelled on how the popular in culture became populist in politics, what follows is the explanation of how the populists (Podemos and Iglesias) became popular as mediated by culture. Accordingly, the emphasis is much less on what made Podemos a populist party and more on how the party conveyed its "popularness" (via Iglesias's leadership), as well as how key ideas of its populism were translated into popular culture, which was in the end at the heart of their successful populist strategy. It all began with Iglesias's antiestablishment orientation and his irruption as a television celebrity, which had echoes in the audiovisual culture of the time and also, crucially, served to craft a political narrative with a new cinematic style, or what will be referred as Podemos's cinematic turn, to wink at the idea of Europe's "populist turn" in the previous decade and to imply the need to understand Podemos's populism beyond a strictly political framework.[9] Accordingly, what follows explores how, first, television signified Podemos's populist leadership not only through Iglesias's newfound role of political celebrity but also via his own audiovisual taste. Second, the chapter looks at how those populist codes, popularized on prime-time television, were translated into popular culture with the help of cinematic language (beyond the party's mediatic strategy). To such ends, given the film's popularity as well as the filmmaker's "popularness" (i.e., his ability to capture and shape Spain's popular consciousness with his cinema), Álex de la Iglesia's *Mi gran noche* (2015) serves as an analytical springboard to explore a key concept in Podemos's populism: *la casta*, or the caste. This idea lays the ground for examining another fundamental principle in Podemos's populism: the need to appear authentic, to be "of the people" in direct opposition to *la casta*. The most transparent and the most substantial example of such a populist strategy can be seen in Fernando León de Aranoa's documentary *Política, manual de instrucciones* (2016). There, both party and leader are cinematically coded as the "realest" political actors at the moment, preparing the stage for their epic journey to "asaltar los cielos" (storm into the heavens) in the name of the Spanish *pueblo*.[10] Finally, Podemos's performance of authenticity opens the door to investigate Iglesias's emotional "realness" as another tool of popular-populist authentication. The performative display of his true emotions is thus understood, politically, with the help of Emmy Eklundh's conceptualization of the visceral and Paul Julian Smith's analysis of filmic emotionality.

Pablo Iglesias's Televisually Coded Leadership

Long before the foundation of Podemos. Iglesias's Gramscian conceptualization of cultural production as a medium to amass political hegemony was assumed to be essential political praxis.[11] Once Podemos entered institutional politics, it simply became commonplace. On Iglesias's weekly show *Fort Apache* (which he hosted and statedly styled as a "civilized" version of the political *tertulias* in mainstream television), one opening monologue—tellingly titled "Fiction and Power"—affirmed: "Why would a figure such as José María Lasalle, state secretary of culture, denounce with apocalyptic affection that Podemos's populist strategy is based on amassing cultural hegemony? Well . . . because he's really referring to Podemos's struggle for power; and as the old Sardinian Antonio Gramsci knew all too well, the *dispositifs* of persuasion at the base of key hegemonic discourses are cultural. Today, we'll talk about one of the most recent and powerful cultural *dispositifs*: television series, which precisely deal with that: power."[12] Podemos's understanding of cultural hegemony became key to the party's approach to the leadership of Iglesias and his performances on television. The objective was to make Iglesias part and parcel of popular culture—in the Gramscian sense of both *popular* and *culture*. In this respect, Antonio Gómez López-Quiñones clarifies: "Suffice to say that the aspect that makes 'culture' into 'popular culture' escapes any empirical description regarding the very object of study (the cultural) or its mode of production (cultural artifacts). . . . In a Gramscian sense, 'popular' (in culture) is all that which managed to become popular (to be popularized) at different moments in history."[13] Accordingly, the televisual figure of Iglesias escapes much of the contingency of television as cultural production and expands to the realm of the popular at large (i.e., that which has been popularized), where his performances are much more effective. With this notion of the popular in mind, Iglesias is defined by the potentiality for stardom that television offers in direct proportion to the way he defines television as a medium. Iglesias's views of the popular in television (i.e., not only what is popular but also and in parallel to what should be popular) are as important as the ways he represents himself in his television appearances—even beyond the way television presents him, which, generally speaking, responds to the more or less uncomplicated commercial logic of mainstream media.[14]

The media persona of Pablo Iglesias was constructed by means of two axes of televisual representation: first, there was the projection of Iglesias as an ordinary man, attuned to the politics of everyday, defined by a (curated) pedestrian honesty that contrasted with the increasingly convoluted justifications of those who somehow still defended in some way the status quo;[15] second, as a direct consequence, Iglesias performed a type of popular authenticity not dissimilar to the authentic selves produced in the framework of reality television—albeit within the new reality-like format of the *tertulias*. The result of these two lines of televisual representation was a political leadership that heavily relied on the affective investment of the public in what became the newfound celebrity status of many political dissidents: "activists, protesters and other marginal figures have migrated into the mainstream, and both emerging and established forms of screen media have granted them a platform through which they can, to a degree, control their new-found cult of personality and, by extension, their political message."[16] To such end, the political project of Podemos had the difficult task of constantly balancing the love-hate relationship intrinsic to the relationship between stardom and fandom.

In retrospect, anyone who revisits Iglesias's televisual performances can see how the two main features of his media persona are, to a great extent, self-evident.[17] However, what is not so apparent is how those characteristics could strike a balance between the authentic, everyday persona of Iglesias and his status as a celebrity politician with an ever-growing evident ambition to acquire institutional power. Iglesias was an integral part of what Graeme Turner had called the "demotic turn" of television, which refers to "the increasing visibility of the 'ordinary person' as they have turned themselves into media content through celebrity culture, reality TV, DIY web-sites, talk radio and the like."[18] The self-construction of Iglesias made use of Iglesias's own "ordinariness" and reversed the translation process between media and media users. Instead of letting television participate in the construction of the identities of their viewers (i.e., a television whose "function is closer to that of a translator or even an author of identities"), Iglesias turned the tables and performed the role of a viewer that would translate the "popular" for those already in television.[19] In other words, Iglesias's performance would project the everyday, the ordinary, the popular into television, which would eventually turn him into a televisual celebrity product that operated as a natural representative of society and occupied the center of symbolic production, thus opening the door for the popular to become populist.

Beyond the content that Iglesias created for his own television shows *La Tuerka* and *Fort Apache*, his celebrity status functioned as a type of televisual programming with a cultural (and political) impact that attempted to shape what was already popular into a new populist form. In this sense, Iglesias's "ordinary" celebrity persona is "not ordinary like the rest of us; what . . . [he] possesses is the capacity to perform a particularly spectacular version of ordinariness in public."[20] And in the demotic setting of television, his performance was inherently seductive in that the role he played within the larger structures of Podemos's dramatic plotlines created an populist affective investment (both negatively and positively) that often ruled over the strictly political investment on the party (i.e., beyond the natural attachments of party members with their political organization). In this sense, as a way to control the balance between emotional and political expenditure in the reality television format that Iglesias and Podemos cohabited, televisual fiction and its potential for political allegory provided an escape valve, projecting the excess of popular-populist desires onto an alternative fictional representation of Iglesias's "real" understanding of politics as well as of "real" leadership. Iglesias's own televisual (and to a lesser extent filmic) tastes became a much less taxing recourse to produce cultural hegemony, one of the main prerequisites of all populist strategies.[21] It is, then, through the rise of on-demand television series and the commentary that Iglesias had produced on the matter that one can analyze how the way Iglesias consumed and read a series of televisual cultural products became an important part of his politics—in a way transcending Podemos's (populist) communication strategy.

At the peak of Podemos's notoriety, *The Wire* and *Game of Thrones* were the two shows most prominently featured by Iglesias and other well-known members of the party.[22] The two can be said to have expressly formed the backbone of Podemos's understanding of how political power can be culturally represented in order to (try to) herd popular imagination in electoral politics. Iglesias's televisual leadership was informed by his own views of these cultural *dispositifs*. On the one hand, *The Wire* was seen as the journey of a few underdogs in their quest to expose and possibly change a system corrupt to the core. On the other hand, *Game of Thrones* spoke to the relationship between personal ambition and political power within the framework of Podemos's realpolitik.

What follows is not a critical analysis of these television products and the allegorical use of them that Iglesias may have made in the Spanish political context. A causal line is not drawn between Iglesias's media appearances and his media consumption. However, their correlation helps to understand Iglesias's visualization of the "popular" in "culture" (in the Gramscian sense), which is the basis of his self-portrayal as (populist) leader as well as Podemos's electoral politics at large. This analysis is the logical extension of Juan Carlos Monedero's thoughts in the prologue to the book on *Game of Thrones* that Iglesias edited: "¿Cine y política? Claro. No solo porque, desde sus comienzos, el cine fuera un arma de propaganda. También porque refleja las claves que hacen que una sociedad se mueva . . . Ahora que viene el invierno. Cine y política." (Cinema and politics? They go together, of course. Not only because since its inception cinema was used as a propaganda tool, but also because cinema mirrors the key elements that move society in one direction or another. . . . And now that 'winter is coming' [in reference to the television series *Game of Thrones*]: Cinema and politics."[23] Iglesias's understanding of the televisual codes in *The Wire* and *Game of Thrones* did inform his political performance as leader of Podemos, which would ultimately influence the evolving relationship of the party with the people.

If there is a common criticism of Iglesias's leadership, it is the allegation that he behaves in the perceived style of alpha-male-like populist leaders of the revolutionary Left. In fact, as early as in the first Asamblea Ciudadana of Podemos (also known as Vistalegre I), at which Iglesias was elected secretary-general, he already had to respond to accusations about his macho persona, to which he replied: "I'm not irreplaceable. I'm at the service of the party's majority. I am a party militant and not a *macho alfa* [alpha male]."[24] Regardless, comparing Iglesias to mainly Latin American leaders such as Hugo Chávez, Evo Morales, and Rafael Correa became in one way or another a commonplace of his "macho alphanness" (even within Podemos).[25] Interestingly, such characterization (which never really left him) ran counter to his own self-portrayal as leader, whose main mission was that of establishing *organically* Podemos's cultural hegemony.[26] To see through these two opposed poles of representation (i.e., the caricature of a macho, populist hyperleadership or, on the contrary, Podemos's equally overblown portrayals of Iglesias as a type of organic intellectual à la Gramsci), Iglesias's professed admiration for David Simon and Ed Burns's HBO show *The Wire* is a fictional window through which one can better gauge the distance between the projection of an image (Iglesias's) and its desired impact (Podemos's electoral gains). Fictional representation is a separate metric that nuances the picture of Iglesias's projected media persona.

One of the main characters in *The Wire*, Lester Freamon (Clarke Peters)—the intellectual-like detective who, being tasked with the wire operation throughout the show, uses only his brainpower to make arrests—contains the televisual codes that would later fit the essence of Iglesias's self-professed leadership.[27] Explicitly, Iglesias projects his admiration onto this character on the basis of, first, Freamon's "ordinary" intellectuality (i.e., his intelligence is relatable and, as such, he is a trusted adviser of other characters in the show) and, second, Freamon's ability to work against the system from within the system. After being ostracized to the police pawnshop unit as punishment for going against the political orders of the deputy commissioner, Freamon proves essential in uncovering the corrupt players who punished him in the first place. In his most iconic scene, Freamon famously asserts: "You follow drugs, you get drug addicts and drug dealers. But you start to follow the money, and you don't know where the fuck is gonna take you."[28] The scene is in turn used in Iglesias's *Fort Apache*'s show (in the episode entitled "Ficción y poder") to discuss how the neoliberal system at the root of the Spanish crisis will eventually fall apart (fig. 4.1). In that entire conversation about Freamon and *The Wire*, there is the sense that the retributory element of Freamon's actions is fundamental to understanding the show's relevance in the Spanish context. Freamon (as the character who exposes the cracks in the system and those who benefit from its corrupt nature) is interpreted as an allegorical catalyzer of Iglesias projected self-image of a popular avenger against societal hierarchy. In this sense, while Iglesias's mission is marred by the contradictions and limitations of real life, fiction allows him to fully project his more or less explicit desire for retribution (or, at minimum, some type of accountability).

Implicit in Iglesias's reading of Freamon's crusade against the corrupt system, there is also a principled incorruptibility that uncomplicatedly defines them both. Freamon's righteous objectives stem from his portrayal as a character determined by an unbreakable honesty, many times to his own detriment. In the same way, Iglesias's attacks against societal hierarchy emanate from his self-representation as an incorruptible political leader who sacrifices his private life for the sake of the public good. To this effect, Iglesias acknowledges the political value of *The Wire* in moral terms: "*The Wire* is a tragedy that has a moral undertone but without falling back to the cynicism found in *House of Cards*. With the tragic in mind, *The Wire* asks its audience if we can live a better life, one without so much pain. . . . That is, *The Wire* is

Figure 4.1. Still frame from the visual excerpt that introduces the discussion on *The Wire* in *Fort Apache's* episode "Ficción y poder," Hispan TV, YouTube video, 0:34, https://www.youtube.com/watch?v=jw_HdJ2Jldo.

an ancient Greek tragedy; the thing is that in the former the gods (as opposed to ancient Greek dramaturgy), the ones throwing lightning bolts, are the economic and political powers that be (as represented) in the connection with police characters."[29] Through this lens, Iglesias projects onto *The Wire* and, thus, unproblematically justifies his role in politics as a moralist enterprise meant to win the moral affection of the people-audience.

Through the moral framework of this premium-cable show (to which ironically the majority of the Spanish population had only restricted access), Podemos's political morality finds a mirror of the popular that somewhat unburdens its project as far as cultural representation is concerned. In the realm of popular culture, Podemos's "pedagogical" construction of a degraded political reality in the process of purification by means of Iglesias's leadership finds legitimacy in *The Wire*'s capacity to represent Baltimore as America's own politically rotten reality. This is a process of cultural legitimization that seeks a much easier route by means of the weight of US cultural hegemony in Spain and, more concretely, by what Smith has termed the "HBO-quality canon" (which makes television critics despise their local television shows and "reverently review new episodes of North American series but ignore their own").[30] When Iglesias projects his leadership and his fight through figures like Lester Freamon, he is also projecting the cultural legitimacy that the HBO canon enjoys.

Similarly, but much more explicitly, *Game of Thrones* is also key to understanding Podemos's politics beyond the party's self-stated goals in its communication strategy, especially in relation to Iglesias's conception of realpolitik.[31] This HBO show "offers a decipherable template to address . . . 'the puppeteers' behind the enactment of political decisions, represented in the series by characters such as Tyrion Lannister."[32] At the risk of being overly psychoanalytical, Iglesias's professed love for Tyrion Lannister (the dwarf aristocrat interpreted by Peter Dinklage) appears, most clearly, to reflect his own self-perception as political leader:

> The character that I love the most is Tyron, because he combines a profound humanism with a certain class consciousness (despite his aristocratic origins). He has a deep love for life and for the oppressed. . . . He has an innate solidarity for all those who face difficulties, and at the same time he is not naive . . . . Tyrion is able to understand the rules of politics; the rules of how power really works. The combination of someone sensitive who loves life . . . with the added dimension of someone who is a stateman . . . is what I like the most. He is the Antonio Gramsci of this television series.[33]

For Iglesias, Tyrion Lannister is the epitome of Machiavellian power as conceived by Gramsci, as "well-intentioned words without claws and fangs are useless."[34] Iglesias grew his "claws" and "fangs" first in the *tertulias* and, after being elected to the Spanish Parliament, in the innumerable media interviews and press conferences he gave. Much as Tyrion was characterized in the show, Iglesias was progressively portrayed by the media as an arrogant politician who had become too big for his britches. He was also depicted as a little political actor—a dwarf in comparison to established politicians—who had developed an insatiable personal ambition. Similarly, Tyrion's character development in *Game of Thrones* went from his being a total outsider, unwilling to play politics, to his acquiring a central role in the fight against his own father's and sister's despotic power.

Iglesias's reading of Tyrion is complemented by his interpretation of the character of Daenerys Targaryen, also known as the Khaleesi (the outcast dragon queen, an archetypical underdog, played by Emilia Clarke). From that perspective, he wonders about the role of charismatic power in politics:

> Slaves don't simply obey Daenerys because she has a whip, but also because she has a type of charismatic power that is granted to her by the mere fact of being their liberator. Yet one should further question that assertion. The

problem . . . is that Daenerys is not simply an individual political animal. She has dragons that are in reality her "claws" and her "fangs." . . . What's ultimately decisive about this character is that . . . apart from her given charisma, her discursive ability and her whip, she has an army, and she has real dragons as real weapons of mass destruction.[35]

If only metaphorically, Iglesias implemented that cosmovision of power when in his first encounter with the King of Spain, Felipe VI, he gifted him a DVD box of *Game of Thrones*—against all established protocol.[36] Beyond a possible ironic interpretation, the image represents Podemos's first attempts to wield cultural power, the only power that the party could have at that moment. Iglesias knew that the image would be culturally marked as powerful at a time when Podemos had very little political capital. Even more boldly, when asked why he breached royal protocol, Iglesias justified the gift by stating that he did so because Podemos identifies with Khaleesi—a character whose only objective in the show is to conquer the Iron Throne.[37]

Iglesias's comparisons to *Game of Thrones* are informed by a sense of realpolitik that understands victory (in Leninist terms) as the primary drive of politics.[38] Thus, Podemos was considered an electoral war machine (i.e., following Íñigo Errejón's conceptualization and the nonapologetic establishment of Iglesias's hyperleadership in a centralized and increasingly vertical party) that would eventually grant Iglesias the "iron throne" of Spanish politics. The stakes were as high as the chosen title of the book on the HBO show that Iglesias coordinated: "Ganar o morir" (to win or to die). Iglesias and Podemos framed themselves as *the* "real" option in the same way that Daenerys "is not simply morally credible and honorable as a character, . . . beyond that, her entire political project is . . . credible, plausible, and ultimately real; one expects a type of certainty from it."[39] And they became a "real" project by way of a political verisimilitude that was cinematically established.

If anything, the figure of Iglesias allowed for revisualizing in color the seemingly unmovable demos conceived at best in black and white since the Transición. Furthermore, the once-reduced color palette for that demos had been transformed with the passing of time into an ideological color blindness—in the form of an enforced neutrality or moderation when it came to political positioning—that had indeed ruled with an iron fist the political imaginary of Spain. The 15-M used such vision deficiency to its benefit and exposed the artificiality of established power. Following that visual metaphor, the movement demanded a total overhaul of the increasingly colorless political system. When Iglesias appeared and referred to a ruling caste that had

been in power for decades to the detriment of the Spanish *pueblo*, a new system of colors forced its way back into the politics (literally and figuratively).
Podemos broke not only conceptually but also visually and then performatively with established politics. The party's color (purple) was the result of
fusing blue, the color of the Popular Party on the Right, and red, the color
of the PSOE (the Partido Socialista Obrero Español) on the (center) Left. The
circle in its logo referred to the assembly structure of the 15-M. It symbolized that "the 'us' takes precedence over the 'avant-garde,' the body over the
head . . . in order to move toward becoming an open movement, which . . .
performatively evokes the construction of a new subject as both contingent
and hegemonic: *the people*."[40]

This sudden (conceptual, visual, performative) alteration allowed the
entire political discursive practice to be resignified. The old metaphors did
not work any longer; the once-coveted political center, the virtuous middle
ground between Left and Right, had become incomprehensible and was
nowhere to be seen. But above all, the political arena had again acquired
distinguishable traits for separating the powerful from the powerless. It was
thus visually possible to know and to judge those on different sides of the
newly color-coded political spectrum. Although political clarity does not
necessarily beget social justice, the visualization of a Spanish caste was the
Trojan horse that the founding members of Podemos had thought would
finally help to purge the country of its extractive elites. And from inside the
wooden horse, the media persona of Iglesias awaited his turn to take over
the throne of Spanish politics via a populist strategy that was as televisual
as it was cinematic.

Television was the medium through which their political message was
first delivered, but cinema was the visual style that shaped that message. So
if television had been the main channel through which Podemos reached
and represented people's unheard demands since the days of the 15-M, the
language of cinema allowed for a more effective presentation of such representative impetus. And that was how Podemos's populist politics were able
to become culturally popular. In this respect, the usage of *cinematic* here is
not meant to be an analytical category (as in the analysis of cinematic representation in contrast to Podemos's mediatic representation in television).
Rather, it refers to the ability of Podemos when engaging the public cinematically (within the aesthetic and the discourse of film) through its media
appearances on television, which projected Iglesias as an empty signifier
within Spain's populist moment. Podemos's cinematic style was to tap into

a particular narrative in popular culture (the heroic epic of the HBO canon), ultimately granting the party's condition of possibility as populist in politics.

Under such a prism, cinema helps us to understand how certain visualities can function as generators of political identities that may give way to the creation of new political realities. This approach closely follows Podemos's construction of a new political reality that can be further conceptualized via Steven Marsh's interpretation of temporality in film as untimely and directly related to the performance of change. As such, Marsh analyzes film against Frederic Jameson's historicist teleology which "has consistently maintained that there is a correspondence between representation and the political reality of its production."[41] In line with such a conceptual distinction, the cinematic presentation of political subjects (e.g., a working-class protagonist) is not only decoupled from its contingent historical representation (i.e., in the Industrial Revolution or during the neoliberal times of deindustrialization) but also is able to (re)produce old as well as new political realities due to its "untimely" nature (e.g., the cinematic presentation of communism and fascism remains mostly unchanged in representations that still inform today's political reality). Podemos's machine of cinematic presentation (or performance) of change aimed to construct a new political reality against the grain of the material reality of its production (just as Marsh has argued something similar in relation to Spanish cinematic production). Thus, Podemos's populist politics visualized (cinematically) a path to victory against all odds and via what was at the time almost unthinkable: the quixotic leadership of Pablo Iglesias fighting against the Spanish elites on prime-time television in the name of the people.

La casta Cinematic

In what was at the time his most watched television interview, Pablo Iglesias defined for the interviewer Pedro Piqueras the meaning of a term revitalized by Podemos that was dominating the vocabulary of Spanish politics—*la casta*: the caste, as in a social caste system: "There are two types of politicians. Those politicians who carry the citizenry's will in the way a mailperson carries people's letters, and those others who are butlers of the rich. The politicians who are butlers of the rich are *casta* and the politicians who act like a mailperson for the citizenry are simply honest people. . . . A very important number of those who have ruled this country have used their popular mandate to enrich themselves and make their friends rich too. And the word *casta* can be used to point the finger at them."[42] As used in the political discourse of Iglesias and Podemos at large, the term *casta* originated in the book *The Caste: How Italian Politicians Became Untouchable*, by the journalists Sergio Rizzo and Gian Antonio Stella. At least since the turn of the twentieth century, the word had historically had currency in Spain with a very similar meaning among prominent figures such as Benito Pérez Galdós, Ramón Pérez de Ayala, and Manuel Azaña.[43] However, its new life in the twenty-first century and patent political effectiveness resided in the concrete usage given by the Podemos phenomenon. *Casta* became so recognizable that it was almost interchangeable with political and economic corruption in Spain. It acted, as Joaquín Valdivielso has noted, like a populist interpellation, discursively constructing the opposition between haves and have-nots, those at the top and those at the bottom, the Spanish people and the Spanish caste.[44] So beyond its discursive impetus, the term was able to generate a readily accessible mental image to make sense of a quite complex set of historical circumstances, as corruption in Spain is rooted in Francoism but also inserted in the neoliberal turn favored by the European Union, for example. When Iglesias speaks of politicians as butlers of the rich in the context of the crisis, the idea of *la casta* projects a visual metaphor that encapsulates the essence of the times. Although Iglesias could be pressed to name who really belonged to that caste (as in the interview with Piqueras), he did not have to identify anyone by name to be extremely effective. Everyone at that time in Spain already had in mind a picture of those in *la casta*.

That is one of the main reasons the word was so effective: it triggered a mental image that belonged to no one and everyone at the same time. The word became a prominent feature of popular culture, as understood by the Spanish historian José Alvarez Junco, in that "the popular avoids official documentation and thrives in the more escaping practice of its sheer diversity."[45] In this respect, the term became collectivized as part of those processes of symbolic representation that favor the unwritten. The visual politics of *la casta* superseded its more specific discursive essence in the creation of collective stories. As images travel faster and more efficiently within the realm of collective storytelling, the word became a type of a visual tool that imposed interpretation and proposed unquestionable evidence for new narrations of a common "us" against a common institutionalized other.[46] Beyond Podemos's political usage, when transposed to its most fluid state—in the practice of its sheer cultural diversity—*la casta* acquired its popular zenith, ultimately granting the term its populist robustness. When Iglesias was at the peak of his popularity, Álex de la Iglesia's *Mi gran noche* (2015) was one of the most popular Spanish films, and it is a fitting platform for exploring the audiovisual practices of *la casta* beyond its most explicit usage.

Mi gran noche's entire plot revolved around the spectacle of television and its relationship with a televisual public whose reality had become completely mediated by television. Similarly, the Podemos phenomenon was built around a televisual spectacle that depended on the construction of an audience mediated by the crisis, whose source of political identification was ultimately the crisis. De la Iglesia's use of television in all his cinema to approach political reality was particularly pertinent to Podemos's televisual construction of its politics. The spectacles provided by De la Iglesia and by Podemos ensued in the understanding that the material reality of a crisis and its artifice (i.e., its televisual representation) were intimately connected. The connection—reality plus artifice—points to what Vinodh Venkatesh, following Stephen Duncombe's theorization of spectacle in everyday life, has referred to as De la Iglesia's use of television as an "ethical spectacle."[47] This type of televisual spectacle avoids pretending that the portrayal of reality in television is real; instead, it makes a pact with its audience and "demonstrates the reality of its own illusions."[48] An ethical spectacle co-constructs "reality" happening on both sides of the screen. The public not only knows from the beginning that the jig is up; they also encourage its irreality and participate in the illusion, because the ultimate goal of this type of televisual spectacle is to create an engaged community with a sense of a shared "reality" (regardless of its realness). From the perspective of the media industry, that engagement is essential for anchoring a loyal audience, and at the same time, it has the potential to produce a type of common sense around which a political bond can be established.[49]

Conceptually, Álex de la Iglesia's *Mi gran noche* reflects on the capacity of television to construct popular realities. The film narrates the television prerecording of New Year's Eve in October 2015. The main plot depicts the precarious conditions of a cast of extras (*figurantes con o sin frase*) who are being locked into working continuously on set for more than a week because of a large protest against television cuts outside the studio. The studio's outside and inside represent a reality vertebrated by the crisis, though a crisis obliquely represented. Similarly, the conceptualization of *la casta* in the film appears explicitly only as a caricature, in the shape of the character of Benítez (Santiago Segura), a corrupt television producer who runs the program both inside (as showrunner) and outside (because the protests are directed at him). However, far from allowing him free rein, his status as *casta* impedes his movements around the television set (he is mostly enclosed to the office area of the channel) and especially in the space between the inside of the studio (where his commands are useless, as he has no technical skills) and the outside (where the protesters could accost him). Equally, all those other characters who benefit in one way or another from the status quo find themselves in the film moving with increasing difficulty *entre bastidores*, constantly negotiating their privileges. So rather than implementing a direct visualization of the Spanish caste, *Mi gran noche* represented the political climate that Podemos's ideation of *la casta* brought about.

While De la Iglesia's cinema is popularly known for its tragicomic horror, his filmic practice—as Cristina Moreiras-Menor has suggested—belongs with Luis Buñuel, Mario Camus, and Jaime Chavarri, as it is directly informed by "a thoughtful critique, highly political, in regard to temporality, privileging in his conception of temporality the present as the moment in (Spanish) history par excellence."[50] Notwithstanding the public's general association of De la Iglesia's filmography with a less explicitly political enterprise (especially when compared with some of his coetaneous filmmakers such as Fernando León de Aranoa or Icíar Bollaín), his cinema has always had the capacity to exude the politics of its time.[51] Yet at the time of its release, *Mi gran noche* was broadly characterized as a mainstream film that was "hardly subversive," which did little to denounce its context of crisis.[52]

This indictment reveals much more than a soft critique of the film. It voices a common understanding at the time that demanded the overt representation of the collective suffering that the crisis had provoked (as explained in Chapter 3). In this respect, Triana-Toribio proposes that "perhaps the real reason for raising these concerns is that the crisis has devastated too many real lives and futures and we cannot avoid the feeling that films in these circumstances could and should do more to denounce."[53] In a time of crisis, when reality became divided by a clear-cut line (e.g., those who endure the crisis and those who benefited from it, those who caused it and those who didn't), De la Iglesia chose to make a film that presented victims and victimizers from an oblique perspective. In this way, as Albritton has suggested, a type of film like *Mi gran noche* may hint at the destruction of capitalist institutions, "albeit safely, on screen, and in a manner so surreal that it has likely lost any potential radicality."[54] Nevertheless, its alleged lack of political radicality does also away with a monologic act of political denunciation that in the context of the film would have been drown in a sea of radical protest (on the screen, in the streets, and in Parliament with the appearance of Podemos). And even though *Mi gran noche* struck a much less explicit political pose, it was able to capture the much more pervasive sentiment of social change as filtered by popular culture. In this sense, De la Iglesia was immersed in the dialogic task of translation that connected the film's politically charged context with its even more politically positioned audience.

Following the Gramscian notion of translatability, the signs that designated Spanish society as in crisis went through a process of translation that replaced those former (political, economic) signs with another set of signs of cinematic representation—this time in the form of De la Iglesia's famous film.[55] At the moment, this act of cinematic translation would have to go through the filter of Podemos's influential interpretation of Spanish society as being dominated by *la casta*. In that way, the term was inescapable and, to a great extent, became a type of cosmovision destined to generate cultural hegemony—as thought by Gramsci. *Mi gran noche* would then imply a task of translation from the social practice of *la casta* (as framed by Podemos) into the cinematic praxis of representing popular reality (as in reality television). Politically, Podemos successfully translated *casta* between languages (from its Italian usage into Spanish), between theories of the political (from Laclauian theory of populism and his ideation of the empty signifier into the practice of Spanish politics to combat a long history of elites' unaccountability), and finally, between publics (from a restricted electoral audience to the mass audiences of television). In *Mi gran noche*, De la Iglesia was cinematically reading from Podemos's translation to implement his own translational process. And in any process of translation, there is always a degree of loss and fluidity of what is translated. So De la Iglesia's film did not explicitly represent Podemos's translation of Spanish political reality; it constructed a visual metaphor of that reality, which, most importantly, had in mind "one of the key aspects of the translational process: the needs of its intended audience."[56] The film paid special attention at the representative relationship between both sides of the screen, between those who see and those who are seen, in a cinematic process of translation from political reality into the reality of television. *Mi gran noche* is in that way an explicit display of metacommentary on the confluence of filmic and televisual representation.

The film blends the inner boundaries that demarcate the separation between televisual and nontelevisual reality. Most prominently, affecting bursts of joy for the camera during nonexistent performances, the extras inside the studio staged their heightened fake emotions as an inversed mirror of the protesters' "real" anger against the television channel in the outside. In the middle of the representation of these two polar-opposite (ir)realities, the "reality" of television celebrities was inserted, with their lives ruled by ruthless and vacuous competitions for the spotlight, which in the end became their only important reality. All of them were ultimately vessels of televisual representation, and thus their realities became the "reality" of television. Nothing escaped the camera lenses: television absorbed the reality of the crisis that accompanied all those lives inside and outside the studio. The crisis was thus overdetermined by the reality of a television also in crisis, rooted in the schism between its public and those who decided what the public needs—a metaphorical conceptualization symbolizing the fissure in Spanish society between the people and *la casta* at the time.

Contrary to the extras' exaggerated performances, *Mi gran noche* portrayed a television in need of a real public that could be complicit with its "reality." Not only was the show completely detached from its present reality—it deals with a prerecording of a future New Year's Eve show, so could not have a real audience in the present—the actual filming of the show was alienating even to its fake audience, the extras, who had been in lockdown on set for more than a week. To top it all off, multiple labor accidents in the studio kept delaying the filming of the show, bringing it to a state of crisis. The only representation of a real audience were the protesters outside the studio, former employees of the channel laid off by Benítez; they were the material representation of the crisis. They were the only ones really engaged with the show, albeit only in a negative manner.

The axis of this televisual crisis did not mirror the crisis of Spanish society exactly. In this sense, the film was not so much structured by the patent inequalities between those at the bottom (i.e., the extras as part of the disposable *precariat* and the protesters as the already disposed unemployed) and those above them (i.e., Benítez and all the rest). The crisis was really scaffolded by the impossibility of stepping out of the crisis of representation that the crisis of television had provoked. This television in crisis demanded constant participation, which obtained through sheer force. None of characters in the film was participating willingly of the televisual spectacle (which was not only alienating to everyone but also had become hazardous), and all of them were bound by the television studio (as they were physically locked on set). The crisis was in that way systemic and so were the lives in crisis of all those characters trapped by the televisual (ir)reality.

The gridlock seemed to be broken only when the film neared the end in what was to be the last performance of the night by the old-timer, once-legendary Alphonso (interpreted by Raphael who himself is an old semiforgotten celebrity). In the middle of his performance, his badly mistreated son and personal assistant Yuri (Carlos Areces) was about to have him shot dead. However, at the last minute, his own hired mercenary, Óscar (Jaime Ordóñez)—a disgruntled fan of Alphonso—refused to execute Yuri's plan professing his unyielding love for Alphonso. While Yuri tussled with Óscar to complete the deed, the following illuminating dialogue ensued:

> Óscar: I live my life the way I want. I am what I am [Óscar is here maniacally reciting the lyrics of Raphael's song "Escándalo" as it plays in the background, while in turn Alphonso (Raphael) performs the lip-sync version of his own song].
> Óscar: I'll shoot him [but does not shoot].
> Yuri: Shoot him!
> Óscar: I can't! I love this song of his!
>
> Óscar: Alphonso is a living legend! He's living history of Spain! And he's also your father.
> Yuri: All the more reason to do so, we need to start from scratch.[57]

Yuri's last words were a not-so-subtle hint at the need to reset Spanish history in order to start completely anew. When put in context, taking into account the different visual cues of the scene, the dialogue actually pointed to the inevitability of a profound change of the existing televisual structure. This was a structure so damaged that its fall would be brought about by the mere (even deranged) pursuit of such a resetting.

The sequence of events produced a domino effect that signaled a visually chaotic series of attempts at eliminating metaphorically the *casta*-like hierarchies that conformed this televisual spectacle in crisis. The first and most obvious one was the giant zero of the hanging numbers that announce the New Year of 2016, from where Yuri attempted to kill his abusive celebrity father. Then, there was how Yuri misfired and instead shot the giant cross (a common symbol of Spanishness in De la Iglesia's filmography) that the extra José (Pepón Nieto) was carrying. The latter had angrily taken the cross from his demanding mother (Terele Pávez) in his only act of defiance in the film. José was ironically saved by the cross, but—tellingly—the cross was then tossed away and forgotten. What is more, as the chaos in the studio increased, Benítez was arrested on corruption charges in a short, anticlimactic scene. Immediately after, Yuri was similarly taken down by the studio security guards, whom earlier in the film he had belittled taking advantage of his more privileged—albeit precarious—position in the channel's food chain. As the extras were being finally let out of the set, Alphonso uncharacteristically offered his helicopter to José, his mother and his newfound love Paloma (Blanca Suárez), an extra who was believed to be jinxed. While the rest of extras were walking out, the scene cuts to Alphonso's helicopter nosediving, about to crash into the ground. The last hierarchy, that of the celebrity star system, had been brought down both literally (in the visualization of the aircraft's malfunction at the hands of the jinxed extra, Paloma, who was heard messing around with the control panel) and figuratively (as the once-marginalized extras were symbolically sharing in the helicopter the space of celebrity exclusivity with Alphonso). The televisual system was cinematically reset. All the old symbols that visualized the established order of televisual representation were gone. Nothing had been put in place instead, and no hopeful future was hinted at; the only allegorical signs of social justice were either unsatisfying (e.g., Benítez's arrest) or ephemeral (e.g., the symbolic equality achieved by the extras was quickly gone in the helicopter's crash). Nevertheless, visually, systemic change had occurred, and the *casta*-like hierarchies were (televisually) out of sight, which did not mean they had completely disappeared. The symbolic visual erasure of the *casta* did not necessarily preclude the advent of a positive change of the system, only the hope for one.

Analogous to that representation of systemic change in the film, the popularization of *la casta* was dependent on a spectacle that symbolically performed its visual disappearance with the appearance of Podemos. In this sense, Iglesias's denunciation of a Spanish caste did more than merely point out the deep political antagonism that the crisis had brought to the surface—in fact, profound hostilities in Spanish politics preexisted Podemos's usage of the term with similar levels of intensity. *La casta*'s popularity was in great part due to the ability of the term to perform an essentialist demand, which could be cosmetically met (especially by television standards). As such, the performances of Pablo Iglesias on prime-time television, battling against the symbols of the Spanish caste, had a take-no-prisoners approach that made them irresistible to watch. The appeal of a young Iglesias in jeans, with a ponytail, berating (mostly) older men in expensive suits provided the ideal televisual framework for the political weaponization of *la casta*. Like the end of De la Iglesia's film, the erasure of *la casta* was an eminently visual endeavor that shamed the old political and economic establishment into hiding (at least temporarily).[58]

Rhetorically, at the level of political discourse, *la casta* served "as a 'negative bonding' . . . in order to capitalize on . . . antagonism as a cohesive factor: 'by knowing them, we know what we want.'"[59] On a visual level, *la casta* interpellated to the dissolution of its own representation: by seeing them, we know we want them gone. The visions that *la casta* provoked went hand in hand with a type of plebeian retribution, which translated political discourse into the visualization of Bastille-like revolutionary action, where the powerful lost most of their glamour (though not their power). Films like *Mi gran noche*, which at most represented obliquely the political ecosystem of the crisis, performed the vanishment of *la casta* and did away with the symbols of the old regime. Iglesias embodied the central signifier of that vision "against other signifiers through images, in people, in performance . . . [which catalyzed] the psychological investment of Podemos supporters."[60] A new iteration in the visual politics of the popular-populist—guided now by Podemos's quest for cultural hegemony—quickly made use of and quickly moved past the collective logic of denunciation that intensified after the 15-M. This time the people were to be the vicarious spectators of a populist performance that had them as protagonists of what will be called Podemos's cinematic turn.

The Cinematic Turn of Podemos

Perhaps counterintuitively at the time, the logic of Podemos emphasized Iglesias's leadership as the missing link between what was popularly known (the lack of a real democracy) and what was seen daily (the perceived inability to effect systemic democratic changes). The media appearances of Iglesias introduced a visual politics key to a new hermeneutics of the Spanish *pueblo* since the 15-M, which had increasingly lost representative transversality by becoming transformed into contingent and increasingly dispersed, albeit powerful, voices of protest. Podemos, however, grasped the relationship between what was made visible—economic injustices, political corruption, huge demonstrations against austerity measures—and what was visually possible: a new cycle of political representation that poignantly asked about the images of protest in relation to their performative and transformative qualities. That is, Iglesias became a conduit of visual representation that connected the scattered images of protest and resignified them as conditions of possibility within a cohesive storyline. What is more, Iglesias's political discourse (that cohesive storyline) was especially effective in visualizing change because it was crafted with the language of cinema; hence, the importance of approaching Podemos cinematically. To such effect, a great deal of party's success rested on its cinematic style of emotional engagement, which would craft an appealing visual narrative of political confrontation—the people who demanded systemic change versus *la casta* who clung to the status quo—with Iglesias as the "realest" representative of the people and the underdog protagonist of Spain's new political melodrama.

The media appearance of Pablo Iglesias can be considered as a moving image that repeatedly asked the viewers, to what extent can boundaries to transformative politics (i.e., the stalemate between social protest and institutional change) be transgressed by the visualization of a new horizon of political success (favored by the new battleground of the television set)?[61] Podemos and its rapid electoral advances were not only an affirmative answer to that question; they also supposed a new wave in the spectacularizing of politics as necessarily embedded in popular culture. Especially with the help of the change in format of *tertulias*, such as *Al Rojo Vivo* or *La Sexta Noche*, which were very similarly modeled after sports talk shows, the party enacted a new political visuality of the plebs that used the figure of Iglesias cinematically as a sort of plebeian avenger for prime-time television. As such, instead of mere demands for real change, the figure of Iglesias connected to "a certain animus of nonviolent, plebeian retribution that was brewing at the time, as people perceived that those at the top had been mocking the citizenry for quite some time."[62] His image and the visual metaphors it conjured did not visualize victims (of the crisis, of a politically corrupt system) in need of recognition. It projected the image of political retribution; a visual politics (stemming from the audiovisual culture analyzed in Chapter 3) by which the politically invisible plebs were not only being visually represented in politics beyond the domain of cultural representation; they were seen at the center of a political victory that could avenge their long time in the shadows and, conceptually speaking, open the door to the making of a new *pueblo*. And what could be more compelling than political vengeance? With the help of this powerful vision, Podemos was to perform the transformation hope into change.

Podemos's visual politics were highly performative "geared toward challenging culturally commonsensical assumptions about how to 'do politics.'"[63] As much as Podemos's performances were often aimed at defying the established political habitus in institutional(ized) spaces (as Sara Martínez Guillem argues), its performative drive was guided by the audiovisual documentation of its performances regardless of the actors' awareness or intentions while being filmed.[64] The appearance of political authenticity was as important as the authenticity of politics. In this sense, there are two aspects that should be further considered: on the one hand, the theorization of Podemos's populism must veer away from its well-studied and self-professed discursive impetus of popular authenticity to incorporate how that discourse was performed (audiovisually) and not simply ideated;[65] on the other hand, relatedly, more attention needs to be paid to how the character role of Iglesias as populist leader in such performance was emotionally constructed and how he fit into the ideation of Podemos's overall cinematic strategy.

Regarding the first aspect, Fernando León de Aranoa's documentary on Podemos—*Política, manual de instrucciones* (2016)—grants extraordinary moments of transparency that allow for further consideration of Podemos's performative impetus. As Fiona Noble argues: "As a documentary claiming spontaneity and immediacy, the deployment of performance with its lexis of rehearsal and staginess creates a tension that exemplifies the constructed and narrativized character of political performativity. The rhetoric of performance permeates both the ethos of the party and the documentary which depicts Pablo Iglesias and fellow Podemos party members backstage and participating in various events including rallies and media interviews."[66] However, it must be stressed that the film won't be here understood as the filmic representation of Podemos's constructed reality. Beyond highlighting "the inseparability of performance and politics within the landscape of contemporary Spanish society," *Política* is important because it is one the most evident examples of how the party used political performativity (in this case, performing their realest selves in front of León de Aranoa's cameras) as another way to appear authentically popular, of the people.[67] It is thus a conceptual window into how Podemos's political discourse (theorized within the parameters Gramscian hegemony and Laclau's populism) was cinematically performed. Even though León de Aranoa never directly dwells on the relationship between Podemos and populism outside Podemos's own conceptualization, the theoretical connection can be implicitly interpreted. In fact, it is first found in the film's very title, which can be interpreted as referring to the script Podemos used to perform the staging of a new *pueblo* as an instruction manual to understand the political in its rawest sense. As the film advances, it becomes clear that the manual has been directly translated from the Latin American populist experiences, as throughout the film images of Podemos's relatively unknown two-week tour in Bolivia, Ecuador, and Uruguay are prominently interspersed, breaking the hard-established linearity of filmic events. But populism in the film is thought beyond its abstract composition. It materializes in the everyday praxis of Podemos in its contradictions as well as in its unspoken limitations. Podemos's populist hypothesis as shown in the film operates as a specific visual metaphor of the vast conceptual range of populism within the practice of Spain's political crisis of representation.

In that sense, populism (as an abstract political theory) is not so much seen in the film as the film allowing one to see Podemos's performing of its populism as part of the party's political practice (presenting the party's main characters as ordinary people that aspired to make democracy demotic again). In other words, it is the filmic documentation of Podemos's populist aesthetic that matters over the populism that Podemos ideates as seen in the film. Thus, the performativity of cinematic representation is of essence when thinking of the performances of Podemos in León de Aranoa's film. Populism is important for Podemos not because it has a more or less precise political use (despite its founding members' assertion of the different practical uses of Podemos's so-called populist hypothesis).[68] Populism is critical in Podemos's politics because it can be seen performed as the realest way of doing politics. Furthermore, the documentation of performance (via film, television, or the internet) is what accounts for the "real" (or popularly authentic) in Podemos's populist politics, and not the other way around. As such, populism does not precede its performance. It is its performance (of belonging to the people) that gives meaning to Podemos's populism. And in the case of *Política*, it is the filming of the performance that substantiate Podemos's populist strategies (e.g., media communication, political organization, electoral marketing). Podemos's populism depended "on documentation to attain symbolic status within the realm of culture."[69] That is, the performance of Podemos's populist practice is in the end constituted through the performativity of the documentation of such praxis.

To further understand how the visual documentation of Podemos's populism was not only essential but also inseparable from the implementation of its own populist practice (as the truest demotic representative in Spanish politics), it is useful to recall at length the words of Iglesias in conversation with León de Aranoa about *Política*:

> For me, there are two separate parts in this documentary. There is one part in which the leaders of Podemos speak directly to camera and we interpret politically what's happening around us. I think that part is quite conventional, but there is another part that is much less so. And, when I rewatched the documentary, that part made me think of how irresponsible we were when we let your film crew film in. We were sharing with you every detail of what was taking place inside the party back then. However, I think that second part, though less politically conventional, is what grants this documentary its cinematic value. Being in the inside of all those political moments—when real politics is taking place—is what's valuable. Because real politics has not to do

with someone talking about his/her politics directly to the camera. Real politics takes place when that someone is caught by the camera living through a political moment, a moment of tension around a political decision.[70]

Iglesias, in this reflection, is artificially separating the theatricality of performance (i.e., when members of Podemos talk directly into camera with a political intention, acknowledging the political presence of their viewership) and the documentation of performance (i.e., the recording of a moment in the film that "caught" the members of Podemos performing their politics without an audience in mind, a moment of supposed political rawness). Nevertheless, as Philip Auslander has argued, the differentiation not only is artificial but also ideologically manufactured: "the *assumption* that in the former mode [in the theatrical category], the event is staged primarily for an immediately present audience and that the documentation is a secondary, supplementary record of an event that has its own prior integrity."[71] There is not an ontological division between the staging of a political thought, which always assumes an audience, and the documenting of an spontaneous political event that reflect "real" political thinking behind the consciously staged political thought. Both are dependent on the interaction with an audience (whether intended or not) and, more critically, the discussions that inevitably spring from that interaction.

As a result, in the case of Podemos, the differentiation between the unfiltered documentation of party politics and its intentional theatricalization is equally performative. It performs a veiled discussion with the public, in which a "real" Podemos—spontaneous, true, popular, of the people—is ideologically as well as preemptively constructed against the inevitable process of becoming less "real" and more like other political parties—since the Podemos leadership in the film already shows a great level of consciousness in regard to their future behavior as part of the political establishment. Underneath the distinction lies the framing of Podemos as a political party with a "real" popular essence, one confirmed in León de Aranoa's behind-the-scenes-like filming of Podemos leadership (of their assemblies, their electoral campaigns, their meetings with political leaders, their successes and their losses). This is the performance of the "organic" side of Podemos that necessitates of its artificial opposite to emphasize with a certain degree of verisimilitude how much more the former is prevalent in this new political party. The division is very much performed "in order to reappropriate [its] symbolic dimensions, blurring the distinction between 'frontstage' and 'backstage' practices."[72] In this respect, Podemos's populism was dependent on that type of performed political "realness" (i.e., one that does not appear to distinguish between what is manufactured to be publicly displayed and what is extemporaneously seen) as much as it relied on its audiovisual documentation to be perceived as "real" (i.e., one that is documented with handheld cameras, linearly filmed, authentic, culturally popular, not apparently highbrow). Nevertheless, the successful performativity of Podemos as a party of the people required much more than documenting verisimilar performances of popular authenticity. It confided in the construction of a political leadership in nonpolitical spaces at a time when political leaders were at an all-time low.[73]

From the vantage point of hindsight, in the interview conducted by Pablo Iglesias with León de Aranoa, the two further reflected on the latter's documentary on Podemos—*Política, manual de instrucciones*—and the unprecedented access the filmmaker was given to record from the inside the newly founded party. In that conversation, Iglesias, then vice president in Pedro Sánchez's coalition government, wondered how they could have been so politically irresponsible by allowing such free rein to the film crew.[74] At the same time, both agreed that the film acquired "cinematic value" only because of the recording of unfiltered moments of tension, outside the protagonists' posterior rationalizations of those occasions.[75] Iglesias finally reasoned that the filmmaker could so freely document the party's internal affairs because, at that time in Podemos, they were more interested in the beauty that cinema could create than in party politics.[76]

What at first might simply seem a superficial remark actually points to a critical moment of political as well as popular representation in the interim that went from the 15-M until Podemos was electorally established. This was a moment specially marked by the need for symbolic reconstruction of people's lives in the political realm. At the height of the economic crisis, when austerity measures were implemented despite the rapid intensifications of protests, the figure of Pablo Iglesias as the personification of Podemos was able to agglutinate myriad political demands into a cohesive symbol of change. Although Podemos's electoral gains were possible only because of the intense groundwork of a panoply of organizations and social movements that preceded the foundation of the party, it was the ability of Podemos's leadership to visualize democratic change as "real" beyond what was deemed possible at the institutional level that initially cracked open the 15-M's "[previous] performative incision, a cut in time, a demarcation in temporality."[77] Podemos understood that the fissure in history produced by the 15-M had also provoked a breach of cultural representation in the realm of the popular, whose meaning was to be intensely negotiated under the new parameters of populism and, especially, Iglesias's populist leadership.

Podemos and Iglesias succeeded in their conceptualization of (populist) leadership because it was first and foremost performed outside the institutional political arena and was not overtly politically coded. It took place at the intersection of the populist and the popular in the realm of the explicitly cultural. At this intersection, even when Podemos formed part of the institutional space, politics were symbolically coded as popular culture. Critically, it was the visualization of Iglesias's (politically constructed) emotions as popular common sense that was at the base of the cultural (re)creation of Podemos's populist leadership. The praxis of this leadership implemented a visual politics beyond the translation of (Laclau's) populism as theory into political practice. Iglesias's performances as leader were also cinematically framed to engage his audience emotionally. In this sense, Iglesias's emotions functioned, politically, through what Emmy Eklundh calls "visceral ties" and, culturally, in a similar way to what Paul Julian Smith terms "emotional participation" in film.[78]

Eklundh proposes that "we conceive of political subjects as created by visceral ties, a type of hegemony, which capture the inherent co-constitutive nature between affect and signification."[79] In the context of Spain's populist cycle, the author uses the idea of the visceral to analyze how a new political subject (a *pueblo*) was "produced by affective investments in empty signifiers" such as the demands for a real democracy in the 15-M or, in the case of Podemos, Iglesias's populist leadership.[80] The mediatic imprint of the latter furthered that political subjectivity within the institutionalized framework of the party, as distinct from the more socially and politically decentralized structure of the 15-M movement. Hence, Eklundh states, "the online and televised presence of Pablo Iglesias as the leader could be seen as visceral ties, the affective investment in an empty signifier," which, I argue, connected the people of popular culture with the people of populism.[81] Politically, Iglesias was the nodal point that reunited the people and their growing frustration around its mediatized persona to foster a new time in Spanish democracy. Culturally, though, the leadership of Iglesias constructed a type of emotional engagement that is better understood by the affective mechanisms of cinema as explained by Smith's investigation on Spain's visual culture.

Broadly speaking, Smith's main argument follows the moral philosopher Martha Nussbaum by way of expanding her contention that emotions cannot be severed from the rationalization of emotions (i.e., the reasons that beget, perpetuate, or dismiss emotions).[82] Following that line of thinking, Smith approaches filmic emotions as a type of cognition. Film can be said to invite its audience to transcend the overt narrative of its plot and engage emotionally with what is visually presented. What is seen on film needs to be carefully examined as the conjunction of what is said and what is felt. More concretely, Smith, via Nussbaum, considers how the act of caring (for someone) is audiovisually narrated as a form of intelligence and, thus, refers to the "emotional imperative" of film as "inseparable from the intellectual goal of understanding subjects and institutions."[83] Iglesias's frequent displays of emotional caring (for the people) are to be embedded as part of his populist style. Iglesias's emotions connect with Smith's emotional imperative in film in that the display of affectivity begets the political narrative that constructs the "us" of populism (not the other way around). This sequence (emotions first, political discourse second) is what bonds the leader-protagonist with the people-audience. And through Iglesias's pathos, Podemos's ethics are thus constructed in cinematic fashion. As such, the audiovisual performances of Iglesias not only aimed at creating a political ethos of authenticity; they invited his audience to transcend the discursive nature of his politics to fully engage with the ways his emotions were displayed. This was an invitation for the people to be affectively invested in Iglesias's leadership similarly to the ways audiences participate in film's emotional architecture.

Just like a film can produce an emotional following beyond its "objective" artistic value, seeing Iglesias's authentic emotions was critical to validate Podemos's popular authenticity, which ultimately supported their ethical discourse on anything political.[84] In this sense, Podemos's populist style can be further understood as a cinematic tool that allowed for the construction of political emotional bonds. An illuminating example was the ceremony of constituting Parliament (i.e., "la sesión constitutiva de las Cortes") in January 2016 after Podemos obtained sixty-nine seats in the general elections. Two emblematic moments reflected the conceptual sequence that unites emotions, authenticity, politics, ethics, and their audiovisual representation. The first took place inside the Spanish Parliament when, instead of succinctly responding affirmatively to the ritual questioning of parliamentary constitution, Iglesias stated that he will accept the constitutional mandate with the objective of changing it and added immediately after in sign language: "nunca más un país sin su gente" (no more a country-government without the people).[85] The second directly complements the first: Iglesias is seen outside Parliament, after the ceremony, crying inconsolably. Finally, the events are resignified and hierarchized as Iglesias, via social media, publicly engages with his own emotionality when he tweeted a news article that captured that moment.

On the one hand, regarding the first moment, Iglesias's words sharply contrasted with the off-camera hissing and booing by opposing members of Parliament. Podemos's actual political message (i.e., the possibility of changing the Constitution) was subsided under a populist demand (i.e., a demand in the Laclauian sense that would make of the image of Iglesias in Parliament the empty signifier which was to authentically and democratically represent the Spanish *pueblo*; a *país* with *su gente*, a government with the people) that was in turn superseded by the performance of Iglesias (i.e., his gesturing and his attempt to make his voice heard in the middle of that hostile noise), which was finally documented audiovisually in stark opposition to normative representations of institutional politics (i.e., traditional decorum in Parliament is seen as the symbol of old politics, whereas the breaking of institutional correctness is perceived as the sign of political change). On the other hand, outside the Parliament building, in the second moment previously referred, the tears of Iglesias became the definite sign of his political authenticity and framed Podemos's politics as emotionally accessible. Ultimately, Iglesias's emotions marked a moment of collective authenticity in that his emotional display portrayed him as a "real" politician (i.e., one who actually cares) but at the same time allowed the emotional participation of the viewers (via the positive or negative connection to Iglesias's performance) in an event that was otherwise designed to produce institutional distance. Similar to Smith's analysis of the emotional imperative in film, both of Iglesias's performances (one premeditated, one spontaneous) were emotionally constructed to "educate the spectator and listener into new structures of feeling whose values and associations are difficult to delimit."[86] The (self-)representation of Iglesias in such a way visualized those structures of feeling in a controlled sequence that was cinematically constructed. This was another performance of the authentic that echoes what Bill Nichols had termed the "performative mode" of filmmaking, which "serves to heighten the sense of emotional engagement" with the audience.[87] Moreover, as previously referred to in the analysis of León de Aranoa's *Política*, it was a mode of being seen that connected with the party's attempts at performing and controlling its own authentic representation across all type of media.[88]

More subtly, Iglesias's own participation in the sequence of events is later politically recoded into a more refined and more beneficial hierarchy of feelings. As earlier mentioned, Iglesias tweeted a news article of the moment. The video was from *Libertad Digital* and entitled "Pablo Iglesias rompe a llorar a la salida del Congreso" (Pablo Iglesias breaks into tears outside of Congress). Iglesias linked to the video in his tweet, in which he wrote: "Orgullosos de que se note lo que sentimos. Orgullosos de no olvidar de dónde venimos. Orgullosos de la gente humilde" (Proud of showing our feelings. Proud of not hiding what we feel. Proud of not forgetting where we come from. Proud of people of humble origins).[89] Iglesias was here linking pride, sentimentality, and his humble origins with the pride of *la gente humilde*, which can also refer to the *pueblo* in general. What could be thought of as Iglesias's merely partisan monologic reaction is in reality the performance of an emotionally stratified dialogue between the people who are *humilde* (i.e., people without lofty pretensions but also, as defined by the Real Academia Española, people who lack aristocratic origins) and those who could be aligned outside as well as opposed to such a people, like those symbolically represented by *Libertad Digital*.

The choice of the video source was not accidental. *Libertad Digital* is a Far Right media outlet founded by the pundit Federico Jiménez Losantos; it was (and still is) especially antagonistic to Podemos. Iglesias's tweet suggests an inverted pyramid led by the *gente humilde*—those who could feel compelled by his speech and his tears—in unstated contrast to those in Parliament who booed him, or to those in *Libertad Digital* who frequently attacked him, or to those who, as the video caption suggests, might interpret Iglesias's tears as a sign of weakness. In the end, the takeaway in Iglesias's tweet is meant to frame those who cannot understand his unfettered emotions and his stated will to change Spanish politics as not *humildes*—in the sense of the fourth entry in the *Diccionario de la lengua española*, which defines humility as those who lack *nobleza* (nobility).[90] The contrast is so stark as to paint the clearest picture of the opposition (*nobleza* versus *gente humilde*) that Iglesias is otherwise referring to only implicitly. That is, while Iglesias's written declaration is not explicitly antagonistic, the conjunction of what is seen in the video and what is known of the video source visualize a conflict that lives in the realm of the unstated, of the unwritten. It is precisely due to this nonverbalized nature (in that one can visualize the issue at hand but not necessarily define it concretely with words) that the conflict can garner political traction.

That ambiguity follows the conceptual trail of Podemos's populist framing of the political, especially in its ideation of the people versus *la casta*, which closely aligns with the antagonistic framework used by Iglesias in his tweet. Beyond that political conceptualization, at a visual level (as theorized by Smith), it is remarkable how Iglesias invites the fusing of emotion and cognition in a filmed event, which eventually becomes a multipurpose visual metaphor (Iglesias's weeping image) of political change. In fact, the Podemos phenomenon is often accompanied by Iglesias's emotional eloquence. This emotional intelligence serves a performative purpose that cinematically orders Podemos's political discourse. That is, it gives aesthetic and ethical preference to a filmed sequence of events that put in practice Podemos's politics of hope and change in the cultural arena. Podemos's new political vocabulary is transformed into accessible visual metaphors that are then resignified in popular culture. Hence, Podemos's ability to style itself as emotionally and politically authentic formed the basis for establishing a series of complementary plotlines—the evil *casta*, the "ordinary" populist leader, the final revenge of the plebeian *pueblo*—that were to popularize the journey of how hope could finally become change.

Conclusion

In this chapter, Podemos is seen tapping into an unmet popular desire that seemed to have initially settled for cultural representation in politics over direct political participation (perhaps as a result of nearly reaching collective exhaustion in the fight against the crisis). The key to the party's ability to meet that desire (in turn the cause of its meteoric success) was in how its political style constructed new cultural imaginaries that quickly connected stories of the people by and for the people. Particularly via Pablo Iglesias's audiovisual representations, Podemos constructed and performed a visual sequence from the new *pueblo* of the 15-M and the unheard pleas for a real democracy to the political battles against the oppression of *la casta*. To such end, the Podemos phenomenon crafted two main thematic lines from the perspective of cinematic and televisual representation: first, there was the tale of a vaguely historicized antagonist, represented in the idea of a privileged caste, which was shamelessly affronting the Spanish people in times of crisis; second, another story was told, with Iglesias as the protagonist underdog who would offer a viable alternative to the crisis and, thus, subvert the hard-established order of political expectations in the caste system. While the first storyline advanced the creation of the second one (in that the construction of an "enemy" necessarily fostered the making of Iglesias's "heroic" leadership), the two converged in a veiled and ambiguous fable of plebeian retribution in the battle for the "throne" of Spanish political power.[91]

Iglesias entered the television screen as a conduit of popular common sense, making comprehensible, cataloging, and prioritizing the varied suffering of people's lives in crisis. He was able to translate the language of political revolution into the language of television with a new cinematic style that engaged audiences in an emotional political narrative (i.e., wielding cinema's "emotional imperative"). Demands for real change stopped being slogans that could be framed as radical politics and became expressions regularly used by talking heads on television screens. The incision that began in the 15-M became a gaping hole when the new diagnosis of Spanish reality—as one in need of a deep transformation—was pushed further by Iglesias's televised performances. Iglesias spoke with a visual language that rapidly captured popular imagination, giving old words a new meaning that was easy to visualize without the need to define them precisely (e.g., *casta, nueva política*). This new terminology was effective because it was not merely used as political spin. It became part of popular culture and embedded within a political melodrama especially designed for the people of television (most of whom had lost the visual anchor that 15-M provided but were still craving the transversal politics, the hope, the representation, and so on, that the movement had created). In those televised melodramatic sequences, politicians and political commentators were cynically inviting Iglesias and any other protesters to form a political party as the real solution to their mounting indignation. In an unexpected plot twist, Iglesias picked up the gauntlet, announced the launch of Podemos, and transformed Spanish politics into a television thriller that visualized tout court how meaningful change could be achieved against all odds.

What is more, millions of Spaniards did not simply follow the (mis)adventures of Iglesias and the rest of the Podemos as cast in their historical attempt to bring real democratic change à la 15-M. A significant number of them became affectively invested in the party's political ethos through Iglesias's populist leadership. Increasingly legitimized by his televised performances in "serious" debates, the figure of Iglesias coherently wove a cinematic storyline that engaged his audience with an unprecedently appealing end in sight: the so-called *asalto a los cielos* (storming of the heavens) and the incredibly bold assertion at the time that Podemos was created to rule the country. Beyond the party's political goals, there was an impetus behind that unprecedented affective investment that could be concretely found in how televisual and filmic representation was fused in the performance of a new political style. It was a journey that went from hope to change, which was made possible to a great extent because that performance was eventually collectivized (i.e., made popular) through the television screen. And while the audiovisual format that gave popular force to Podemos was television, the crafting of a political heroic identity that emotionally connected (with) many people was to be understood through the prism of cinematic representation.

That's why, rather than the crafting of visual narratives through the medium of film, the use of cinematic representation has here alluded to how the televised images of Iglesias became an everyday signifier that permitted the cohesion of fragmented political contingencies (e.g., the multiple and varied lives in crises after the 15-M) into a timeless identity (Podemos as *podemos*; similar to the famous "yes, we can"). Podemos was an identity that directly spoke to the people in the visual language of the people; for instance, through the images of Pablo Iglesias as the popular-populist HBO-like hero of Podemos, in the filmic translation of *la casta* into one of the most important films of the year (*Mi gran noche*) by one of the most renowned Spanish filmmakers (Álex de la Iglesia), and via the performed authenticity of their populist politics as visualized by León de Aranoa's documentary on Podemos as well as by the curated online persona that Iglesias had crafted. That's how, against all odds, the populists became popular among the Spanish populace.

The fusion of television, as the chosen medium to speak directly to the people in the language of what Turner called "ordinary" celebrities, and cinema, as the visual aesthetic to engage people's emotional investment, opened a new chapter in Spanish politics beyond traditional forms of representation. Podemos's cinematic turn is accordingly conceived in this chapter beyond the reproduction (through television or cinema) of a verisimilar political reality. The cinematic turn of Podemos is poised to be a timeless representative force born of the ability of televisual as well as cinematic (re)presentation to generate cultural imaginaries that engage (with) large swaths of the public. It is thought as an extraordinary synchrony between the viewers' projected reality (with their heterogeneous political desires) and the illusory projections they see on the screens (big or small), with Pablo Iglesias as heroic protagonist speaking in populist tongues. The supposedly culturally lowbrow television and highbrow cinematic aesthetic merged thus into Podemos's new audiovisual narrative of the people. This was a transversal collapsing of two worlds onto each other that opened the door to the materialization of hope into change. What is more, while the door was opened, Podemos shifted the stage from the squares and the streets—where the people had restricted access to institutional politics and were amassing plebeian complexity in terms of their political "unconstitution"—to the television sets, phones, and even movie theaters. With Podemos as catalyst, these media platforms helped to revisualize the plebs and, eventually, perform their demands in the voice of the authentic *pueblo*. The party created to that effect a new political style marked by the representative impetus of popular cinema (beyond the mere spectacularizing of politics or a sophisticated communication strategy) within a feedback loop of political hope fueled by the construction of a "real" change much like real democracy was constructed during the 15-M. In this respect, Podemos and its rapid electoral advances proved that politics could be transformed through popular culture such as television, HBO series, and blockbuster films. But because all cinematic plotlines eventually need to finish, Podemos's melodramatic thriller would have its grand finale with the end of populism in Spain.

5

Parodying Podemos

A Memetic Journey toward the End of Populism

Not long after its Hollywoodesque rise, Podemos and its brand of populism waned, giving way to the despairing postfascism now coloring the Spanish political landscape. While Podemos's populist bid was to order in a series of gripping cinematic sequences the somewhat disperse, transversal, anti-ideological idea of the people that stemmed from the 15-M, in parallel, populism's radical division between a popular "us" and antipopular *casta* was inadvertently preparing the ground for the remake of the historical plotline of Francoism, whose fascist conceptualization of politics bifurcated society into the Schmittian enemy-friend paradigm.[1] In this sense, Podemos's Schmittian side encountered the truest face of Schmitt's politics in the postfascist party Vox as the former lost relevance to the rise of the latter.[2] The visualization of the people that accompanied Podemos's cinematic turn became cornered by the sectorial, ideological unearthing of a popular antagonism anchored in the old leftist-rightist axis of political confrontation. The moving sequence of a "people" from below who opposed those at the top hoping for future systemic changes mutated into a still image of two confronted peoples, completely uncoupled from a populist style that depended on the transversality of its symbolic representation, away from the traditional ideological imagery of the Spanish Left (related in one way or another to the Second Republic) and of the Spanish Right (mostly associated with symbols of Spanish nationalism, whose representative impetus connects inevitably with a vague but deeply rooted Francoist patrimonialization of the nation). As populism lost

its visual force, the political confrontation became divided in two clear factions: one on the "real" Left, purportedly represented most authentically by
Podemos, and one on the "real" Right, whose most authentic self-appointed
representative was Vox. With that change of vision, the people of Podemos's
populism became less and less visible until the party finally disappeared.

The reasons for this disappearance are varied, but the most salient is
Podemos's inability to further move cultural identities (or subjectivities) in
politics beyond the leftist imaginary. To be fair, Podemos was aggressively
pressured from all sides to conform to the long-established ideological
spectrum of leftism in Spain, which namely supposed the abandonment of
the populist top-bottom axis of political confrontation for more traditional
frameworks under the wide umbrella of European democratic socialism.
While the pressures from the Right were a given, it was the Left—very broadly
speaking—that exercised the most effective sway.[3] As such, the political force
of Podemos changed from the party's ability to make a blockbuster out of
Iglesias's heroic populist leadership to the parodic framing of that leadership. In this last stage, the leaders of Podemos were progressively losing the
capacity to control the coherence of their hero's storyline by way of social
media's double-edged sword identity politics.

This was not a sudden change. It was a progressively self-assumed and
inadvertently implemented shift. To read between the lines of what was said,
what was known and what was seen, one needs to resort to the realm of the
implicit and the symbolic. Initially, the Podemos phenomenon took advantage of social media's essence as "a site of populist practices of articulating
a claim to 'the people,' because of these platforms' ability to blur the line
between elite and popular power."[4] As the phenomenon inevitably evolved
closer to institutional politics, the capacity to articulate the popular into the
populist dwindled, so much so that the party went from being an agent of
a popular common sense in politics to being at the mercy of a maddening
electoral logic always with an eye on what was the most electorally suitable.
Parallel to that strategical shift, online parodies were becoming a refuge for
the increasing discontent with institutional politics in general and, more
particularly, with the evolution of Podemos; which at some point was veri-
similarly represented as indistinguishable from traditional political actors,
as just fixated on election results. These parodies were a revealing symptom
of the eventual ending of the populist moment in Spain, largely symbolized
by how Podemos's representations journeyed toward the symbolic universe
of the Left.

The figure of Iglesias—as a synecdoche of Podemos—had been at the
center of parodies since the party's inception. Parodies of him are critical

to understanding the fluctuations between the popular, in the Gramscian sense, and the populist, as framed by Podemos's reading of Laclau. That is, when what has been popularized (e.g., the intrinsic corruption of Spanish elites) coincided with a populist stimulus (e.g., Iglesias's usage of *la casta*), a window for structural change opened, and parody was an instrument of horizontalization for the populist leader to be perceived as on a level with the people. Nevertheless, when the popular began to disassociate from the populist, structural change was abandoned, partial reforms were readily welcomed, and populism's symbolic universe became an object of parody, even ridicule.[5] Importantly, these fluctuations point to the eventual impossibility of controlling the processes of populist representation from above, which in turn lies at the heart of Podemos's loss of political influence.[6]

The evolution of Podemos and its relationship with the people from an ambiguously populist relation to an expressly electoral one was most visibly represented in the confluence of parodic humor and the internet's ability to create new cultural frameworks through what has been generally referred to as memes. Critical to understanding how Podemos evolved in such an online context, we must first clarify that it's not that memes' existence were a deciding factor in the shifting fortunes of Podemos's populist bid; it was the early success of Podemos's populist strategy, as institutional power was acquired, that changed the party's relation to memetic culture. That is, memes were an important part of political expression in popular culture before, during, and after the Podemos phenomenon. Memes did not change Podemos's politics, but Podemos changed its political relationship to them. In this sense, taking into account that political memes have become an inextricable part of populism on social media, as Podemos's connection with populism transformed, so did its relationship to memes.

On social media, the populist moment produced dual identities by means of "both highlighting the voices of 'the people' and styling oneself on 'the people.'"[7] That's why memetics—as the study of collaborative, participatory online "performative acts" also known as memes—help to disentangle the complex processes of representation that occurred between Podemos, Iglesias, and their parodies.[8] From Twitter hashtags to YouTube videos, the memetic media analyzed in in this chapter follows a rationale guided by representative value and not so much by participatory value. Memes have the capacity to visualize a shift in a set of already-established political norms and, thus, open the door to realizing change in political culture. The performative nature of these memes implies that what is actually changed in politics stems from a negotiation between what is real and what is not in the realm of popular culture. Parody marks the frontier between the authentically popular (hence, viably populist) and the popularly inauthentic (thus, inadmissibly populist). Through the cultural intertextuality and intrinsic visuality of memetics, the end of populism can be both seen and argued outside a strictly political causality.

The end of populism could be explained in the Laclauian sense by the "repletion" of Podemos's empty signifier, namely, Pablo Iglesias. This was a process that, despite being essentially political, was more clearly seen in the cultural sphere. Consequently, if rhetorically Podemos (currently Unidas Podemos) could be still somehow framed under the parameters of populist discourse, popular culture's visual cues painted a party distanced from its initial populist impetus, increasingly closer to the traditional Spanish Left.[9] Iglesias lost his popular "ordinariness" and became "repleted" with either positive or negative ideological signification depending on where one stood on Podemos's politics. The party surrendered most of its political ambiguity and thus was resignified (at best) as a party to the Left of the social-democratic PSOE. What is striking about these processes of resignification is not so much that they signaled the further unviability of Podemos's populist hypothesis, but that they indicate the much less studied, and even dismissed, role of popular agency when separated from political leaderships in populism. The trajectory of how Podemos and Iglesias in particular became signified tracks with how the popular undertakes control over its own signification outside the preestablished discursive impetus that tries to shape, order, and make sense of it in the populist bid to access far-reaching institutional powers. For the popular to achieve a degree of emancipation from top-down populist ways of seeing, parody is the most obvious tool.

As Podemos was being "repleted" with signification, Iglesias went from being an empty signifier in politics to a memetic signified in culture. This was a shift favored by the horizontalization of popular agency that Podemos's cinematic enterprise had previously allowed via Iglesias's television appearances. It was also a change that, once implemented, was more difficult to govern. While the Hollywood-like plot of Podemos's *asalto a los cielos* was more easily enacted within the confines of television, the memetic—much harder to regulate—had the ability to confer (in)authenticity outside the more or less expected causality of the party's self-produced cinematic experience. Memetics suppose a type of collective identification that as much as it allows the identification *with*, in this case, a political movement, party, or leadership, it can also determine the identification *of* that very same movement, party, or leadership. Because memetic identification heavily relies on the replication of a series of visualities, leaving the discursive as background support or as a conceptual given, the potential for creating a much more rapid and effective popular common sense is greater. With this in mind, what follows is the analysis of the memetic development of that common sense: how it started primarily as an online discursive incursion in the occupied squares of the 15-M; how it later agglutinated in the many visions of Iglesias's populist leadership, only to be progressively disaggregated with the institutionalization of Podemos; and finally, how it was returned to its fragmented original state with the restoration of a leftist-rightist way of seeing. Such a chain of dominoes is what marks the end of the populist moment in Spanish politics, a concatenation of events that played out visually through the sharing of memes on the internet.

Emptying the Signifiers

The 15-M marked a generational reconfiguration of a new cultural community of mostly young, primarily urban, and economically precarious people whose identity was decidedly political. This generation was accultured in the codes of social media and informed by the short and direct messaging of Twitter, the main social media platform used during the 15-M and subsequently perceived in Spain as an eminently political network. From the very beginning, their communication was memetic. In Richard Dawkins's original, biologically determinist formulation, memes were cultural units—like catchphrases, jokes, nursery rhymes, and so on—that competed for attention to be replicated and, thus, passed on from generation to generation in the cultural history of humanity. Later adapted in the fields of cultural studies and anthropology to explain the media ecology of the internet, and especially social media, memes became understood as metaphorical artifacts that explained the spread of online media both in terms of their virality (following Dawkins's terminology) and as part of what Limor Shifman has called the "(post)modern folklore, in which shared norms and values are constructed."[10] Memes eventually became shorthand for a wide array of complex cultural practices on the internet that, far from being static, are constantly changing and developing over time.

Memes are fundamentally based on catalyzing user interaction, ordering participation in different online communities, and creating communal identifications via the multiple anonymous reappropriations of online media. Memetic representation does not simply dwell on the meme as "an expression of existing social-cultural norms[;] it is also a social tool for negotiating them."[11] In that sense, memes are small acts of performance that negotiate ongoing norms as well as they establish adherence to what is supposed to be "natural" in the collective culture of the internet. They are part of a process of negotiation between what is "natural" or authentic and what can be ridiculed as no longer culturally acceptable. Although humor and parody are essential to memetic representation, "memes also fulfil deeper gratifications than simple laughs, having implications for identity building, public discourse, and commentary through collaborative action."[12] Since the global climate of protest generated after the financial crisis of 2008, they have become unavoidable symbols of political participation. Their political value resides in their ability to visualize common sense through the promotion of self-convinced audiences or, contrariwise, their capacity of persuasion when adapting, recycling, (re)appropriating, and parodying a once-established logic via "interdiscursive, intertwining, multiple texts and commentaries into complex collages."[13]

In regard to the crisis, the 15-M's communication promoted an established common sense that was inclusive of a popular "us" and hence transversally populist. It easily allowed the participation of high numbers of people who would in turn encourage others to participate with very different degrees of commitment. Beyond these already well-known characteristics that informed the "viral" participatory reach of the 15-M, the movement's ability to influence political discourse from the bottom up, leaderless, and without the help of established social actors was exceptional in the history of Spanish democracy. Particularly important in regard to the highly influential politics of the 15-M was the usage and popularization via Twitter of catchphrases (many of them analyzed in Chapter 1). Given the nature of that social network at the time, it is also important to note that in the early memetic communications during the 15-M, those slogans were qualitatively different, with visual content that was eminently discursive, from the later iterations around Podemos and Pablo Iglesias, which were more decisively marked by parodic imagery. Irrespective of their degree of textual or visual orientation, there's no doubt these expressions became popular for their ability to project culturally a vivid image of the politics at hand.

The first ones originated from the very name of the organizations responsible for much of the initial logistics in the square occupations, such as Democracia Real Ya and Juventud sin Futuro. But some of the most famous and colorful ones started as impromptu chants or were casually written on handmade placards that later became hashtags on Twitter: the chant "¡PSOE y PP la misma mierda es!" (PSOE and PP [the two big parties in Spanish politics] are both the same shit) would become PPSOE, for example, and—humorously echoing of Monty Python—the placard that read "Nobody Expects the Span-ish Revolution" would change into #SpanishRevolution (or vice versa, as it is impossible to know which iteration came first). As the movement grew in popularity, all these catchphrases lost their more overt tone as political demands in order to flourish as folkloric articulations of conventional wis-dom. They became more than a temporal memetic disruption attached to an ad hoc protest. They surpassed the temporality of the 15-M's encampments and kept their transversality, inclusivity, and virality well after the movement dwindled its public visual prominence. They were becoming memetic repre-sentatives of a popular, soon to be populist, common sense. Important not only for their memetic qualities, these phrases were essential tools for dele-gitimizing the status quo. In their parodic essence, they were above all an affirmation of people's power.

In the realm of politics, memes intertwine the popular and the populist because they facilitate the participatory creation of accounts by the people, for the people, and of the people; or what Ryan M. Milner terms "polyvo-cal public commentary."[14] Protests today tend to be much less ideologically defined by a party, a union, or even a class and much more politically contin-gent in relation to a concrete event or concatenation of circumstances per-ceived to need change. In the age of social media, protesters can more easily attune to broader discussions in popular (online) culture to try to convey the figure of a populist counterpublic that could both provide support or exer-cise an opposition in the name of the people.[15] This is a "vernacular mode of public conversation" that allows a type of resignification as well as a political reappropriation that is inherently transversal, because it is equally postideo-logical.[16] One can speak of memetic signifiers in a way similar to Laclau's take on empty signifiers in his theory of populism. Referring to memetic signifiers in the Laclauian sense, Paulo Gerbaudo writes that "the virality of Internet memes is largely down precisely to their ostensible simplicity, if not outright 'emptiness.'"[17] Their lack of prescribed ideological character grants a type of political inclusivity that promotes popular-populist identifications. Moreover, their public significance surpasses peer-to-peer network relation-ships, as Manuel Castells had once theorized in his conceptualization of the 15-M as a network of networks. Their significance is found in their capacity to construct identities and, especially, to promote common sense, which given its viral character can make those identifications very quickly perceived as inherently popular. When it comes to protests, the popular can easily become populist because "imitation elicits imitation, in a sequence that in waves of popular enthusiasm can acquire huge proportions, and the growth of the protest movement can be recorded from people's timelines."[18] Memetics can thus explain how and why certain online symbols become popular-populist icons of political engagement and political belonging.

A paradigmatic example of that delegitimizing yet affirming popular power was the 15-M catchphrase *no hay pan para tanto chorizo*. The expression came to public prominence sometime between the first weeks of the encampments and the subsequent aftershocks of protest toward the end of 2011. In the following years, as the Rajoy government was inundated by the long-standing cases of the Popular Party's political corruption, it became one of the most visible slogans. "No hay pan para tanto chorizo" literally means "there is not enough bread for that many sausages." The meaning is, however, visibly layered: *chorizo* is both a type of sausage in Spain and also slang for thief, which in this case is really a metaphor for corruption. The slogan semiotically activated a communal framework of protest—against an established corrupt other—while also asserting the unviability of corruption in Spain any longer; Nicola Montesano Montessori and Esperanza Morales-López concluded that "the basic layers of society cannot carry the weight of the new elite with its greed, bonuses and antisocial behavior, a claim made by, for instance, Andrew Sayer in his recent book *Why We Can't Afford the Rich*."[19] Although never fully developed in their argument, the reference to Sayer's book point to the most important part of the catchphrase. It implies the construction of an antagonism—the "we" versus the "rich" in the title—that is predicated more on the reinforcement of the common "we, the people" than on the rejection of the confronted corrupt "they, the rich." This conceptualization of the people is bound together by parody and humor. The humorous undertone in Sayer's book title is made explicitly parodic and ultimately politically enhanced in the famous expression originated during the 15-M.

It is the parodic along with the memetic that allows the popular—in this case, the visualization of a corrupt Spain ruled by *chorizos*—to be bridged by the populist, particularly when one thinks of how close these *chorizos* are to *la casta*. The memetic quality of the phrase is in line with Gerbaudo's analysis of "protest avatars" as memetic signifiers during and after the 15-M. Gerbaudo argues that the banners adopted by internet users in their profile picture as a sign of solidarity with a protest movement are a temporal visual disturbance of the memetic ecology that is highly effective in creating the perception of mass support "due to the way in which protest avatars turn the immense diversity of visual content normally seen in various social media conversations into visual unanimity."[20] Consequently, the fragmented individualities of the internet can be seen temporarily as a uniform mass that

Figure 5.1. Picture of a demonstration after the 15-M in which the slogan "No hay pan para tanto chorizo" can be read. Picture taken on May 15, 2011, by ACido Zítrico, https://www.flickr.com/photos/acido/5724063649.

facilitates what the design collective Metahaven has called online activism's "reality-management."[21] The catchphrase's humorous component further replicates a homogeneous amusement among all those who think of themselves as "the people."

A general distrust of elites and their characterization as inherently corrupt or, in this case, *chorizos*, at another time might have passed as an uneventful common place. But in this context, what can be simply regarded as part of a more or less accepted stereotype garners a special type of replicability that allows the popular to be politically performed as populist across multiple media. The phrase is able to jump and develop from the political discourse in the squares to the internet to then multiple other types of (audio)visual media. This implies a political transversality that is greatly enhanced by the phrase's potential to have several political purposes: it can be a humorous statement in the background of a large climate of protest (figs. 5.1 and 5.2), or it can be used as a more direct challenge to the economic and political system when, for instance, adopted by the hacktivist group Anonymous.[22] It can form part of a more conventional mode of political satire, such as the one espoused by *El Jueves* or as seen in a famous sketch for the television show *Vaya Semanita*.[23] Such is the phrase's capacity of memetic representation that its various functions ultimately align with what Rancière termed a new distribution of the sensible, "new modes of sense perception . . . [that] induce novel forms of political subjectivity."[24] The *chorizo*, then, is popularly framed

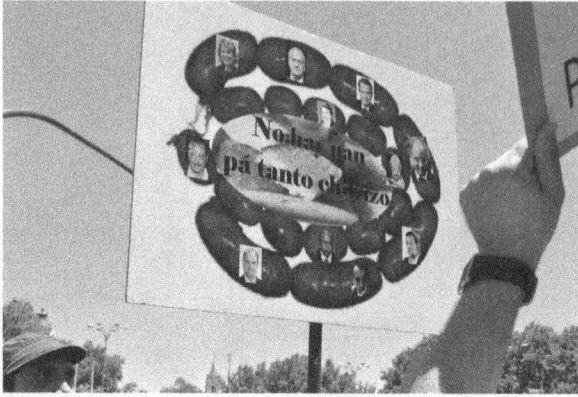

Figure 5.2. Sign in a demonstration, in which the slogan's humorous sense—the double entendre of *chorizo*—can be seen more clearly. Picture taken on June 19, 2011, by Rafel Robles, https://www.flickr.com/photos/rafaelrobles/5854195504.

as an elitist "other" that is increasingly distanced from what is to be essentially popular, of the people. Then, when attached to politicians, it has the capacity to delegitimize the source of their representative power. Add to that both the potential for ideological and media transversality, and the *chorizo* can be considered a memetic signifier that has been "emptied" of political specificity and so able to generate a new political subjectivity sustained by a new political visuality or a new way of seeing the political. And this new way of seeing that generated a new political subjectivity—which is memetically representative, culturally popular, and politically populist—was another key feature in popular culture (apart from the cinematic momentum explained in the previous chapter) that prepared the ground for the successful irruption of Podemos.

Parodying Podemos

As the parodic humor emblematized by the memetic expression *no hay pan para tanto chorizo* was slipping into frustrated cynicism, Podemos and Pablo Iglesias jumped onto the political stage. Their appearance absorbed the most cynical visions of the people since the 15-M's retreat from the squares. It served to recatalyze the popular (the need for a *democracia real ya*) into the populist (Podemos). After three years of intense protests, not much had changed in terms of actual policy. Despite sustained representations of populist

antagonism in Spain's (audio)visual culture that went along with an environment of popular empowerment (seen in the successes of the Plataforma de
Afectados por la Hipoteca, the different *mareas ciudadanas*, and the popular
legal action against Bankia and Rodrigo Rato by the anonymous collective
15MpaRato), political frustration did not appear to find a clear outlet for hope.
In fact, there was an increasing sense that an opportunity had been lost and
that the country had regressed politically, as the implementation of Rajoy's
austerity measures was in full swing despite widespread popular opposition.
Under these circumstances, parodies became closer to representations of a
kind of political disillusion that invited political inaction (a common trope
in Spanish history), moving away from their initial usage as tools for popular
unity and social activism.

However, when Podemos entered the picture, parodic humor picked up
its former memetic essence and kick-started the original framework that had
been almost abandoned—this time, for the advent of populism. The parodies
of Podemos and Iglesias served to establish a symbolic structure of authenticity in their populist politics. Their memetic characteristics were premised
once again on the negotiation of what a "real" political change would look
like—the logical extension of the 15-M's *democracia real ya*. On the one hand,
as established in the previous chapter, Podemos used Iglesias's "ordinary"
celebrity status on television to perform a politics of the people legitimized
by the party's popular authenticity. On the other, when it came to its online
media presence, Podemos introduced a subtly different version of the authentic: the memetically authentic.

Memetic authenticity, according to Limor Shifman, can be a way to bridge
the personal and the political or a reflection of "a cynical awareness that
everything is constructed and a craving for 'authentic' politics."[25] Shifman
understands this type of authenticity split into an external "objective" one,
factual and scientifically measurable, as well as an internal "subjective" one,
individualistically framed as "staying true to oneself."[26] Paradoxically, because
anything authentic is thought as anathema to anything copied, memetic
authenticity is based on "overt imitation and emphasized constructedness"
through what Shifman refers to as "hypersignification" or "a conscious highlighting of meaning-making processes."[27] The hypersignified is authentically
replicated most effectively through parody, because the parodic (regardless
of the seriousness or triviality of the content) is in essence a tool to establish
the (in)authenticity of what is parodied. The more something is hyperboli-
cally (re)signified through its constant imitation on social media, the more
powerful the parodic effect becomes and the more the object of the parody

can be perceived as real (e.g., the previously marginal underdogs can parody their way into the realness of the mainstream) or phony (e.g., the mainstream can be parodied into the margins and become perceived as out of touch with the "real" everyday reality).

Memetic authenticity relies less on the perception that a given memetic representation is authentic or not and more on the widespread realization that the target of the parodied representation has been successfully reappropriated as (in)authentic, depending on the parody's purpose. For instance, on the first anniversary of the 15-M, in an effort to connect the Arab Spring, the Indignados, and Occupy Wall Street, a memetic campaign was relaunched across multiple social media platforms with the already-famous slogan "We are the 99 percent." This instantiates what Shifman has called a testimonial rally, which in this case depicted protesters "with handwritten signs outlining their life narratives and struggles as part of a protest against the uneven division of wealth."[28] Despite the political seriousness of the matter, the catchphrase was replicated similarly to the ways "no hay pan para tanto chorizo" was used after the 15-M. In the context of the global bailouts of banks and the implementation of austerity measures, online testimonials were ridiculing the idea that the "system" was in need of help.[29] The parodic essence of the testimonies was based not on their ability to convey a humorous tone but on their capacity to represent political reality as laughable. Accordingly, the parody's object was the representation of the status quo (the metaphorically implied 1 percent) as inauthentic vis-à-vis the authentic testimonies of people claiming that "We are the 99 percent." This tension between disputed authenticities—apart from being at the core of how parodic humor works—is what granted replicability in this memetic context.

Podemos used that notion of memetic authenticity but through a different memetic strategy, one that was overtly humorous and promoted Iglesias's (self-)parody to establish the "realness" of the party's political challenge. Most of the memes were characterized by what has been termed *reaction photoshops*—which can be defined as "collections of edited images created in response to a set of photographs which may be labeled as memetic photos" to expose the (in)authentic elements of what is being represented.[30] The most famous one was a cutout picture of Iglesias behind a tree that was later modified to feature the leader of Podemos creeping up on the powerful.[31] Although the picture of Iglesias was originally produced without irony and as part of a campaign of staged authenticity during Podemos's first electoral campaign, his memetic authenticity did not suffer. The popular impetus of the Podemos phenomenon was strong enough that it made Iglesias's politically marketed photo shoot a memetic representation of realness. His picture was so campy that it became popularly "real" and still positioned Iglesias on the side of authentic people and against the inauthentic *casta*.

With Podemos's savvy handling of social media, it was quickly understood that parody would further attune the party to popular culture and authentically frame its populist politics. That being the case, not only were parodies of the party welcome; self-parody was (and is) happily promoted.[32] At this early stage of Podemos's evolution, when the party was seen as a refreshing outsider, Pablo Iglesias was often at the center of parodies though rarely their target. In fact, he was used as a parodic tool that would memetically authenticate Iglesias as a political figure that "stays true himself" (in regard to what Shifman had previously argued) and Podemos as a party of the people. This memetic framing established them both outside the institutional inauthentic sphere which, at that time, was unequivocally characterized by the presence of *chorizos, la casta*, and the 1 percent.

Once Podemos entered the sphere of parliamentary politics, its memetic authenticity significantly devolved. Consequently, Iglesias went from being at the center of what was parodied to be the object of parodies that emphasized the constructedness of his authenticity, particularly in relation to his perceived extraordinary political ambition.[33] Although this was a particularly cynical type of criticism, the parodies of Iglesias's thirst for power were a first sign of Podemos's Achilles' heel in their memetic journey from relentless outsiders to domesticated insiders. To that end, Iglesias became portrayed as betraying his past authentic self, characterized by an uncompromising political stance. Although a certain loss of freshness was expected as part of the party's natural evolution in parliamentary politics, Podemos's original authenticity was put into question almost immediately after being elected to Parliament. Podemos's more or less diversified memetic realness ceded way to increasingly homogenous representations of the "real" party as revolving around a power-hungry Iglesias, who would compromise his ideas for any position within government, a characterization that started after the failed negotiations to form a government with the PSOE in early 2016 and has not stopped since.[34] Regardless of the somewhat perverse political reasons to paint such a convenient picture, it was in the realm of popular culture, via the feedback loop between traditional media and memetic participation, that Podemos's politics were cornered: from being a synecdoche of collective change to being pigeonholed as the metonymy of an egocentric leader.

Iglesias's politics had been part of the whole that was Podemos's populism, and then the whole of Podemos's populist politics became the part that was Iglesias's perceived narcissistic populist leadership.[35]

Notwithstanding the concerted efforts to smear Podemos and Iglesias, the main reason for such a loss of authenticity was due to the impossibility of further constituting Podemos's political representation outside the cultural parameters of the Left.[36] In this sense, Iglesias's parodies on the internet evolved closely linked to the challenges from the Left regarding Podemos's populism. At a discursive level, the shift germinated between the decision to formally integrate the traditional leftist party Izquierda Unida within Podemos in 2016 and the ideological split over the so-called populist hypothesis during the party's second statal assembly in 2017, also known as Vistalegre II, in which Errejón's populist strategy was virtually vanquished.[37] During that time, the party adopted a language that was at minimum decisively recognizable by the Left. Daniel Rueda, however, argues that the result of Vistalegre II was not the ideological choice between the defeat of populism and the victory of a leftist strategy but the establishment of two postpopulist alternatives.[38] The victory of Iglesias in the assembly would simply signal the adaptation of Podemos's populist strategy to a new political contingency. Along similar lines, Alexandros Kioupkiolis speaks of two versions of populism: one led by Errejón, who "stood for a middle-class populism, which speaks broadly to the people 'beyond left and right' and is more moderate," in contrast to Iglesias's "neochavismo, because it mirrors the leftist radical and plebiscitarian populism of Hugo Chávez in Venezuela."[39]

While according to these scholars Podemos may be still defined under the parameters of a new type of leftist populism, it is here argued that the explicit divorce with Errejón (the main proponent of a Laclauian populist strategy) marked the beginning of the end of populism as a viable choice in Spanish politics. That is, it was not so much that the party chose to stay away from a certain type of populism (Errejón's) and favored a more recognizable leftist populist version (Iglesias's), but that populism stopped being a viable electoral alternative altogether. When looking at the visual evolution of the party in (online) popular culture, it is increasingly evident that the populist window was closing on Podemos, which was what ultimately forced the overhaul of the populist hypothesis. The party's electoral decline and its widespread visualization as (radical) leftist in culturally progressive circles on the internet was one of the first symptoms of the end of populism overall as a political moment. Regardless of the definition of Podemos's politics as postpopulist or otherwise, the heart of the matter resides in the progressive unviability of populism itself as visualized by the memetic ecosystem that evolved subsequently. To know how populism ended, one should pay less attention to what was said by and about the party and look more attentively at the images and messages in viral circulation.

Repleting the Signifiers: Podemos's Popular Decline or How Populism Lost its Foothold

Although taking social media's pulse on politics as a way to fully understand a phenomenon as complex as Podemos could be certainly problematic (if not outright wrongheaded), the online world is acutely aware of certain dynamics and impressions (especially negative ones) containing kernels of truths that are symptoms of much larger historical forces at play in popular culture. In this respect, the shift in how Podemos's populist politics were perceived online aligns with the particular calvary of the Left when it came to dealing with its stereotypes and reveals a deeper incapacity when it comes to managing popular attitudes toward leftist politics in general. And if there are three common clichés that have served to caricature the Left internationally, those are its perennial internal conflicts and divisions, the purge of dissidents, and the eventual selling out of the working class once leftist leaders are in power. These stereotypes run historically deep across the wide spectrum of the Left and can be traced as far back as the Hague Congress of the First International in 1872, which saw a bitter fight between Bakunin's anarchists and Marx's communists and resulted in the expulsion of the anarchist wing from the organization. In Spain, these commonplace assumptions are a blend of Francoist propaganda and the cultural consequences of the very particular history of the Spanish Left. With the advent of the Cold War, leftism in Spain was caught in a bind between Franco's staunch anticommunism and the Soviet Union as the sole image of the international Left. To this point, historian Antonio Cazorla-Sánchez makes an illuminating argument worth quoting in full:

> As the Cold War made its appearance, the New State [of Francoism] understood that publicly creating the impression that the only political alternative were the communists would be of double benefit: it would reinforce the regime's international image as a champion of anti-communism, and it would intimidate not only the more politically moderate among its supporters but even the

backers of centrist and moderate Left parties. Ironically, the Spanish Communist Party was doing its best to fit just that role by presenting the other opposition groups as traitors "bought by Imperialism" and informers of the Spanish police. When the Americans, the last hope of the democratic forces in Spain, decided that Franco, for all his defects, was the lesser evil for their interests, everybody understood that the battle for democracy had been lost in Spain.[40]

While Francoism naturally perpetuated the most vicious stereotypes of leftists, it was the Left's peculiarly "impossible" position that legitimized and even enhanced many of its best-known stereotypes. The most pointed criticisms of communists—rather cynically—coupled an overtly unnuanced understanding of the Soviet Union with long-held leftist clichés, helping to solidify the broad identification of the Spanish Left with the evilest side of Soviet communism.

Such a caricature was preserved during the Transición. Politically, as part of the new geopolitical context that favored the social democrats of the PSOE to contain the Spanish Communist Party before its expected legalization, the characterization of leftists as dangerous members of a secret society that would rekindle the old forgotten violence of the Civil War was greatly enlarged.[41] Culturally, Ken Loach's internationally acclaimed film *Land and Freedom* (1994)—whose main plot revolved around George Orwell's accounts of the clashes between anarchists, socialists, and communists in *Homage to Catalonia*—was inadvertently another brick in the wall alleging how the "pure" Left (dangerously radical and homogeneously communist) was to be seen during a time in Spanish politics that had been long singing the praises of centrism and moderation. That's why, for instance, the most prominent films on the Spanish Civil War after the end of Francoism, from Luis García Berlanga's 1985 *La vaquilla* to David Trueba's *Soldados de Salamina* in 2003, are in essence a warning against political extremism. And because the Right in Spain had appropriated all notions of political moderation during the democratic transition, it was the Left that was more easily dismissed with the habitual commonplaces.[42]

This mixed bag of clichés and historical facts eventually ensnared Podemos most evidently during Vistalegre II, when those in attendance were shown on prime-time television and on every news channel bursting into shouts of unity between Pablo Iglesias and Íñigo Errejón. Furthermore, the fact that Podemos had decided to change its name to Unidos Podemos (literally, "united, we can"—it later changed it again to Unidas Podemos) while it was more disunited than it had ever been in its short history was a cruel irony that reinforced the stereotypes even further. The caricatures of the Left were catching up with Podemos's populist attempt precisely to get rid of all those leftist clichés, which had haunted the history of progressive change in Spain until their irruption in 2014.

Podemos's attempt to resignify the idea of *patria* ("fatherland," in etymological relation to patriotism) illustrates the difficult balance between populism and the influence of leftist symbolism in Spanish politics. The conceptualization of *patria* was indeed intrinsic to Francoism and, hence, generally alien to the Left. However, in the run-up to the general elections of 2016, Podemos began using and associating the term with the idea of a functional welfare state. To that end, the slogan "La patria eres tú" (the *patria* is you) was ideated "to engage in a counter-hegemonic struggle with the Right and to contest its monopolization of the nation."[43] Being patriotic was to mean rehabilitating Spain's decimated welfare system, and increased taxes for the rich were the main tool to show patriotism. Nevertheless, even though the ideation was theoretically promising, it never stuck in practice beyond its use as a valid political point. Despite its argumentative potency, the difficulty in using *patria* in such a way lay in its excessive discursive significance. That is, the term could work in a political debate but was useless in the realm of popular culture (in the realm of the unwritten, of the performative and the visual, where most concepts stage their emptiness at their best).

Naturally, popular culture required of a notion such as *patria* the usage of its visual-performative mirror, the national flag. Although Podemos could successfully articulate the idea politically, the display of the national flag was viscerally anathema to most in the party (all of whom came from different traditions on the Left). The discursive resignification of the old Spanish *patria* was one thing; the total uncoupling of the Spanish flag from the Francoist legacy in the eyes of great many leftists—who also formed the main electoral base of party—was quite another. This was yet another indication of how much tighter the populist window of opportunity was getting and, on the contrary, how much more comfortable the electoral room was within the symbolic universe of Spanish leftism. Eventually, it seemed almost unavoidable that the party would fight the battle for political renewal and cultural resignification (of the Left and the many clichés that haunted it) away from populism.

When Podemos faced being characterized by the common tropes of the Left, its claim to a singular popular authenticity had to be renegotiated. The framework of what was popularly authentic had shifted from the novel political style of Iglesias and Podemos's irreverence to a political environment ruled by pragmatism, electoral tactics, and the old ruthless quest for institutional power. As Podemos was inevitably institutionalized, so was its authenticity. Because much of what was authentic in Podemos had to do with the populist framing of conflict in regard to how the people had been marginalized from decision-making processes in the institutional sphere versus *la casta* who had co-opted all democratic institutions, the conceptualization was harder to sustain once the party was part and parcel of the institutions it had previously attacked.

More decisive was how Podemos's politics became necessarily partial, perceived as only directed to a part of the electorate, of *its* people. The party's once-populist empty demands were being repleted (in the Laclauian sense) with electoral demands. Podemos faced an electoral environment that required a programmatic specificity that ran increasingly counter to the construction of Iglesias as an empty signifier. Hence Podemos had to replete Iglesias's figure with an electoral meaning that could not eventually be attached to new empty signifiers beyond the already-well-spent ideation of *la casta*. In comparison to how *la casta* was popularized, the attempt to resignify and reappropriate the idea of *patria* was tellingly ineffective: it ended up strictly confined to the realm of politics and had almost no impact on popular culture. *Trama* and the so-called *tramabús* glaringly suffered the same fate.[44] The linked concepts did not only not stick politically or culturally but were ridiculed from all ideological sides.[45] In this respect, to emphasize the increasing incapacity of Podemos to exert political influence beyond its established electorate, the well-known leftist historian and sociologist Emmanuel Rodríguez opined: "Suffice to say that if anyone has choked with laughter when seeing for the first time the *tramabús*, it surely has nothing to do with the accuracy of the action's political conception or because the concept [of the *trama*] didn't have interesting effects in terms of political communication (that is patently true and visible). The real problem is that the action is at heart inane and impotent; because it can't go beyond its own auto-referentiality."[46] Podemos was basically preaching to the choir. It was effective in communicating its political message only to its already-convinced voters and was thus unable to further move a popular logic into the party's populist framework. The inability to popularly enact a populist discourse was the most obvious sign that the problem at hand was not really with the way Podemos's strategic discourse was being implemented (i.e., the discursive usage of *patria* or *trama*) but with the discourse of populism itself. These were the first indicators that the populist moment was coming to end in Spanish politics.

Although discursively the end of populism was reflected in Podemos's inability to popularize a new empty vocabulary, visually its populist politics were being repleted with leftist signifiers. This was done in three stages, coinciding with the three main stereotypes of the traditional Left (as previously mentioned), and memetics was the field of representation that most prominently visualized such repletion. The first stage, the visualization of internal conflict within Podemos, was critically preceded by the implicit parodying of populism through the explicit parodying of Errejón. As such, the memetic representations evolved from Errejón being humorously depicted as the intellectual nerd of Podemos to his repeated condescending portrayal as the childlike figure of his own political party.[47] The parodic became, then, the ideal ground to establish a type of playful ambiguity through which criticisms could never be regarded as such. Errejón's infantilization was simply framed as lighthearted jokes, which otherwise enabled the political delegitimization of populism within Podemos in a much more subtle way than the repeated attacks from outside the party.

What is more, it was the Podemos leadership in the memetic sphere that catalyzed such a delegitimizing process. In the run-up to Vistalegre II, when the split between Errejón and Iglesias reached its climax, the two started divulging their political differences in the shape of memetic exchanges. The exchanges were later discursively situated within the framework of what was referred in the previous chapter as "ordinariness." As such, their online playful arguments were not to be understood as a type of passive aggressiveness but as a kind of jest that should be taken as part of their "ordinary" relationship. However, this playfulness was, on the one hand, embedded in an increased mediatic attention on Podemos's real internal conflicts, and on the other, it was increasingly influenced by the rapid acceleration of its memetic representation under the parameters of leftist clichés. Podemos's "realness" was thus folded into two realities: one externally objective and one internally subjective, that were being "hypersignified" out of its control (following Shifman's argument on memetic authenticity).[48] No matter how the relationship between Iglesias and Errejón was spun, neither could not escape the new representative framework. Their memetic authenticity was leaving populism behind while returning to Left-Right axis of reference in popular culture.

In fact, the men's own self-parodic attempts at representing Podemos's internal conflict as "ordinary"—far from enacting a popular-populist "emptiness"—would eventually point to their specific ideological differences. For instance, in a tweet referencing the famous Monty Python sketch "The People's Front of Judea," Iglesias utilized the (visual) language of the Left while Errejón resorted to the populist *casta* (the reference to the Monty Python sketch is particularly well known in Spain and quickly situated the two leaders as clichéd representations of the traditional petty quarrels within the Left beyond the content of their dispute).[49] Whereas the clash could be objectively understood in that it was informed by an actual ideological diversion within Podemos, it was mostly subjectively construed that their "real" selves were opened to anyone's interpretation. And what had been an internal tension typical of all political parties became highly mediatized as a personal schism between the two leaders, which in turn gave way to two irreconcilable factions—the so-called *pablistas* and *errejonistas*. In the shape of a self-fulling prophecy, the memetic play of their political differences marked two confronted constructions of realness informed by two differentiated political selves vis-à-vis two different conceptualizations of the people. Contrary to Podemos's expectations of once and for all settling its populist politics into a widely popular "winning framework" (i.e., the much-touted *marco ganador*), the result was the progressive hypersignification of Podemos as a party that was less *of* the people and more of *its own* people.[50]

The specificity of Podemos as a party of its people would increasingly visualize it alongside stereotypical representations on the Left, but it would also enhance memetically its ugliest political side, within the leftist tradition. After the proposal of Errejón was defeated in Vistalegre II and he was forced to work under Iglesias's leadership, their relationship still maintained the previous memetic playfulness. The main difference was that their conflict became influenced by patriarchal dynamics that reconnected with accusations of the party's toxic masculinity at the leadership level. Even though this was an old complaint mostly exploited by the Right and born of Iglesias's first representations as Podemos's alpha male, it was effectively being linked to the deep-seated dynamics that had been nurtured by long-held habits of male chauvinism and mansplaining on the Left. Although previously, Podemos's perceived excessive masculinity could be superseded by the populist framing of Iglesias, the same perception was being attached to the party's overall inauthentic status at the popular level (regardless of the representation's truth before and afterward).

Aligned with such a logic, Podemos leadership was represented as a patriarchal family in crisis. The patriarch Iglesias was portrayed as in charge of the well-being of the childlike members of his family, of Errejón, but also by extension the rest of Podemos (electorate included). In this regard, when the 2017 BBC interview of the (male) professor interrupted by his children on live television went viral on the internet, the popular late-night show *Late Motiv* recycled the video memetically representing the new role of Iglesias as patriarch of Podemos.[51] Iglesias praised and retweeted the parody.[52] Shortly thereafter, the original video was parodied from a feminist viewpoint (*New Zealand Today* reenacted the scene with a woman as interviewee who, instead of rejecting her children, is able to take care of them on camera without stopping the interview), and then the parodied version of Iglesias began again to resonate with old accusations of *machismo*.

It is, however, important to note that this series of online actions was not memetically significant because of the content of the parodies and the analogies that could be drawn (explicitly and implicitly) in relation to Podemos's feminist blindside. The importance of the actions' memetic replicability largely lies in what the representative framework of the meme says about the evolution of the Podemos phenomenon. If it is not hard to imagine how Iglesias and Podemos at an earlier time could have been parodied as the naughty children (in representation of the people) that interrupted their father (in representation of *la casta*), the new way of seeing Podemos represented the party's leaders as a parody of themselves. Far from being seen as a threat to the system (and parodied accordingly), Podemos was reentering the popular imaginary as a threat only to itself, as a party fitting the traditional commonplaces of the Left.

Its "realness" was being reconstructed outside Podemos's control. This was due mainly to the ability of the online parodic to *perform* political delegitimization in a playful tone that could not be fully exacted so was much harder to counteract. This is a type of parody that enables "campaigns to criticize an opponent in a way that is different from 'going negative' as is traditionally seen in attack ads."[53] A quintessential example thereof was the viral image of Pablo Iglesias, Íñigo Errejón, and Ramón Espinar, behind whom the word *nosotras* was displayed as a staged sign of the party's new feminist turn.[54] This had become a type of staged authenticity that did not have the capacity to be memetically authenticated positively in a populist way. If initially the cutout image of Iglesias behind a tree (which was also part of a campaign of staged authenticity) represented the "realness" of his populist challenge, this time the image was used to reveal the inauthenticity of its politics of the people or, opposingly, the authenticity of the politics of *its* people, connecting with stereotypes of historical machismo on the Left. The increasingly negative parodying was effective because it was not a direct attack from the Right. In fact, the most successful parodies of Podemos originated in online spaces that can be regarded as culturally progressive. That's precisely why they were the most effective in changing Podemos's memetic status from authentically popular-populist to stereotypically leftist.

The second stage, the political purge, was the logical consequence of the first, internal conflict, which coincided with the increased hostile environment within the party. Besides the especially difficult political circumstances in Podemos's electoral run, it was the confluence of an external "objective" reality and its "subjective" counterpart that pushed the party into a tight representative framework detrimental for the expansion of its electorate. Its "realness" was being negotiated with less and less room to maneuver under the pressing influence of the long-established perceptions of the Spanish Left. Once the framework was assumed, the dispute around Podemos's authenticity took place mostly between the leadership—increasingly represented as the party's vanguard—and the party's people, the leftist electorate. Moreover, because the most successful parodies were coming from the Left, the attacks from the Right could be more easily legitimized.

From Vistalegre II in 2017 to Errejón's exit from the party in 2019, the two major press outlets most clearly on the Right openly characterized Podemos on their front covers with the ancient language of the Cold War and the clichéd views of Soviet communism.[55] Those media caricatures in another time would have been regarded as innocuously passé and mostly out of touch with reality—in fact, this had been the case with previous characterizations of all kinds of progressive politics in Spain. However, Podemos's new frame of representation on the Left legitimized those criticisms from the Right. Pablo Iglesias was perceived as the absolute "communist" leader of the party not for an objective (factual) portrayal but because that "objectivity" was filtered and validated memetically by the subjective sphere of the internet's parodic humor. The two main outlets of political satire in Spain, *El Jueves* and *El Mundo Today*, are culturally aligned with the Left and memetically represented Iglesias as a megalomaniac with an authoritarian strain.[56] The fact that the many parodies of Podemos did not "go negative," playfully appealing to an audience that was culturally progressive, made the "subjective" perception of Iglesias's true self function as an "objective" characterization—of Podemos as a "real" Soviet communist party—and vice versa.

What is more, if Iglesias had previously functioned as the empty synecdoche of Podemos and a visual metaphor of collective change (whose parodies could enhance his political self-centeredness but would not override Podemos's populist challenge), just a few years later, most of Podemos's representations (memetic and otherwise) were being absorbed by the totality of

Iglesias's leadership. Change had thus been individualized. Iglesias stopped being a synecdoche of the party to become represented as *the party*. Accordingly, most parodies were directed at reflecting such operation of substitution—a caricature of a party so profoundly purged of dissidents that ended up having Iglesias as sole member. Regardless of the actual efforts in purging the so-called *errejonistas* from positions of leadership, this was primarily a "subjective" operation that had Podemos replaced as an agent of popular-populist change. It was a representation that favored the common understanding of politics as dependent on the (in)abilities of political leaderships. Podemos was seen as a mere a generational replacement of political representatives on the Left, who at most would try to channel the interests of its electorate (their people), reestablishing old hierarchies of parliamentary representation. The most direct consequence of such an assumption was the abandonment of any previous hope of a systemic overhaul at the institutional level. In turn, any talk around structural change was redirected through the parodic, automatically triggering comparisons of Podemos's political evolution with the historical defeats of the Spanish Left, which had often served to justify citizens' perennial disappointment with all sorts of progressive movements.

The purging of traitors stereotypically foresees the treasonous inclinations of those in charge of the purge, and Iglesias was finally represented as a sellout. In the same way that the idea of "we, the people" was inextricable from its daily performance in the occupied squares during the 15-M, Podemos's parliamentarians had to embody "being the people" in their daily performances inside and outside parliament. Because a great part of their political capital was spent on being perceived as belonging to such new political culture, they had to perform a political style and a lifestyle that made them objectively and subjectively different, distinguishing them from *la casta*, from old politics, from the status quo—both factually, in regard to their proposed policies, and idiosyncratically, always showing their "real" image as regular people doing politics and not as politicians posing as regular people. Podemos's political change needed to be perceived as "lived" in both private and public. It could not be merely enunciated as part of their politics or simply theatricalized in parliament. In this sense, "for instance, many of Podemos's new deputies gave up their right, as members of Congress, to use an official government car, and chose instead to walk or ride their bikes to Congress."[57] This was a type of "lived" change that required political performance to be a permanent performative state. The performative thus became analogous with the politician's authentic political life—in this case, a life that must stay true to oneself and to what one preaches politically.

When it was revealed that Iglesias and his partner, Irene Montero, another prominent member of the party, had bought an oversized country house in the upscale municipality of Galapagar, the old allegation that spoke of Podemos's leadership as part of *la casta* came once again to the fore.[58] Many in the party tried to justify the purchase in all sorts of ways. However, and despite the often-unethical essence as well as certainly hypocritical nature of the criticisms, the fact that Iglesias had banked politically on his popular authenticity—an "ordinary" person, part of the *gente humilde*, living in the working-class neighborhood of Vallecas—only emphasized his perceived betrayal.[59] Moreover, given the ever more recognizable characterization of Podemos as leftist, Iglesias's "treason" was classified as a class-based one. Framed under the all-too-common trope of the betrayal of the working classes by the very working-class leaders who should defend them, this final memetic representation of Iglesias was implicitly assuming an anticlass neoliberal message, that is, a message aimed at affirming the absurdity of working-class solidarity by enhancing the "natural" supremacy of the logic of neoliberal self-betterment (emblematically portrayed in Iglesias's and Montero's purchase). However, at an explicit level, these memes simply laughed at the historical "contradictions" of leftism without any pretense of sophistication.[60] The explicitly subjective, the parodying of Iglesias (and Podemos at large), was then solidifying the implicitly objective, the resilience of the neoliberal logic.

Conclusion

In their visual ethnography of protest signs during the 15-M's square occupations, Luisa Martín Rojo and Carmelo Díaz Frutos analyzed how protesting went beyond the linguistic uttering of political slogans in public. The many signs visualized during the occupation were radically changing the uses of urban space into a linguistic landscape (or *paisaje lingüístico*) where the discourse of the common good was not only a matter of political speech but also at the heart of the movement's political practice: "The many placards and banners in the squares did not simply serve to attract people to the protest camps. They served to transform the perception of what public space was to be used for, changing the common tendency to see it only as a space for private usage [i.e., the space of advertising]. Instead, it became a new site for the commons."[61] Once the protest camps, with all their protest signs, had retreated from the squares, that linguistic landscape finally switched to the internet space, first, in the form of hashtags (discursive in nature) and, later, in the shape of memes (intrinsically visual). The shift in the perception of the common good (from private to public) and its dual online-offline reception fostered a political culture dependent on collective participation from below. The people (as thought by populism) were thus to be interpreted from another angle of cultural interpretation: that of memetic signification, which allowed for the rapid creation and faster replication of new cultural frameworks online that had the ability to profoundly shape political discourse offline. Podemos perfectly understood and successfully made use of these new feature of Spain's political culture after the 15-M. Parodic humor was at the center of that success. It was the most effective way to foster the online replicability of the new populist common sense that began in the 15-M, and the party took it new heights of popularity. Yet as demonstrated in this chapter, such memetic logic swiftly turned against Iglesias's party. The very particular pigeonholing of Podemos as the party of Spain's institutional Left meant not only that Podemos lost its capacity to culturally summon the will of the people (of populism) as its most authentic political representative; it also signaled that the end of the populist cycle was near.

Through the figure of Iglesias, who had consciously acted as the synecdoche of Podemos, the populist phenomenon fell trap to the immediacy and volatility of its own transversal political aspirations. The evolution of Iglesias's memes pointed at the unsolvable tension between, on the one hand, achieving immense popularity as being authentically of the people (hence viably populist to quickly amass political-cultural capital), and on the other hand, being able to establish ideological depth beyond that superficial representation (a superficiality so transversal that opened the door to Iglesias's popular-populist bid in the first place). Within this conundrum, the memetic representation of Iglesias, as the only source of Podemos's "realness," visualized how the two sole representatives of Spanish populism at the time went from being "of the people" (in populism) to being "of *their* people" (in leftism). Thus, outside his electoral base, Iglesias ended up branded as part of those "inauthentic" leaders of the Spanish Left, whomever they may be—a caricature of how power corrupts even the most honest politician. This was an implicit message destined to encourage cynicism and political inaction, because Podemos had supposedly demonstrated that "all politicians are the same." It was a rationale that followed the still-prevalent logic of neoliberal technocracy and connected with Francoist endemic apoliticism. It was a push to put the popular back to its original place before the crisis of 2008–2011. In the hope that the people would return to that more manageable place, the same forces in the status quo who (before and after every election since

2011) spoke of the necessity of a coalition between the two major parties on both sides of the ideological spectrum (the PSOE and the PP) finally found Podemos (mediatically and memetically) backed against the wall of radical leftism. The result, however, was not the restoration of the more docile citizenry previous to 15-M and the Podemos phenomenon. Much to the contrary, with the apparent electoral neutralization of Podemos and the definitive recuperation of the Left-Right axis of political confrontation, a new iteration of antagonism arose. The figure of Santiago Abascal and Vox took on the role that Iglesias and Podemos had had; only this time around, Vox implemented a type of antagonism that was dangerously reminiscent of Francoist fascism.

VOX'S POSTFASCISM AND THE MEMETIC RECONSTRUCTION OF NATIONALIST ANTAGONISM

I'd rather be called Fascist than be praised by Pablo Iglesias

—SANTIAGO ABASCAL

While Podemos's populist style required the "emptying" of conceptualizations such as the people or *la casta* through the ordinary, vulgar, or bad-mannered leadership of Iglesias to start constructing a productive antagonistic frontier (e.g., between "we, the people" and "they, *la casta*"), the antagonism promoted by Vox's far-right-wing positions depended on the opposite political machination. Apart from being stylistically similar to the historic figure of the good-mannered, paternalistic, Francoist *señorito* of Spain's landed class (or *latifundistas*), Vox's mode of political expression needed to be as ideologically specific as possible, defined by a historically defined *pueblo* with its very precise ideological enemies—in this case, the perceived enemies of the Spanish people.[1] What follows is a recounting of how the popular-populist impetus born of the 15-M and taken to new heights by the Podemos phenomenon became replaced by the qualitatively different political and cultural impetus of Vox. To that effect, this chapter takes the shape of an epilogue as an allusion both to the end of the populist narrative recounted throughout this book and to the definitive end of the populist moment in Spain, which the visualization of Podemos as a party of the Left has just advanced.

Importantly, Vox's momentum, despite being animated by the era of Trumpism and Steve Bannon's right-wing populist strategy for Europe (who did indeed meet with Vox's leaders to establish a Trump-like figure in Spain), was more dangerously and directly shaped by the political ghosts of Franco-ism, which were reincarnated in the party's aspirations to "Make Spain Great Again"—beyond what that Trumpian slogan may evoke.[2] Vox is not like its European right-wing populist counterparts. Although the party is certainly riding the favorable populist wave, Vox's leader Santiago Abascal does not fit the mold of the right-wing populist leader who uses being popular in culture as a tool to become populist in politics (especially regarding the ability to be electorally transversal). In this respect, the social anthropologist Lynda Dematteo offers a paradigmatic comparative example to further understands how Vox needs to be approached from a nonpopulist angle of interpretation. She explains right-wing populism in Italy through the Northern League political party and its uses of the popular as populist. First, Dematteo refers to its former leader Umberto Bossi, who embodied the stereotype of the Italian "idiot" from the North "to better seduce the voters at the expense of traditional elites."[3] Dematteo's main argument centers on how populist leaders like Bossi use popular culture as a mask "to take possession of the others . . . to assert themselves by making the needs of the crowds coincide with those they express."[4] Bossi needed to put on masks (e.g., the mask of the ridiculed northerner, of the honest peasant, of the forgotten industrial worker) to pass as ordinary at political rallies or in parliament but also on televised interviews and on Facebook, Twitter, and so forth. The medium of popular culture gave the populist leader direct access to the masses, toward whom they hold up a mask-mirror that allows for politically unmediated representation between the leader and the people. And in the case of Italian populism, this game of masks allowed the elected populists to take "symbolic revenge on their opponents" in the name of "liberating their supporters from their complexes."[5]

The successor of Bossi—since 2013, leader of the Northern League and in close ideological proximity with Vox's Santiago Abascal—symbolically portrays himself as "the stupid son of a concierge" whose humble (ordinary) origins allow him to tell it like is, according to Dematteo.[6] Thus, for instance, Salvini can incorporate into his political persona a veneer of cultural ordinariness, which has allowed him to popularize the idea that everyday Italians should not be ashamed of their fascist past (in the same way he was not embarrassed by his own past as an ordinary man), freeing them from the "political correctness" imposed by urban elites.[7] Salvini, then, was not only entirely normalizing "the Italian fascist heritage"; he was able to do so precisely because fascism was performed as a trait of his ordinary Italianness, as a mask that was supposed to truly reflect the life story of everyday Italians. And there, in the way fascism was performed and seen as culturally ordinary (full of low passions, bad mannered, with an underdog essence), in the political style that Salvini enacted when pitting the ordinary people of the North against the Italian elites of Rome, one can find the key difference between Vox's postfascist politics and the Northern League's right-wing populism.

Vox lacks popular "ordinariness" in its political as well as ideological essence of the people, which is conceptualized closer to the parameters of the nation.[8] Instead of a popular-populist antagonism, which would oppose an ambiguous people against a vaguely defined elite, Vox proposes a national(ist) antagonism that centers on defending a traditional conception of the Spanish nation and Spanishness, culturally linked with what has been termed *sociological Francoism*, which is the idea that "'Franco's regime . . . became a way of life for all Spaniards" well after the dictator died.[9] Vox is simply the stark reminder that such "a way of life" is still latent in sectors of Spanish society who tend to see politics in marked nationalist dichotomies (i.e., true Spaniards versus anti-Spaniards). Initially, Vox's antagonism was directed mainly against the historical role of peripheral nationalisms in Spanish politics. Of particular importance for the reconstruction of the antagonistic frontier was then the Catalan bid for independence and, especially, the incidents around the "referendum" of October 1, 2017. Vox's nationalist antagonistic framework (embedded in nationalisms' general conceptualization of the popular) rapidly evolved into a type of national antagonism (specific to the history of Francoism and Spanishness), which divided Spain's population between its legitimate defenders and its undesirable enemies.[10] Catalanists and the rest of non-Spanish nationalisms—but also immigrants, feminists, leftists, and even allegedly "wimpy" rightists—became otherized in a way that resonated with Francoism's historical divisions of the Spanish people. As such, Vox spoke of a "living Spain," or *España Viva*, that posed a dichotomic divide between "a patriotic alternative or an agreement of betrayal. Either the disaggregation or the historical continuity of our homeland. Either socialist misery, or the prosperity of our children and grandchildren. Either the progressive dictatorship or freedom for the Spaniards."[11] To put it another way, as José Rama and others have argued, Vox's leaders may not express an explicit rejection of current democratic values in contrast to their apparent nostalgia for a better past, but they "adopt many of the positions of the Francoist regime in terms of the defense of traditional moral values exalting the alleged past grandeur of Spain."[12] So if it hadn't been clear before, this shift in the construction of antagonism from popular-populist to national-nationalist definitely indicated the end of populism and announced the beginning of what historian Enzo Traverso—who specializes in European totalitarianisms—has called "postfascism."[13]

Traverso distinguishes fascism, neofascism, and postfascism. The first is the ideology that informs the historical events of interwar years (namely, Italian *fascismo*, German Nazism, and Spanish Francoism). The second denotes the posterior attempts at the revival of historical fascism by different groups in different geographies under different political circumstances. Although there is a conceptual continuity between the first two, *postfascism* describes "a phenomenon in transition, a movement that is still in transformation and has not yet crystallized."[14] Postfascism applies to a series of movements on the extremist Right that, despite having a (neo)fascist background, have transformed their ideology to the extent that one cannot claim there is an ideological continuity between (neo)fascism and postfascism. In this sense, postfascism is a phenomenon decidedly marked by our current political uncertainties: "Postfascism belongs to a particular regime of historicity—the beginning of the twenty-first century—which explains its erratic, unstable, and often contradictory ideological content, in which antinomic political philosophies mix together."[15] The historical fascist roots cannot be ignored, but postfascism is more defined by its ideological metamorphoses and, especially, by the political direction the different movements under such a label are moving toward. In this sense, postfascist phenomena are best described by their very similar political objectives rather than by the heterogeneous conceptual or different historical pathways to achieving such goals. Under that definition one can then put in the same bag Marine Le Pen's National Front (later, National Rally), Forum for Democracy in the Netherlands, and Santiago Abascal's Vox.

Most prominently, one of the common ambitions of postfascism has been the visualization of a homogeneous nation easily identifiable in racial, cultural, or religious terms.[16] Given the extraordinary obsessions of Francoism with the unity of the Spanish nation, Vox's politics are particularly influenced by the necessity of a cohesive national imaginary. The party maintains a vision of Spain that directly stems from Franco's regime. However, its image of Spain is not so much based in the recovery of the Spanish nation's past (at least, not explicitly); instead, it emphasizes the need to recuperate a strong national identity that appears to be no longer possible in the present. The focus is thus less on the nation and more on the national, because nationalist ideology matters much less than the creation of an easy-to-demarcate national identification: the construction of a cohesive national discourse that fit into an imagined, symbolic, political, and historical framework simply is not as urgent as the creation of a mechanism of exclusion-inclusion via an (un)recognizable national identity. Vox's process of national identification functions most effectively in negative terms, that is, in relation to everything that is *not* Spanish, without having to resort to ontological, historicist, or "objective" demarcations. For instance, the particular usage of the national imagery made by Vox is not aimed at reinforcing a common hegemonic discourse of the Spanish nation and its people, but it is mostly directed at discriminating "true" Spaniards from their confronted others. It is a preliminary visual cue that, while indicating belonging into Spanishness by means of national symbols, expels from such symbolic regime what does not fit into Vox's antagonistic political structure.[17] This is a type of antagonism that directly follows the steps of Francoist conceptualization of the nation and its successful patrimonialization of national symbols.

The fascist conception of Spain began right after the 1936 coup when Franco's army nominated itself as the *bando nacional*. The self-nomination followed the main justification for the military uprising, which was "predicated on the notion that Spain needed an emergency to restore order and traditional values to the nation."[18] Such gestures anticipated the establishment of a cohesive symbolic project for Spain characterized by what Luis Angosto-Ferrández has called a "muting multivocality."[19] That is, in the process of cementing a fascist idea of Spain, Franco's forces erected symbols of national unity that were dependent on the literal and metaphorical death of any association with the Spanish Second Republic and its citizenry. After the war ended—as Pablo Sánchez León has argued in regard to the history of Spanish patriotism—Francoism constructed a "new state" for the "true" Spanish *patria*, which was not only "originally disengaged from the narrative on citizenship building"; its raison d'être was found on "the suppression of basic constitutional rights upholding the exercise of citizenship."[20] Franco had violently decoupled the conceptualization of democratic citizenship from the notion of *patria* by treating any political position that was not aligned with the basic tenets of the dictatorship as extraneous foreign agents (operatives of Soviet communism or emissaries of a Jewish-Freemason cabal). Francoist foundational violence "erased the opacity that facilitates polyphonic multivocality" when creating a national project and therefore muted all other expressions of Spanishness.[21] In this sense, one can argue that Franco's dictatorship did not really aim to rewrite the past; it broke with the past, because it wrote new rules of existence based on a new national symbolic project eminently void of words that could not be comprehended or followed rationally. The 15-M, first, and Podemos, later, was an attempt in the opposite direction, a bid to expand the idea of citizenship into the *patria* through the backdoor of the *pueblo* as thought by populism. It was, however, a complex historical operation that involved much more than simply recuperating an alternative democratic memory to the Francoist legacy. Because Franco's regime lived on in the democratic period thanks to the socialization of forgetting, implicitly making all Spaniards complicit, the popular transformation of the present instinctively carried on with the amnesty of the past by obsessively focusing on what the future might bring. As such, the ghost of Francoism remained unexorcised, more clearly seen in the impossible coupling of *patria* and citizenry that Podemos had tried. Given the unremitting force of history and the much-weakened position of Spanish politics when it comes to historical memory, Podemos's failed resymbolization of the *patria* was a paradigmatic example of the obstacles ingrained in the political present.

A great part of the difficulties of the present when dealing with the past has to do with how Francoism developed a symbolic structure to explain itself, the country, and its people that ultimately replaced political discourse with "gestures, images, emotions, colors, rituals, sounds, and cries."[22] As most notably argued by Walter Benjamin in his "Theories of German Fascism," fascist aesthetics were to become a "primal experience" imbued with a "mysticism . . . [that] crawls forth on its thousands unsightly conceptual feet."[23] This conceptual matrix was ultimately aimed at elevating the people into "a higher realm of politics that they would experience sensually."[24] Francoist aesthetic aspirations went beyond mere insertion of recognizable fascist symbols. They created a national project that demanded an existential break from the immediate democratic and republican past. Such a break was not so much conceived of from an ideological standpoint as it was conceptualized as a new way of life that would be lived even after Franco had passed.[25] Before and after Franco's death, Francoism was a reconceptualization of the people that heavily relied on a symbolic structure that needed to be felt and was rarely conversed. As such, any new political project was dependent on creating a parallel symbolic structure unconnected to old leftist rationalizations, which incidentally explains the initial success of the 15-M as well as the posterior loss of influence of Podemos—albeit only as far as popular culture is concerned.

Franco's Spain was ultimately determined by the performative qualities of Spanishness. It was a performance based on what Jo Labanyi has called a "melodramatic representation of history," by which token one was given the fatal choice of belonging to a national healthy body or, on the contrary, siding with a foreign red malaise.[26] In choosing existence over extermination, the Spanish people were also incorporated into "an all-inclusive national culture based on an organic concept of 'the popular.'"[27] Francoism's ultimate success was the progressive securing and manufacturing of a popular consent that was subservient to the establishment of a cultural matrix, in which its varied representations were directed at the occupation of the entire symbolic field. Political resistance was muted, especially because it was never allowed to dispute the Francoist symbolic spectrum of Spanishness. Anti-Francoism was in this way pushed to a discursive plane completely out of tune with the regime's hegemonic project for the Spanish people. In other words, the few in the opposition who survived Francoist repression were obliged to craft rational responses to an irrational system of oppression and expression. Anti-Francoists were largely made incomprehensible at a symbolic and emotional level within Spain. As much as their words could be understood by anyone—especially those in the international community, where anti-Francoists found most of their support—they were completely surpassed by the emotional architecture of Francoism. Vox came to be the direct inheritor and best interpreter of that Francoist framework, as revamped through a new cosmetic of Spanishness, directly attuned to a very important part of Spanish popular culture.

And that is exactly why Podemos's ideation of *patria* did not really work. The more the party was being discursively as well as stylistically codified under the parameters of the traditional Left (full of political reasons and progressively out of tune with emotions in popular culture), the more room there was in the popular to reconstruct an opposition movement to the Podemos phenomenon. Vox was politically reborn in that impasse.[28] In the 2018 regional elections in Andalusia, Abascal's party was first put on the electoral map with 11 percent of the votes. Only a year later, Vox turned into the third-most-voted-for party in the national general election, winning over 3.5 million votes and fifty-two seats in the Spanish Parliament. Conversely, Unidas Podemos reaffirmed its electoral debacle by losing thirty-six seats and more than 2 million votes. Although saved by the historical coalition with the PSOE, which finally saw Iglesias's party gain governmental power at the national level, it became ever more obvious that the Podemos phenomenon had given way to the rise of Vox.

Precisely because Spanish politics had returned to its original Left-Right spectrum, Vox could take advantage of the dynamics inherent in such a divide. To begin with, the heightened political divisions between perceptions on the Left and on the Right meant the final disbandment of what was left of the ideological center. The so-called political moderation, an anti-ideological construct born during the Transición, no longer reaped enough electoral benefits. Consequently, political parties were, above all, in a battle for their "real" essence. Although this contention had subsided on the Left with the definite establishing of Unidas Podemos to the Left of the PSOE, the ideological identity wars had just begun on the Right. In this respect, Vox famously labeled the Popular Party—and to a lesser extent the Center-Right party Ciudadanos (the so-called conservative version of Podemos) because of their increasing lack of electoral influence—as the *derechita cobarde*, the little wimpy cowards of the Right.

At a time of increased polarization, ideological identity was of utmost importance. Vox took decisive advantage of this identitarian push, favoring what Stuart J. Turnbull-Dugarte has called "disloyalty on the Right," which in practice meant that over two-thirds of the votes for Vox came from those who had previously preferred the Popular Party and Ciudadanos.[29] The main reason for such a switch in allegiances was not Vox's toughest position on a series of specific right-wing policies (e.g., stronger anti-immigration stance, openly antiabortion position). It was, however, a broad conceptual shift, largely driven "by their [voters'] Left-Right ideological preferences as well as . . . nationalistic concerns."[30] Among its adversaries, Vox was easily identifiable as the "real" option on the Right. Contrary to the Popular Party's historical efforts to appear as a moderate, centrist conservative party, Vox's position was crystal clear on the Right. It could maintain its purist political identity because it had not gone through any major process of public accountability. Thus, it could easily reposition its identity from marginal actor on ultra-rightist circles to truth teller of the mainstream Right. And one of the fastest ways to realize its "pure" essence was by aggressively identifying the Left as the enemy. To that end, the Left was not only a political enemy but also a national threat.[31] Under these parameters, Vox solidified an essentialist view of national politics that thrived in the simplicity of memetic representation.

If Iglesias had functioned memetically as the synecdoche of Podemos's populism, Vox became the synecdoche of Spanishness as conjured by post-fascism. In terms of memetic authenticity, Abascal's party became immune to negative parodic humor much as Iglesias had initially been. The more Vox was ridiculed, the more its antagonistic agenda was activated, reinforcing Vox's idea that there were only two confronted essences, those who were part of the "real" Spain (defended by Vox) and those who were posing a threat to the Spanish nation (confirmed by their attacks on Vox). Because Vox's main political identity was unequivocally based on the defense of Spanishness, parodying the party was taken as an attempt at parodying Spain. As a way to expose the laughability of these online attacks, humorless parodies were preferred over parodic humor. Thus, Vox often used a type of memetic parody that would aim to expose the anti-Spanishness of its enemies vis-à-vis any other lesser identities.[32] In this sense, the parodic would not establish a dispute between different authenticities, as had been the case with the 15-M's version of real democracy and Podemos. It aimed to settle the undisputed realness of the Spanish identity. Vox's memes merely reaffirmed Vox's essence as the mirror of "real" Spanishness, such as one famous meme that photoshopped Abascal's face into the muscular protagonist of the film *300* surrounded by Spanish flags, under which it read: "Spain first."[33]

Beyond Vox's secondary identity projections (in this case, an unapologetic toxic hypermasculinity), its memetic representations were in essence positioned to create one solid identification. Vox's memetics produced an identification *with* the party and an identification *of* the party that mirrored each other. In that regard, there were not to be any discrepancies between what one knew of the party, what the party said it was, and how the party was seen memetically. The very essence of Vox was predicated on the absolute coherence of this process of political identification. This was key in allowing the antagonistic understanding of Spanish politics under a truly Schmittian friend-enemy paradigm (and not simply an operational conceptualization as it had been argued in regard to Podemos).[34] The populist performance of transversal political change was being substituted by the visualization of a very specific Spanish *pueblo*, whose main objective in politics was the recuperation of the "true" essence of the nation. Conceptually, the popular had gotten rid of the populist and was returning to a dangerous historical place shaped by a (post)fascist identity.

Nevertheless, Vox's apparent nostalgia for a fascist past of strong national unity and masculinist patriots was not the most dangerous aspect of its politics (despite what many commentators in the media have claimed). In fact, such longings had always been part and parcel of the Spanish Right: not by chance was the founder of Vox, Alejo Vidal-Quadras, a prominent member of the Popular Party, as was Abascal. A more pernicious side of Vox is how the party has enabled the impossibility of visualizing hope into change. Vox has set politics looking back into the past: Spanish politics are currently embroiled either in a fight to conserve what little Spaniards have—a struggle not to regress in terms of acquired civil, political, and economic rights— or in a battle to recuperate what they have supposedly lost, namely, their

Spanishness. If the 15-M opened a utopian window of opportunity, in which the "impossible was demanded," Vox shut it tightly closed. Most alarmingly, Vox has unearthed a dystopian dynamic that, just like Francoism did after the end of the Civil War, is making political hope its most precious prisoner. It has implemented a politics of despair that might be counteracted only by the visualization of a new utopian horizon, a utopian vision that is still awaiting to be seen and performed beyond the temporary occupation of squares, the periodic heightening of mass protests, and the unavoidable restrictions of electoral politics. But above all, this new utopia should be able to look at the past to finally exorcise the ghosts of its present when hoping for a more equitable future. That is a utopian impetus based on what Alison Ribeiro de Menezes has termed as disruptive memory: "a Rancèrean [sic] harnessing of memory as a productive dissensus . . . [that] aims not only to examine the present but also to demand new ways of dissenting politically by envisaging a differently ordered world."[35] From thousands of miles away, necessarily confined by the walls of academia, one can only hope that this book is a small step toward at least starting to look in that direction.

THE JOURNEY BACK
FROM POPULISM

This book has been a selective intervention into a populist moment to high-light the evolving role that visuality and performativity played in the forma-tion of popular-populist identity during the decade of the 2010s in Spanish politics. It has endeavored to visualize the story of how Spanish populism and its conceptualization of the people emerged in the occupied squares during the 15-M, matured with the Podemos phenomenon, and were finally put to rest when Vox resuscitated old Francoist mannerisms from a past that ap-peared to have been mostly overcome. Important for the recounting of that story has been how different visual parts heterogeneously shaped the Spanish populist cycle. Because of it, populism's political narrative needed to be ap-proached from the vantage point of cultural analysis. Culture has offered a window of interpretation to better comprehend how populism took hold of Spain's political imagination beyond its most explicit politics, thriving in the more ambiguous but more effective realm of its cultural practice.

More concretely, Chapter 1 focused on how the protesters in the 15-M visu-alized a public political voice for "real" democratic change as seen through a number of textual images (in placards but also in the radical reshaping of advertising in the occupied squares), which would give form to a new pop-ulist identity that quickly became part of Spain's popular culture. In Chap-ter 2, that new political and cultural identity was further explored through a series of documentaries that showed "the people" through the implicit as well as explicit contrast between the identarian silhouette of the "real" people of the 15-M and their confronted elitist other. Ultimately, these films were visual documents of an ongoing clash between the inside and the outside of the movement in an effort to settle who the most authentic representative of the people in Spanish democracy was, thus visualizing the protesters inside the camps performing new ways of doing politics (e.g., in the assemblies, on the internet, through their own audiovisual propaganda) pitted against those (un)elected power brokers in politics who were increasingly seen as illegitimate in culture. Chapter 3 analyzed that conflict as it developed during the years after the 15-M retreated from public sight and splintered into smaller, more issue-driven causes, showing how that division did not mean that the 15-M's ethos lost any political or cultural steam. Much to the contrary, as political frustrations expanded, the people who were in the squares performing a "real" democracy—commonly visualized as constructors of a new democratic time—were progressively seen through the lens of an antagonistic pathos fueled by the economic crisis and the ongoing austerity measures. To such end, a series of fictions films was used as a paradigmatic example of how people's increasing antagonist political logic was best encapsulated culturally. The films analyzed in the chapter proposed in one way or another a sharp populist duality born out of the 15-M: "us," victims of the crisis, versus "them," elite responsible for the crisis. Yet differently from the more constructive political appearance at the onset of the 15-M, the us-people in these films evolved to be portrayed with increasingly destructive, bad-mannered, populist traits in culture. That was a cultural anger that Podemos later capitalized on for its own political success. Chapter 4 turned the page on the 15-M to focus directly on the Podemos phenomenon, which noncoincidentally characterized itself with different degrees of explicitness as the movement's direct inheritor. The chapter dwelled on how the party used television as one of the main platforms to popularize its populist politics, effectively channeling people's growing indignation. It also analyzed how Podemos's message was not simply made popular thanks to television and its capacity for mass communication; the party conveyed a cinematic aesthetic in its political style that successfully visualized its audience as "the people." Podemos thus used the language of cinema to culturally construct Iglesias's populist leadership and frame him as a relatable, "ordinary," political celebrity. Chapter 5 followed the trails of Podemos and Pablo Iglesias in regard to their online presence, the other key platform for their political success. Through the evolution of how the two were characterized on the internet, the chapter narrated how the Podemos phenomenon was first able to agglutinate the 15-M's varied online hashtags into a new memetic identity that made use of parodic humor to establish the authenticity of their populist politics. Nevertheless, as the time passed and Podemos became part of Spain's political institutions, both its memetic identity and its populist politics lost cultural force until they eventually disappeared. Podemos devolved into a party of its people, a markedly leftist party, as opposed to being a party of the people, transversally populist. Yet this shift was not due to a decisive change in political strategy (beyond Podemos's strategic blunders), as much as it was the signal that populist politics and the populist cycle were coming to an end. With that in mind, the book's last chapter was shaped to metaphorically certify the death of Spanish populism and, literally, ended the book's arguments on Spain's populist moment. This was a brief incursion into the advent of the Far Right's Vox party and how its postfascist politics initially bypassed mainstream media with the help of the internet. Vox's online presence was the clearest visual evidence that confirmed the journey of the people back from populism, which in turn gave way to a new political-cultural battle inserted in a dangerous friend-enemy paradigm.

Overall, from a broader transdisciplinary perspective, this book has also attempted to demonstrate how culture (especially popular culture) represents (directly and indirectly) its version of the political and decisively contributes to make politics—as far the mass propagation of ideas and even the creation of new collective identities are concerned. From the 15-M movement to the height of the Podemos phenomenon, it has been necessary to examine how politics affected not just the political sphere, whereby a new political culture was created, but also how those political moments were represented by different cultural artifacts, which were also *presented* as part of a new popular culture that saw and performed the power of the people as a new style of doing politics. That's why the book's main investigative vector has been following the trace of how the people were seen from different angles of presentation (as authentic, bad mannered, plebeian, parodic) performing a new way of doing politics in different formats (in memes, protest signs, films). Ultimately, within the varied presentations of the people, this book wanted to show how the popular and the populist became inextricably connected in a series of images (moving and still) for a limited period of time (from the occupation of squares in 2011 until the decline of Podemos's populist bid and the irruption of Vox's postfascism less than a decade later).

The Last Visual Incursion into the Unbecoming of Spanish Populism

As an alternative and more playful way of closing the book's arguments, this section revisits the connection of the popular and the populist, but this time against the grain. It explores not so much how the popular in culture becomes populist in politics (or vice versa), but how a specific visuality—the picture of a "ponytail-less" Pablo Iglesias, the once-populist leader par excellence—despite being one of the most culturally relevant images at the time in Spanish politics, was the ultimate proof that the popular was completely disconnected from the populist, which ultimately is evidence of the mutual dependence between the two (as this book has argued all along). To reframe the analysis, it is important to reinstate the connections of the popular and the populist, on this occasion with the help Susan Sontag's famous writings on popular culture.

Susan Sontag, in "Against Interpretation," forcefully argued the case for the popular to be included in whatever notion of culture one might have. The popular was understood very much like populism, in essence, has been here conceived, as an uncomplicated, aesthetically low, and even superficial mode of cultural expression. Thus, Sontag opened her 1964 essay with a telling quote by Oscar Wilde: "It is only shallow people who do not judge by appearances. The mystery of the world is the visible, not the invisible."[1] These words relate to a fundamental first impulse of this book: examining how what is visible and obvious to everyone could be a door to the inner workings of complexities about the everyday, the ordinary, the basic, where constitutional humors of politics and culture might be found. It is in the realm of the visible that popular culture resides and where its twin sister in politics, populism, can be *seen*. When it comes to the act of seeing, the choice of words is here important, because to see intentionally signals a conceptual separation from the act of making something seen or—more simply put—the act of interpreting. By opening with Wilde's quote, Sontag was also pointing out a similar idea. That is, she was stressing the importance of seeing meaning against tendencies to obscure it by way of imposing one's interpretation over a certain formal intention behind creative content. Yet it must be emphasized that seeing as opposed to interpreting was a metaphorical conceptualization that did not mean to exile the interpretation of form and content. It was simply warning against elitist interpretative frameworks that concealed the subjective experience of meaning (i.e., its "visibility" in relation to lay individual interpreters). In other words, Sontag's stance against interpretation was, above all, a stance against cultural elitism.

On the one hand, Sontag was writing against the inclination from those at the top of the hermeneutic pyramid (art and literary critics, intellectuals, powerful brokers of the knowledge industry) to force their way of interpreting onto the rest of society, who lacked the necessary means to legitimatize their interpretations. That's why Sontag positively saw the irruption of popular art, which would suppose an escape from a top-down hermeneutic framework due to its intrinsic artistic legibility, by virtue of being "so what it is."[2] On the other, Sontag was not defending popular or low culture against high Culture with capital *C*. At the most essential level, she was arguing against the illusion of separating art form from art content, which was what made possible the imposition of interpretation (formal, contextual, historical, political) over the meaning of the interpreted object in the first place. Only when content was separated from form could those with the acquired power to interpret institute their interpretation of the "special" relationship between content and form. Oppositely, when the two were understood as intrinsically connected such hermeneutic tendency disappeared, favoring the democratization of meaning based on content's "transparence" or visibility (using Wilde's schema), which would ultimately be "the most liberating value in art."[3] Thus, for Sontag, popular culture (especially the cinematic experience) was, when she was writing in the 1960s, the great liberator of meaning in society.[4] If form and content became hermeneutically indistinguishable (what you see is what you get, and vice versa), elitist impositions of meanings would be culturally unviable and cultural meaning-making processes could be democratized.

Similarly, the study of populism has often endorsed interpretative impositions of content (discursive, ideational or ideological) over—and virtually separated from—populist form. In this respect, it has not been uncommon to paint with a broad theoretical brush the immense diversity of populist moments while also neglecting the extensive analysis of populist styles. Nevertheless, in a bid to connect the theory of populism with the specificity of its political expression, new scholarly approaches are recognizing the importance of populism as a political style, such as the studies carried out by Marino, Tormey, Moffit, and Ostiguy referred in earlier chapters. These new ways of understanding populism have emphasized the artificiality of separating populist ideas from the way those ideas are presented by populists. In other words, populism's representative capacity relies on the force of its presentation skills, on the ability of populist leaders and movements to present themselves as the most authentic representative of the people or—more simply put—as the mirror of the people themselves. In connection with Sontag's argument, such power of (re)presentation is thus tied to the inherent transparency of the popular in culture that mirrors the way populist ideas are styled as politically transparent, as a type of people's common sense that is apparent in both form and content (hence rendering the division invisible). The evolution of Pablo Iglesias's image is the perfect example of how his political leadership became disconnected from the transparency of the culturally popular despite his enormous popularity in both politics and culture. Such visual unfolding can be condensed into one simple question around another "viral" moment of Iglesias, when he was photographed for the first time after resigning from his political positions in the government and in Unidas Podemos with his new haircut reading a book. Why can that photograph of Iglesias be said to have lost its popular-populist force despite signaling an undisputable crucial moment in Spain's politics and Spanish popular culture?[5]

The photograph in which Iglesias was seen for the first time without his iconic ponytail was published by *La Vanguardia* as an exclusive scoop by the renowned cultural journalist Pedro Vallín, more recently reassigned to the beat of political reporting. Apart from covering Podemos's politics, Vallín was known to Iglesias as his guest on *Fort Apache*, *La Tuerka*, and his short-lived cultural show *Spoilers*. In these shows, the two shared a similar approach to reading politics through culture, especially in cinema and television. That's why it wasn't by chance that, in the picture of Iglesias published by Vallín, Iglesias appeared holding Vallín's book *Me cago en Godard: Por qué deberías adorar el cine americano (y desconfiar del cine de autor) si eres culto y progre* (Fuck Godard: Why you should love American cinema [and distrust film *auteurs*] if you are cultured and are a progressive). Apart from the simple explanation given by Vallín—Iglesias texted the photo to the journalist to let him know that he finally had time to read his book, two years after the former interviewed him in *La Tuerka*—both the political context of the photographic composition and the symbolism of the photograph pointed to a more deeply layered commentary.[6] And it is in the invisible layers of that commentary, in its restricted invisibility or, more simply, in its unapparent visibility, that one begins to see why Iglesias's photo couldn't be seen as populist and, by the same token, one can also realize what it takes for the popular to become populist.

To dig deeper into the unsaid angles of interpretation within the picture (which might indeed be multiple, as Iglesias is well known for teasing the public with hidden cultural and political messages) is beside the point. The picture's relevance here lies in its inability to enact a populist visuality, one that remits to an emptied signification. On the contrary, Iglesias's image is characterized by the "fullness" of its meaning. The layers of signification that hide underneath the (intentional or not) symbolism of the picture fill it with meaning, making it part of Spain's popular culture but only in the sense that is part of Iglesias's online virality. That is, its popularity lies solely in its replicability, signifying Iglesias as someone who "goes viral." Moreover, because the picture is full of meaning, connoted by the interpretation from Iglesias of Iglesias himself as a political icon, its populist characteristics are annulled by the homogeneous depth of its political interpretation (as opposed to the superficial heterogeneity that populism demands of popular signification). The political context as well as Iglesias's consciously acquired political dramatis persona as leftist icon forces one to see the image within the visual codes of the cultural Left. In this sense, only someone who understands those codes can "correctly" interpret Iglesias's message. Iglesias can maintain the popular only thanks to his "virality" and not his apparent identification with the people, which otherwise would have "emptied" his persona in the photograph by loosely equating heterogeneous political demands with the instantaneous cultural "transparency" of Iglesias's visuality, authenticating him as "ordinary" (as discussed in Chapter 4), of the people, thus inserting him in the tandem popular-populist. Yet this picture of Iglesias is "repleted" with political and cultural tropes of the new Spanish Left that the ex-leader of Unidas Podemos seems to be fostering himself.

In that respect, Vallín's book title is particularly significant. At one level, profanity is ironically positioned (as opposed to, for instance, the discussion on Carminism's bad manners in Chapter 3) in the title (*Fuck Godard*). The vulgar in conjunction with the symbol of elitism that the allusion to Godard signifies positions Iglesias not as part of the *vulgo*, the ordinary, or the plebs. Much to the contrary, it anticipates and links with the subtitle, *Why you should love American cinema (and distrust film* auteurs) *if you are cultured and are a progressive*: being seen reading Vallín's book associates Iglesias with those that "have culture" and are *progres* (a somewhat negative identification of progressives or more generally leftists in Spain). After reading Chapter 5, it should be clear that Iglesias's populist "emptiness" was abandoned for a consciously ideological identification with the Left. This picture reinforces again such a shift not only because of the explicit connections between Vallín's book and Iglesias ideological projections but also because of what is no longer seen in the latter's political performance within this visual composition: his populism. Because for Iglesias to be *seen* as populist, he'd need to *perform* being of the people.

In that photograph, Iglesias is, however, theatricalizing his "extraordinariness" rather than his former "ordinary," populist persona. After his grand exit from institutional politics, he is performing his grand entry into public life within the controlled environment of the visual and the symbolic, where Iglesias culturally thrives and politically moves best. From the perspective of how Iglesias is self-represented in the image, his performance is at the service of the extraordinary, visualizing a political leader who has made history, someone who knows full well that by virtue of getting a haircut he becomes politically relevant, and so he exploits his relevance by posing symbolically in a picture like a fallen Samson of the Left, now retreated into a life of the mind, and away from the (increasingly fraught) everyday culture of the people and the messy politics of the popular. Such an assertion, far from being negative, points to the main message of this book: the act of seeing the people is consubstantial to the act of performing populism, performing being of the people. The photograph of Iglesias simply shows that the once-iconic populist leader had shed his populism at long last. Because in the end the difference between whether to be or not be populist lies in the (in)ability to *present* the popular as populist.

NOTES

INTRODUCTION

1. Santiago Alba Rico, "Podemos in Spain: Limits and Possibilities for Change," in *Spain after the Indignados/15M Movement: The 99% Speaks Out*, ed. Óscar Pereira-Zazo and Steven L. Torres (New York: Palgrave Macmillan, 2019), 83.

2. Bryan Cameron, "Spain in Crisis: 15-M and the Culture of Indignation," *Journal of Spanish Cultural Studies* 15, nos. 1–2 (2014): 2.

3. Óscar Pereira-Zazo and Steven L. Torres, "Introduction: After the 15M," in *Spain after the Indignados/15M Movement: The 99% Speaks Out*, ed. Óscar Pereira-Zazo and Steven L. Torres (New York: Palgrave Macmillan, 2019), 4.

4. Pereira-Zazo and Torres, 5.

5. Pereira-Zazo and Torres, 7.

6. In the media and also in some intellectual circles of the Left, the 15-M's protests were at the time labeled as "events," contingent to their immediate present fueled by the immediacy of the internet, rather than inserted in the established political tradition of a social movement with a sense of history. As Katryn Evinson has argued, they were criticized for their "presentism" as well as their fundamental incapability to challenge the overall capitalist structures because of their supposedly myopic view of problems at hand: "According to these criticisms, they are presentists for operating in the very coordinates made possible by neoliberalism. They fail to articulate a project outside of the neoliberal fragmented experience of time. But driven by an urgency to challenge austerity politics, a fundamental feature of neoliberal capitalism, it seems more accurate to view these mobilizations as reacting right where they could: in the precariousness of their here and now." Katryn Evinson, "The Generative Politics of Presentism in Post-15M Spain," *boundary 2* 48, no. 3 (2021): 174.

7. That publication, with its focus on the democratic transition, revealed another important feature of the 15-M's historical significance. As such, many of the central critiques to the movement were in reality a veiled defense of

the so-called Moncloa Pacts and the Transición, which the 15-M was questioning as not a fully democratic transition given the ties of some economic and political elites to the Francoist establishment. For a full discussion of the turbulent relation between the movement and the defenders of the Transición, see Kostis Kornetis, "'Is There a Future in This Past?' Analyzing 15M's Intricate Relation to the Transición," *Journal of Spanish Cultural Studies* 15, nos. 1–2 (2014): 83–98.

8. Pereira-Zazo and Torres, "Introduction," 5.

9. For a detailed discussion on the 15-M and the myth its spontaneous irruption and novelty, see Cristina Flesher Fominaya, "Debunking Spontaneity: Spain's 15-M/Indignados as Autonomous Movement," *Social Movement Studies* 14, no. 2 (2015): 146, 158–59. Rubén Díez García and Enrique Laraña, in their exhaustive investigation on the 15-M, point out that there was an explicit connection between the "alterglobalization movement" and the Spanish *indignados*, which coalesced in the particular type of protest that took place during the spring of 2011 across Spain. Moreover, apart from referring to Flesher Fominaya's work, they provide a comprehensive list of social movement scholars who have also demonstrated similar links, such as Eduardo Romanos, Ignacia Perugorría and Benjamín Tejerina, and Marianne Maeckelbergh. Rubén Díez García and Enrique Laraña, *Democracia, dignidad y movimientos sociales: El surgimiento de la cultura cívica y la irrupción de los "indignados" en la vida pública* (Madrid: CIS, 2017), 321.

10. Cristina Flesher Fominaya, *Democracy Reloaded: Inside Spain's Political Laboratory from 15-M to Podemos* (New York: Oxford University Press, 2020), 12.

11. Alfonso Pérez-Agote, "The 15M Movement and the Crisis of Conventional Politics," in *Crisis and Social Mobilization in Contemporary Spain: The 15M Movement*, ed. Benjamín Tejerina and Ignacia Perugorría (New York: Routledge, 2018), 151.

12. All translations are mine unless otherwise noted. Antonio Gómez López-Quiñones, "Introducción. En el laberinto del populismo: Algunas claves históricas y teóricas," *Arizona Journal of Hispanic Cultural Studies* 21 (2017): 106.

13. Flesher Fominaya, *Democracy Reloaded*, 12.

14. Marta Montagut and Nereida Carrillo, "Estrategias de espectacularización en las tertulias políticas televisivas. Caso de la cobertura de las elecciones municipales de Barcelona de 2015," *El Profesional de la Información* 26, no. 4 (2017): 622.

15. Ignacio Orivio and Gemma Saura, "A los 10 años, el 15-M deja un país distinto: También al que soñó," *La Vanguardia*, May 16, 20021, https://www.lavanguardia.com/politica/20210516/7457171/10-anos-15-m-pais-distinto-sono.html.

16. Javier Moreno Barber, "15-M: Esperanzas frustradas," editorial, *El País*, May 16, 2021, https://elpais.com/opinion/2021-05-15/15-m-esperanzas-frustradas.html.

17. The most interesting examples are found on the leftist spectrum of mainstream media. *La Sexta* remembered the movement in an audiovisual piece that almost exclusively focused on its effects on party politics, concluding, "Ten years later, the 15-M's power can be found in its cultural value, a landmark for a generation, rather than being something that has materially produced an effective political transformation." Marta Espartero, "El 15M, diez años después: Qué queda de aquel movimiento que vino a cambiar la política," *La Sexta*, May 15, 2021, https://www.lasexta.com/noticias/nacional/15m-diez-anos-despues-que-queda-aquel-movimiento-que-vino-cambiar-politica_20210514609eb4b95f3ee80001a4ce5c.html. Another representative example is a column in *El País* titled "El archivo que almacena los sueños del 15-M" (The archive that keeps the 15-M's dreams), the overall message of which emphasizes the movement's dreams in contrast to the stark material political (grim) reality of Spain in 2021. Elisa Tasca and Diego Estebánez García, "El archivo que almacena los sueños del 15-M," *El País*, May 15, 2021, https://elpais.com/espana/2021-05-15/el-archivo-que-almacena-los-suenos-del-15-m.html.

18. Even though such a narrative has been questioned by social scientists like Flesher Fominaya—whose book *Democracy Reloaded* rethinks what political change looks like by tracing a continuous genealogy from the 15-M movement to Podemos that goes back to the days of *asamblearismo* and the global justice movement in the 1990s, a great deal of political analyses as well as their cultural representations still run on a version of the 15-M's spontaneity and novelty but ultimately lack of effectiveness.

19. The famous radiobroadcaster Carlos Alsina and his opinion on the movement on the eve of its tenth anniversary is a paradigmatic recounting of the most conservative views on the 15-M. While Alsina's opinion ends up being shrouded by ad hominem, circular arguments typical of rightist commentary of social movements in Spain, his story nonetheless distills the same essence around the 15-M's political inconsequence than the more progressive accounts in *El País* or *La Sexta*; in this case, according to Alsina, the movement's failed politics are due to its infantile diagnosis of Spanish reality that impeded activists to be pragmatic enough to effect political change. Onda Cero, "Alsina analiza el décimo aniversario del 15-M," YouTube video, posted May 14, 2021, 3:40, https://www.youtube.com/watch?v=UmfHs7iaa-0&ab_channel=OndaCero. Similarly but from the opposite ideological spectrum, in a column for the "Babelia" section, Joaquín Estefanía, one of the most established progressive voices of *El País*, reviewed a series of books on the 15-M

commemorating its tenth anniversary. He included his own commentary, which also followed the common accounts on the movement's ultimate lack of real political impact. Joaquín Estefanía, "¡Hasta siempre 15-M1," *El País,* May 15, 2021, https://elpais.com/babelia/2021-05-15/hasta-siempre-15-m.html.

20. Informe Semanal, "La década del 15-M," *Radio Televisión Española,* video, https://www.rtve.es/play/videos/informe-semanal/decada-del-15/5904672/.

21. For a detailed analysis of the different political tropes used against the irruption of Podemos and the negative uses of populism in such a context, see Bécquer Seguín, "Podemos and Its Critics," *Radical Philosophy* 193 (2015): 9–19.

22. Flesher Fominaya's genealogy of autonomous social movements comes first to mind, but also key are Ramón Feenstra's work on the new social movements' relationship to liberal democracy and Miguel Martínez's insights into the relationship between the squatter movement and state governments, just to mention a few of the many scholars who have contributed to a deeper understanding of the politics and political culture of social movements.

23. The 15-M was mainly resisting a historical perception forged during the transition to democracy from Francoism, strongly linked to the newly established parliamentary monarchy system and the bipartisan political leaderships since the 1990s. It was the manufacturing of a popular consensus around the idea that Spain had to necessarily forget its discordant past under Franco's dictatorship to guarantee a stable future as a (neoliberal) middle-class nation in Europe. To such end, as Luis Moreno-Caballud has established, that consensus enabled the acceptance of iniquity in the same way that Franco's dictatorship had to be accepted: unequivocally. It was the continuity of a way of life rooted in inequality that went hand in hand with a process of civic depoliticization, which was fundamentally thrown into question only with the irruption of the 15-M's newly acquired political identity. Luis Moreno-Caballud, *Cultures of Anyone: Studies on Cultural Democratization in the Spanish Neoliberal Crisis* (Liverpool, UK: Liverpool University Press, 2015), 33.

24. For a further conceptualization of the distinction between in and through culture in the context of new social movements, see Nico Carpentier's analysis of active and passive audience participation and communication rights in his book *Media and Participation: A Site of Ideological-Democratic Struggle* (Bristol, UK: Intellect, 2011), 64–68.

25. Emphasis in original. Luis Alegre Zahonero, "'Populism' as the Task of Constructing a People for Change," in *Spain after the Indignados/15M Movement: The 99% Speaks Out,* ed. Óscar Pereira-Zazo and Steven L. Torres (New York: Palgrave Macmillan, 2019), 68.

26. Bécquer Seguín, "Introduction: A Decade of Indignation," *boundary 2* 48, no. 3 (2021): 2, 4.

27. Pereira-Zazo and Torres, "Introduction," 2.

28. Wim Weymans, "From Marianne to Louis: Three Ways of Representing the (European) People in Democratic Societies," in *Popularisation and Populism in the Visual Arts*, ed. Anna Schoeber (New York: Routledge, 2019), 32.

29. Weymans, 32–33.

30. Weymans, 41.

31. Weymans, 42.

32. Brian L. Ott and Robert L. Mack, *Critical Media Studies: An Introduction* (Chichester, UK: Wiley, 2014), 115.

33. Ott and Mack, 115.

34. Winfried Nöth, "Visual Semiotics: Key Features and an Application to Picture Ads," in *The SAGE Handbook of Visual Research Methods*, ed. Luc Pauwels and Dawn Mannay (London: SAGE Publications, 2011), 303–4.

35. Ernesto Laclau, *On Populist Reason* (London: Verso, 2005), 69–70.

36. More than a decade later, the term is still very much in dispute, and in 2005, Francisco Panizza issued the following warning in his introduction to a collection of articles on populism: "It has become almost a cliché to start writing on populism by lamenting the lack of clarity about the concept and casting doubts about its usefulness for political analysis." Francisco Panizza, "Introduction: Populism and the Mirror of Democracy," in *Populism and the Mirror of Democracy*, ed. Francisco Panizza (London: Verso, 2005), 1.

37. Gómez López-Quiñones, "Introducción," 106.

38. Expanding Ernesto Laclau's theorizations, Chantal Mouffe has a working definition of populism that condenses the core political principles of the definition used here. Mouffe defines populism as "a discursive strategy of constructing a political frontier dividing society into two camps and calling for the mobilization of the 'underdog' against 'those in power.' It is not an ideology and cannot be attributed a specific programmatic content. Nor is it a political regime. It is *a way of doing politics* that can take various ideological forms according to both time and place and is compatible with a variety of institutional frameworks." Although Mouffe's definition of populism frames the people theoretically as the result of a political encounter (between the underdogs and the elites), I understand the people as the cultural practice of such theoretical rendezvous. Chantal Mouffe, *For a Left Populism* (London: Verso, 2018), ch. 1.

39. Cristóbal Rovira Kaltwasser and Cas Mudde, "Populism," in *The Oxford Handbook of Political Ideologies*, ed. Michael Freeden and Marc Stears (Oxford: Oxford University Press, 2013); Marcus Morgan, "A Cultural Sociology of Populism," *International Journal of Politics, Culture, and Society* 35, no. 2 (2022): 180.

40. My emphasis. Angela Marino, *Populism and Performance in the Bolivarian Revolution of Venezuela* (Evanston, IL: Northwestern University Press, 2018), 166–67.

41. Marino, 10.

42. In *On Populist Reason*, Laclau made a conscious effort to clarify that populism was not simply a political typology or a type of political movement but a political logic that undergirds the very structure of all politics. To such end, he further explains: "What do we understand, however, by a 'political logic'? . . . While social logics consist in rule-following, political logics are related to the institution of the social. Such an institution, however, as we already know, is not an arbitrary fiat but proceeds out of social demands and is, in that sense, inherent to any process of social change. . . . This in turn involves, as we have seen, the construction of internal frontiers and the identification of an institutionalized 'other.' Whenever we have this combination of structural moments, whatever the ideological or social contents of the political movement in question, we have populism of one sort or another." Laclau, *On Populist Reason*, 117–18.

43. Pierre Ostiguy and Benjamin Moffitt, "Who Would Identify with an 'Empty Signifier'? The Relational, Performative Approach to Populism," in *Populism in Global Perspective*, ed. Pierre Ostiguy, Francisco Panizza, and Benjamin Moffitt (New York: Routledge, 2020), 48.

44. Marino, *Populism and Performance*, 167.

45. Benjamin Moffitt, *The Global Rise of Populism: Performance, Political Style, and Representation* (Stanford, CA: Stanford University Press, 2016), 4–5.

46. Moffitt, 45.

47. Laclau, *On Populist Reason*, 217.

48. "Presentación del libro de Daniel Bernabé: *La distancia del presente*," YouTube video, posted December 9, 2020, 25:45, https://www.youtube.com/watch?v=9qFHretEabg.

49. Most significantly, Bernabé gives the 15-M almost a liquid shape in opposition to the much greater solid shape given to governmental (counter)forces. The 15-M is understood more in terms of its political immateriality and, hence, its intrinsic inability to actualize change. It is an event that culminated in an era marked by a certain neoliberal naïveté, which would eventually fragment into many small political pieces that shaped the conflation of identitarianism and postmodernism, which the author treats as synonyms. More concretely, he argues that "the 15-M was a spontaneous moment of protest. It was not a social movement. Its root causes had not to do with a planned political strategy, because it was probably its spontaneous nature that allowed

it to happen in the first place. . . . In this sense, the 15-M was the beginning of many different things but, above all, was the [symbolic] climatic end of a decade: the happy-go-lucky first years of the twenty first century." Daniel Bernabé, *La distancia del presente: Auge y crisis de la democracia española (2010–2020)* (Madrid: Akal, 2020), 142, 46.

50. Podemos's populism falls under what Chantal Mouffe describes as a "left populist strategy . . . to launch a political offensive in order to establish a new hegemonic formation . . . for the recovery and deepening of [liberal] democracy" and is not so much a truly transversal "populist regime" whose ideological contours are much harder to make out. In fact, in the context of Spanish politics, the mere conceptualization of that regime comes with the added obstacle of being highly dependent on a national populist impetus, which makes it a problematic political strategy from the outset given the troubled history of nationalism in Spain. Chantal Mouffe, *For a Left Populism* (London: Verso, 2019), conclusion.

51. Enzo Traverso, *The New Faces of Fascism: Populism and the Far Right*, trans. David Broder (London: Verso, 2019), 6–7.

CHAPTER 1

1. Ramón A. Feenstra et al., *Refiguring Democracy: The Spanish Political Laboratory* (Abingdon, UK: Routledge, 2017), 6.
2. "Barómetro de junio," *CIS*, no. 2905 (June 2011), http://www.cis.es/cis/export/sites/default/-Archivos/Marginales/2900_2919/2905/Es2905.pdf.
3. Cristina Flesher Fominaya, "Debunking Spontaneity: Spain's 15-M/Indignados as Autonomous Movement," *Social Movement Studies* 14, no. 2 (2015): 158–59.
4. Flesher Fominaya, 159.
5. Quoted in Flesher Fominaya, 148.
6. Paulo Gerbaudo, "Feeds from the Square: Live Streaming, Live Tweeting and the Self-representation of Protest Camps," in *Protest Camps in International context: Spaces, Infrastructures and Media of Resistance*, ed. Gavin Brown, Anna Feigenbaum, Fabian Frenzel, and Patrick McCurdy (Bristol, UK: Policy Press, 2017), 92.
7. Gerbaudo, 101.
8. Spanishrevolutionsol, "#Badcop: ¿Es esto lo que se aprende en la Academia de #Policía? #15M," YouTube video, posted June 16, 2011, https://www.youtube.com/watch?v=AsxxYt10Dzo&ab_channel=spanishrevolutionsol.
9. For a more comprehensive documentation on police abuse of protestors in Spain, see Amnesty International's 2014 report that documents new and old

patterns of abusive policing during political demonstrations. "Spain: The Right to Protest under Threat," *Amnesty International*, April 24, 2014, https://www.amnesty.org/en/documents/EUR41/001/2014/en/.

10. These types of police behaviors were so commonplace that were also part of popular culture. As such, one of the most famous songs by the rap group Los Chikos del Maíz stated that "políticas policíacas estado de excepción ocultan sin vergüenza el número de placa" (police-state policies under a state of exception their police identification they hide shamelessly). The song "El miedo va a cambiar de bando" (Fear will soon change sides) was included in what the band called the "political project" of Riot Propaganda. The "project" was done in direct reaction to and support of the climate of protest during and after the 15-M. This song was so popular it was later picked by Podemos and Pablo Iglesias (a close friend of the band) as one of the unofficial anthems of the party. Riot Propaganda, "El miedo va a cambiar de bando," January 6, 2013, https://riotpropaganda.bandcamp.com/track/el-miedo-va-a-cambiar-de-bando.

11. The full manifesto in English can be read in "How to Cook a Non-Violent Revolution," *Take the Square* (blog), July 15, 2011, https://takethesquare.net/2011/07/15/how-to-cook-a-pacific-revolution/. Regarding media interventions, a simple way to see the centrality of that commitment is found by searching the number of news articles dedicated to the issue of nonviolence between June 15 and 16, 2011. A simple refined search finds a plethora of documented testimonies by 15-M participants that either staunchly advocated for nonviolent protests or condemned any actions that could be construed as violent.

12. Original: *Hay una frase bastante interesante que se dijo durante este verano cuando hubo todos esos episodios de violencia policial y de gente, se decía que no es que los policías pegaran más ahora, sino que los móviles son mejores. El hecho de grabar en vivo todos estos episodios que fueron sucediendo fue clave para despertar a gente a un pensamiento crítico de la realidad política que vivimos.* José Manuel Robles et al., "El movimiento 15-m en los medios y en las redes: Un análisis de sus estrategias comunicativas," *Empiria*, no. 32 (September–December 2015): 54.

13. For Laclau, the political process of signification in populism occurs through what he called empty signifiers, which privilege "the people" as the nodal point in the construction of new political collective identities. The key to understanding how the empty signifier functions in populism does not have to do with the idea that its meaning or signification is literally void. What makes the signifier empty is the fluid relation between its constitutive parts,

the *particular* political demands from which its meaning derives (e.g., wealth redistribution, the end of fiscal austerity, abolishment of the two-party system) and its object of reference, the universal populist logic that its meaning points to (e.g., the sovereign people or its representative in the shape of a populist leader). Further, the conception of the people in populism is not reduced to a mere process of symbolic association, between people's multiple demands and a populist signifier (a leader or an overarching idea such as the 15-M's "real democracy now"). But the relevance of the populist bid can be found in that everyone and each of those demands can retain their particularity and their singular potency while simultaneously being reduced to a process of identification that homogenizes or "empties" them within a populist signifier in opposition to a larger system of (perceived) oppression. That is what Laclau termed the *equivalential logics* of populism. Laclau, *On Populist Reason*, 69–70.

14. Óscar García Agustín, "The Aesthetics of Social Movements in Spain," in *Street Art of Resistance*, ed. Sarah H. Awad and Brady Wagoner (Cham, Switzerland: Springer International Publishing, 2017), 326–27.

15. Julia Ramírez Blanco, *Artistic Utopias of Revolt: Claremont Road, Reclaim the Streets, and the City of Sol* (Cham, Switzerland: Springer International Publishing, 2018), 154.

16. Ramírez Blanco, 134.

17. Ramírez Blanco, 135-137.

18. Initial image of the Hyundai billboard taken on May 19, 2011, by myr rius, Flickr, https://www.flickr.com/photos/lamyr/5758211522/in/pool-spanish-revolution/. Billboard's modified image taken on May 21, 2011, by якrd, Flickr, https://www.flickr.com/photos/ricardopizana/5745534965/in/pool-spanish-revolution/.

19. Ramírez Blanco, *Artistic Utopias*, 134.

20. "Encara penses que els polítics no ens timen?" *La pulga y la locomotora: Anónimos y cabreados* (blog), May 22, 2011, https://lapulgaylalocomotora.wordpress.com/2011/05/22/encara-penses-que-els-politics-no-ens-timen/.

21. Original: *La plaza fue reclamada por el* pueblo. *El ruido también ha sido reclamado por el* pueblo. *Ruido físico, el de la cacerolada de arriba. Y ruido ideológico, en cualquiera de los actos y espacios, en cualquiera de los rincones de Plaza Catalunya.* [. . .] *Es, simplemente, ensordecedor. Y nadie quiere para.* [. . .] *El otro ruido, el ideológico, suena confuso, pero por fin se oye. Es un maremoto de imaginación descontrolado: Dichos, viñetas, eslóganes, reclamaciones, propuestas . . . todo lo que sacan de sus entrañas aquellos a los que no se ha hacía caso.* [. . .] *Se titularía algo así como "Aparten los granujas, ahora nos toca a nosotros." Letra*

y música: El Pueblo. "¡Ruido para todos!" *La pulga y la locomotora: Anónimos y cabreados* (blog), May 21, 2011, https://lapulgaylalocomotora.wordpress. com/2011/05/21/%c2%a1ruido-para-todos/.

22. Ignacia Perugorría and Benjamín Tejerina, "Politics of the Encounter: Cognition, Emotions, and Networks in the Spanish 15-M," *Current Sociology* 61, no. 4 (2013): 432–33.

23. "Qué es la jornada de reflexión," *Newtral*, May 3, 2021, https://www.newtral. es/que-es-jornada-de-reflexion/20210503/.

24. "La Junta Electoral prohíbe todas las protestas del sábado y el domingo," *El Mundo*, May 20, 2011, https://www.elmundo.es/elmundo/2011/05/19/ espana/1305840030.html.

25. For the edited version, see Spanishrevolutionsol, "Acampada Sol: Minuto de Silencio." YouTube video, May 22, 2011, https://www.youtube.com/watch?v= Zx5giakLhP8.

26. Ramírez Blanco, *Artistic Utopias*, 141.

27. Ramírez Blanco, 141–42.

28. Perugorría and Tejerina, "Politics of the Encounter," 433.

29. Perugorría and Tejerina, 433, 435.

30. Flesher Fominaya, *Democracy Reloaded*, 287–88.

31. Flesher Fominaya, 289.

32. Carmina Godoy et al., "La representación visual de los indignados: Aproximación a un análisis visual sobre la caracterización de los participantes del movimiento 15-M," *Nómadas* 47, no. 1 (2016), www.redalyc.org/ pdf/181/18153280001.pdf.

33. Francisco Fernández Segado, "El estado de excepción en el derecho constitucional español," *Revista de Derecho Privado: Documentación Administrativa*, Madrid (January 1978): 476.

34. Amador Fernández-Savater, "El nacimiento de un nuevo poder social," *Hispanic Review* 80, no. 4 (October 2012): 678.

35. Pablo Sánchez León, "Pueblo, oligarquía, clase media y plebe: Combinaciones para pensar históricamente el populismo en la España contemporánea," *Arizona Journal of Hispanic Cultural Studies* 21 (2017): 142.

36. Sánchez León, 142.

37. The visible push against alcohol consumption in the camps contrasts with the more relaxed attitude Spaniards (especially younger generations) have around drinking alcohol in public spaces. While multiple *anti-botellón* laws have been passed since 2002 with the objective of curtailing the very common activity of massive outdoor gatherings for the only purpose of drinking alcohol, drinking in public spaces was and is still today an activity not infrequent

and barely socially sanctioned. That's why it was striking at the time to see a massive gathering of mostly young people condemning and prohibiting the very activity those youth would normally do when they got together in public squares. For an updated account of the legal developments around *botellón* in Spain (i.e., gathering in public spaces for the sole purpose of socializing while drinking), see Jesus Espinosa, "El botellón en la calle, una actividad prohibida en gran parte de España con multas que se han endurecido por la pandemia," *Newtral*, May 9, 2021, https://www.newtral.es/botellon-prohibido-espana-multas-pandemia/20210509/.

38. Moreno-Caballud speaks of the 15-M's "cultures of anyone" as the rejection experts, the ones who used to manufacture cultural and political realities generally subservient to the status quo, in favor of the *cualquiera*—the anyone in his ideation of "cultures of anyone." As such, the 15-M put the anonymous citizens at the center of cultural production in the politics of the popular. Luis Moreno-Caballud. *Cultures of Anyone: Studies on Cultural Democratization in the Spanish Neoliberal Crisis* (Liverpool, UK: University of Liverpool Press, 2015), 2.

39. Fernández-Savater, "El nacimiento," 679.

40. Precise examples of these expressions are so many that compiling a detailed reference list here seems like a tautological exercise. Watching any of the many film documentaries on the 15-M will give the reader direct testimonies of how all these terms were used. The next chapter features a list of the most important audiovisual documents on movement that can also serve as reference.

41. Original: *Somos personas normales y corrientes. Somos como tú: gente que se levanta por las mañanas para estudiar, para trabajar o para buscar trabajo, gente que tiene familia y amigos. [. . .] Unos nos consideramos más progresistas, otros más conservadores. Unos creyentes, otros no. Unos tenemos ideologías bien definidas, otros nos consideramos apolíticos . . . Pero todos estamos preocupados e indignados por el panorama político, económico y social que vemos a nuestro alrededor.* "Manifiesto Democracia real ya," *Revista Paz y Conflictos* 6 (2013): https://revistaseug.ugr.es/index.php/revpaz/article/view/786.

42. "13N cambio de modelo ya. Movilización estatal. Manifiesto completo," posted by Grupotransversal, October 16, 2011, https://madrid.tomalaplaza.net/2011/10/16/13n-manifiesto-completo/.

43. Sánchez León, "Pueblo, oligarquía, clase media y plebe," 142.

44. Josep Maria Antentas, "Spain: The Indignados Rebellion of 2011 in Perspective," *Labor History* 56, no. 2 (2015): 147.

45. Jordi Évole's famous docuseries *Salvados* had an episode entirely devoted to the ideation of the middle class. The episode "Viva la clase media" (long live

the middle class) that aired in November 2015—well after the 15-M—opened with a group of university students in class discussing the significance of the middle class in Spain. Most strikingly, as the professor asks who in the room identifies with the label "middle class," all the students raise their hands. Not coincidentally, the students chosen for this episode are part of the political science program at the Universidad Complutense in Madrid, the program from which many organizers of the 15-M and later the founders of Podemos were politically socialized. In this sense, the statement of Évole's episode seems clear: "we are all middle class" even if we don't (want to) know it.

46. José Saturnino Martínez García, *Estructura social y desigualdad en España* (Madrid: Catarata, 2013), introduction.

47. Jim McGuigan, *Neoliberal Culture* (New York: Palgrave Macmillan, 2016), 22.

48. Jim McGuigan, *Cool Capitalism* (New York: Pluto Press, 2009), 6.

49. Alfonso Amador, *50 días de mayo (Ensayo para una revolución)* (Valencia, Spain: Lovers Film, 2012).

50. "Universidad del Barrio. Historia: La crisis del sistema a través del 15-M," YouTube video, posted April 23, 2015, 4:50, https://www.youtube.com/watch?v=oGfAceuOHGM.

51. "Universidad del Barrio," 11:05.

52. "Universidad del Barrio," 34:30.

53. Amador, *50 días de mayo*, 33:00.

54. Amador, *50 días de mayo*, 34:00.

55. Original: *Yo quiero decir solo una cosa más. Se ha dicho varias veces que no somos unos anarquistas . . . Esto me duele personalmente porque aquí sí que hay unos anarquistas y unos comunistas y una gente que fuma porros y unos perroflautas y una gente jipi. ¿De verdad queréis que nos levantemos y nos vayamos todos los anarquistas, los comunistas, los sindicalistas, los perroflautas, los jipis y la gente que fumamos porros? ¿De verdad?* Amador, *50 días de mayo*, 34:30.

56. Amador Fernández-Savater, "Emborronar la CT (del 'No a la guerra' al 15-M)," in *CT o la cultura de la transición: Crítica a 35 años de cultura española*, ed. Guillem Martínez (Barcelona: Debolsillo, 2016), 49.

57. Fernandez-Savater, 49.

58. Fernandez-Savater, 51.

59. Luis S. Villacañas de Castro, "Chavs, chonis, y el nuevo socialismo (si lo hubiera)," *Res Pública: Revista de Filosofía Política* 29 (2013): 93.

60. Flesher Fominaya, *Democracy Reloaded*, 216.

61. Santiago Alba Rico, "Podemos in Spain: Limits and Possibilities for Change," in *Spain after the Indignados/15-M Movement: The 99% Speaks Out*, ed. Óscar Pereira-Zazo and Steven L. Torres (New York: Palgrave Macmillan, 2019), 82–83.

62. Sánchez León, "Pueblo, oligarquía, clase media y plebe," 147.

63. Sánchez León, 148.

64. Guillem Martínez, "El concepto CT," in *CT o la cultura de la transición: Crítica a 35 años de cultura española*, ed. Guillem Martínez (Barcelona: Debolsillo, 2016), 14–17.

65. Quoted in Flesher Fominaya, *Democracy Reloaded*, 28.

66. Fernández-Savater, "Emborronar la CT," 38.

67. This is particularly relevant to the appearance of Podemos and its frequent labeling as the direct inheritor of 15-M's indignation. The party's condition of possibility was precisely due to the impoverishment of the middle class and the growing environment of hopelessness regarding the truncating of middle-class aspirations. And after the 15-M, Podemos was able to remobilize the public through (implicit, vague) promises of recuperating a middle-class way of life. For instance, as Vicente Rubio-Pueyo argues in his analysis of Podemos's first national electoral platform: "[Podemos's 2016 electoral manifesto] portrayed the candidates . . . in a format imitating the catalog of the Swedish low-cost, do-it-yourself furniture company IKEA. The first thing the casual observer might find problematic is what appears to be an equivalence between the civic action of voting and an object from the universe of consumption. At the same time, the catalog revealed what was in front of everyone's eyes: that under the neoliberal technocratic management of democratic institutions, voting had already been stripped of its civic meaning and reduced to a gesture of consumption." Vicente Rubio-Pueyo, "A Populist Experiment in Spanish Political Culture? On the Cultural Politics of Podemos," *boundary* 2 48, no. 3 (2021): 155.

68. In fact, most of the 15-M's economic proposals, such as raising the minimum wage and the *dación en pago* (deed in lieu of foreclosure), were actually quite pragmatic and specific. The 15-M's most important economic recommendations by the Grupo de Trabajo de Economía de la Acampada Sol are a paradigmatic example of the 15-M's strategic economic pragmatism. They can be read in the online document "Propuestas abiertas del grupo de economía (Acampada Sol-15-M)," last modified June 23, 2011, https://madrid.tomalaplaza.net/2011/06/23/propuestas-abiertas-economia-sol/.

CHAPTER 2

1. The influence of the Arab Spring, particularly the Egyptian Revolution, on the 15-M is already well established in scholarly studies. Most notably, in a short book published the same year the 15-M took place, Carlos Taibo speaks of the great "symbolic echo" that the Arab Revolution had on the occupation

of Spanish squares during the eclosion of movement. Carlos Taibo, Nada será como antes: *Sobre* el Movimiento 15-M (Madrid: Los Libros de la Catarata, 2011), 26–27. Also, Javier Toret was one of the first who investigated the online-offline connections between the Arab Spring and the 15-M main organizations. Javier Toret Medina, *Tecnopolítica y 15M: La potencia de las multitudes conectadas. Un estudio sobre la gestación y explosión del 15M* (Barcelona: Editorial UOC, 2015), 54–58. Similarly, Cristina Flesher Fominaya demonstrated the interconnectedness of those movements (despite their differences) and the transnational dimension of social justice mobilizations for democracy and against austerity after the global financial crisis of 2008–2011. Cristina Flesher Fominaya, Social Movements and Globalization: How Protests, Occupations and Uprisings Are Changing the World (Basingstoke, UK: Palgrave Macmillan, 2014), 6.

2. The prime minister at the time, José Luís Rodríguez Zapatero, avoided fatalist discourses by focusing on the idea that the country was in reality "a prosperous country and, also, a decent country, because it balances the distribution of wealth that it generates." Francisco Collado Campaña and José Francisco Jiménez Díaz, "Discursos políticos ante la crisis económica: Estudio del líder del PSOE," Revista Castellano-Manchega de Ciencias Sociales 14 (2012): 53.

3. These demands for real democracy stemmed from the name and the spirit of Plataforma Democracia Real Ya, which, along with Juventud sin Futuro, organized the first protest in the Puerta del Sol that would later crystallize into the 15-M.

4. These ideas were forged during the Transición, especially after the so-called Moncloa Pacts did not fulfill expectations of deeper democratic change. In this regard, the examples are many, and the topic is too broad to be summarized in a few lines. Gonzalo Wilhelmi's book *Romper el consenso* gives a detailed account of the myriad revolutionary organizations that attempted to establish an alternative constitutional framework beyond the democratic reforms later codified in the Constitution of 1978. The sixth chapter is particularly illuminating. Gonzalo Wilhelmi, *Romper el consenso: La izquierda radical en la Transición española (1975-1982)* (Madrid: Siglo XXI, 2016), 225–60.

5. This is best encapsulated by the historical pursuit of the political center, or *centralidad*, in Spanish politics, which basically argues that any political idea beyond a moderate or centrist position runs the risk of being considered radical, extremist, or simply not politically viable. The renowned journalist Esther Palomera explains the Spanish political class's obsession with being perceived as centrist in the following way: "all of the candidates for the presidency in this electoral campaign have set their aspirations to conquer the votes in that imaginary universe they call political or ideological center." She

further extends that desire to the majority in the Spanish political ecosystem: "There's an obsession among political leaders, journalists, and analysts to overemphasize the battle for the political center, as if it were the mother of all battles in every election." Esther Palomera, "La dudosa existencia del centro ideológico: El 30% de votantes por el que pugnan los partidos," *El Diario*, October 5, 2019, https://www.eldiario.es/politica/centro-existio_1_1331306.html. What is more, the search for the political center is key to understanding Spain's political status quo, because it speaks to the core of Spanish democracy's origin story. As argued by the political scientists José Vidal Pelaz López and Jorge Lafuente del Cano, "the role of the political center is one of the great protagonists of that period [the *Transición*], which is still essential to understand Spanish democracy today and the freedoms the transition brought about then," given that it allowed Spanish politics to renounce to its ingrained *guerracivilismo*; as such, the political center can be defined as "an abdication of maximalist politics from both sides of the ideological spectrum in order to create a shared project of Spain based on two key ideas: reconciliation amongst Spaniards and an understanding that democracy can only flourish under the protective shadow of Spain's constitutional monarchy." José Vidal Pelaz López and Jorge Lafuente del Cano, "Presentación: El centro político en la Transición y los problemas de España," *Memoria y Civilización* 23 (2020): 289–90.

6. Here the use of "real" (within quotation marks) and, hence, the demand for a "real" democracy do not concern democracy in Spain as simply supposed or not really occurring in fact. The term refers specifically to questions around its authenticity. That is, issues surrounding the extent to which the transition to democracy was real or really stemming from the will of the people. In this sense, authenticity has to do with the dispute over Spanish democracy's (in) authentic origins as established in the Transición.

7. Anne Davies, "The Spanish *Femme Fatale* and the Cinematic Negotiation of Spanishness," *Studies in Hispanic Cinemas* 1, no. 1 (2004): 6.

8. Davies, 7.

9. Davies, 8–9.

10. Davies, 7–8.

11. José Manuel Robles, Rubén Díez, Antón R. Castromil, Arturo Rodríguez, and Mildred Cruz, "El movimiento 15-M en los medios y en las redes: Un análisis de sus estrategias comunicativas," *Revista de Metodología de Ciencias Sociales*, no. 32 (September–December 2015): 39.

12. While *Banderas falsas* dealt with where the people could be seen, the second part, *Falsos horizontes* (2013), focused on the "word," or how the 15-M offered

an opportunity to simply *tomar la palabra* (literally, "take the word," but better translated as "take the floor" when speaking in public in an assembly). The second film is visually erratic and does not establish a coherent narrative, thus producing a series of aimless discursive iterations of different people who were part of Acampada Sol in 2011.

13. Gonzalo De Pedro Amatria, "*Banderas falsas*, de Carlos Serrano Azcona," *Otros Cines Europa*, April 8, 2015, www.otroscineseuropa.com/banderas-falsas-de-carlos-serrano-azcona/.

14. Alberto Medina, "De flujos, lugares y peceras: Mutaciones y permutaciones del cualquiera en el 15-M," *Journal of Spanish Cultural Studies* 16, no. 3 (2015): 293–94.

15. Carlos Serrano Azcona, dir., "BANDERAS FALSAS - FALSE FLAGS (Eng Sub) Dir. Carlos Serrano Azcona," YouTube video, posted February 24, 2017, 0: 34 https://www.youtube.com/watch?v=pYWt6uZZN-A&ab_channel=CarlosSerranoAzcona.

16. This conceptualization closely follows Ernesto Laclau's views of the populist moment and the inherent antagonism in populist politics, which ultimately Laclau connected the political logic of hegemony. Concretely, in *On Populist Reason*, Laclau's theory of populism does not attach the capacity to obtain political power to one group. It understands that hegemony is generated through the solidification of heterogeneous social demands within one political conflict. Hegemony is not the capacity of an institutionalized political body to exert power over other groups. On the contrary, hegemony is the capacity of vastly different petitioners to define what a political conflict is regardless of their petitions' specificity. It is in this sense that one can make use of empty signifiers such as the people or *el pueblo* to agglutinate difference into commonality but, more critically, to establish the political separation or an "internal frontier" between "us" (the people) and an institutionalized "other" or "them" (opposed to the people). Laclau, *On Populist Reason*, 74.

17. This assertion stems from the reading of postmodern political theorists such as Chantal Mouffe. Specifically, Mouffe pitted Habermas's conceptualization of the public sphere as the base of deliberative democracy (in which political conflicts need to be resolved through rational deliberation) against what she would later call populism's agonistic politics (in which conflict and affects are part and parcel of an endless political game between adversaries, rather than enemies). Chantal Mouffe, "Deliberative Democracy or Agonistic Pluralism?" *Social Research* 66 (1999): 746.

18. Medina, "De flujos, lugares y peceras," 308.

19. Rancière understands society, or what he calls "social distribution," as cut by the logic of dissensus. As such, he further argues: "The essence of politics is

dissensus. Dissensus is not a confrontation between interests or opinions. It is the demonstration (manifestation) of a gap in the sensible itself. Political demonstration makes visible that which had no reason to be seen; it places one world in another—for instance, the world where the factory is a public space in that where it is considered private, the world where workers speak, and speak about the community, in that where their voices are mere cries expressing pain." Jacques Rancière, *Dissensus: On Politics and Aesthetics*, trans. Steven Corcoran (New York: Continuum, 2010), 38.

20. Medina, "De flujos, lugares y peceras," 309.

21. Stephen Luis Vilaseca, "The 15-M Movement: Formed by and Formative of Counter-Mapping and Spatial Activism." *Journal of Spanish Cultural Studies*, 15:1–2 (2014): 120.

22. In a similar way to the film's didactic rethinking of public space, Sebastiaan Faber has explored the audiovisual constitution of a popular common sense that is no longer guided by experts when referring to Jordi Évole and the docuseries *Salvados* as follows: "[Évole's approach] is framed within an adapted notion of 'popular wisdom.' This attitude is more important that what it may seem at first, because it helps to *constitute* the role for the citizenry. The questions asked by Évole—it is suggested—are simply those that any ordinary citizen could ask." Sebastiaan Faber, "*Salvados* como periodismo populista: en busca de un sujeto nacional-popular," *Arizona Journal of Hispanic Cultural Studies* 21 (2017): 247.

23. Manuel Castells, *Networks of Outrage and Hope: Social Movements in the Internet Age* (Cambridge, UK: Polity Press, 2015), 134.

24. Luis Moreno-Caballud, *Cultures of Anyone: Studies on Cultural Democratization in the Spanish Neoliberal Crisis* (Liverpool, UK: Liverpool UP, 2015), 2.

25. Notably, *La plaza* represents collaboration against the grain of most recorded experiences in the encampments, and, more prominently, Alfonso Amador's *50 días de mayo (Ensayo para una revolución)* (2012), which filmed the tumultuous inner workings of the *asamblea* in the encampment of Valencia from its first day to its last (analyzed in Chapter 1).

26. Original: *Llevo aquí desde el segundo día. Primero hice veintisiete horas que creía que era mi record de trabajo ininterrumpido, pero lo logré batir con uno de cuarenta y nueve horas de trabajo ininterrumpido; para que luego vengan a decirnos que somos unos perroflautas.* Adriano Morán Conesa, dir., "La Plaza: La gestación del movimiento 15-M," YouTube video, posted June 16, 2011, 16:05, https://www.youtube.com/watch?v=jyGE4HCTI6c&ab_channel=zahoryclub.

27. Original emphasis. Álvaro Sevilla-Buitrago, "Outraged Spatialities: The Production of Public Space in the #spanishrevolution," *ACME* 14, no. 1 (2015): 93.

28. Bryan Cameron, "Crowd Control: Populism, Public Assembly, Institutional Crises, and Pere Portabella's *Informe General II: El nuevo rapto de Europa*," *Arizona Journal of Hispanic Cultural Studies* 21 (2017): 160.

29. Isabel Estrada, "Re-politicizing Documentary Footage from the *Transición* in Spain: Images, Representation and the Digital Age," *Bulletin of Spanish Visual Studies* 2, no. 2 (2018): 268.

30. The myth has been adopted by several European institutions. Most prominently, it can be seen in a mosaic in the European Parliament's Paul-Henri Spaak building in Brussels.

31. Portabella's approach to documentaries in relation to how the genre allows subjectivity to vampirize reality is at the heart of the filmmaker's trope of the vampire. The most explicit reference in Portabella's cinema can be found in his 1971 film *Cauadec, vampir*, an "eerie evocation of a fascist state that had already outlived its natural lifespan, with Christopher Lee's Count Dracula as a vampiric image of Franco." Jerry White, "The Changing of the Age: Pere Portabella on *Informe General II*," *Cinema Scope*, no. 67 (Summer 2016): 15.

32. Cameron, "Crowd Control," 161.

33. Núria Araüna and Laia Quílez Esteve have pointed out in their analysis of *Informe General II* that Portabella approach documentary filmmaking as a way of questioning the film's own mechanics of representation, "as such, his work acquires a relative reflexive dimension and activates the questioning of his own representational regime." Núria Araüna and Laia Quílez Esteve, "Crisis económica, transformación política y expresión documental: Crónica del anhelo (más que del cambio)," *Journal of Spanish Cultural Studies* 19, no. 4 (2018): 437.

34. Jaume Duran Castells and Josep Torelló Oliver, "*Informe General* (1976) de Pere Portabella: Un estado de la cuestión cinematográfica sobre la Transición española," *Archivos de la Filmoteca*, no. 73 (October 2017): 217.

35. Moreover, Grueso's film was ideally positioned to act as a new representative, as it was part of the platform 15-M.cc, a "trans-media, collaborative, copyleft, and not-for-profit project" to foster collaborative actions under the umbrella of "freeing culture in the era of the digital and its corresponding ethos of 'Do It Yourself,' which blurs the boundaries between producers and consumers in order to bring about a hybrid conceptualizations such as 'prosumer' and 'conducer.'" Alejandro Alvarado Jódar and Concha Barquero Artés, "Un despertar revulsivo: Prácticas colaborativas en el documental sobre el 15-M," *Fonseca, Journal of Communication* 6 (2013): 307.

36. Stéphane M. Grueso, dir., "15M 'Excelente. Revulsivo. Importante' v.1.6," Proyecto15Mcc, YouTube video, posted February 1, 2013, 68:30, https://www.youtube.com/watch?v=cBouuM-64Ik&ab_channel=proyecto15Mcc.

37. Grueso, 68:48.
38. Grueso, 69:00.
39. Grueso, 70:00.

CHAPTER 3

1. After the square occupations ended, the neighborhoods' *asambleas* (splintered working groups from the 15-M encampments established in city districts and townships), along with spinoffs from the 15-M founding platforms, had held prominent public protest actions such as *rodea el congreso* on September 25, 2012, and the *marea ciudadana* on February 23, 2013.
2. Moffitt, *Global Rise of Populism*, 45.
3. Laura Grattan, "Populism, Race, and Radical Imagination," in *Populism in Global Perspective*, ed. Pierre Ostiguy, Francisco Panizza, Benjamin Moffitt (New York: Routledge, 2020), 138.
4. Grattan, 138.
5. Europa Press, "Báñez: 'España ha vivido por encima de sus posibilidades,'" YouTube video, posted May 22, 2012, https://www.youtube.com/watch?v=EZvDXRcukrw.
6. In literature, writers come to mind such as Belén Gopegui and her novel *El comité de la noche* (set in a Spain in crisis, with an unemployed protagonist that joined an underground group to fight the "system") and Isaac Rosa and his *La habitación oscura* (a metaphorical account of political change that narrates how a group of hedonic young people decided that was time to change their reality). In theater, the initiative of El Teatro del Barrio and its very successful plays, such as *Masacre: Una historia del capitalismo español* and *Autorretrato de un joven capitalista español*, made quite the splash outside alternative circles. In cinema, the fourth film of Santiago Segura's blockbuster saga Torrente, *Torrente 4: Lethal Crisis* (2011), dealt head-on with Spain's economic crisis. In television, the most notable example was how one of the most watched sitcoms in Spanish television history, *Aída*, portrayed in its last two seasons (2011–2013) the economic crisis as an ever-present feature in the characters' lives (e.g., several of them became chronically unemployed or their business had to shut down for lack of clients).
7. Núria Triana-Toribio, "Spanish Cinema of the 2010s: Back to Punk and Other Lessons from the Crisis," *Hispanic Research Journal* 20, no. 1 (2019): 16.
8. Triana-Toribio, 11.
9. Triana-Toribio, 12.
10. Dean Albritton, "Prime Risks: The Politics of Pain and Suffering in Spanish Crisis Cinema," *Journal of Spanish Cultural Studies* 15, nos. 1–2 (2014): 102.

11. Sarah Thomas, "Primed for Suffering: Gender, Subjectivity, and Spectatorship in Spanish Crisis Cinema," *boundary 2* 48, no. 3 (2021): 216.

12. Ivan Villarmea Álvarez has also defined these types of films as austerity cinema (*cine de la austeridad*), grouping them temporally from 2008 to 2016. Significantly for this chapter's argument, he concludes that in all those films, "violence is the only impulse able to unlock the characters' paralysis." Iván Villarmea Álvarez, "Rostros y espacios de la austeridad en los cines ibéricos (2007–2016)," *Iberoamericana* 18, no. 69 (2018): 32. Marta Álvarez has a similar argument when recounting how different films portrayed the crisis; she concludes that many of their characters became outlaws, against the system, in a bid to change their extremely precarious lives in crisis. Marta Álvarez, "De la reivindicación a la ira: Espacios de crisis en el cine español contemporáneo," *Iberoamericana* 18, no. 69 (2018): 83–85.

13. Benjamin Moffitt and Simon Tormey, "Rethinking Populism: Politics, Mediatisation and Political Style," *Political Studies* 62 (2014): 392.

14. Moffitt and Tormey, 392.

15. Moffitt and Tormey, 392.

16. Argyro Kantara, "Populism as Mainstream Politicians' Political Style during the 2012 Greek Election Campaign," in *Discursive Approaches to Populism across Disciplines*, ed. Michael Kranert (Cham, Switzerland: Springer International, 2020), 409.

17. A detailed analysis of how political violence was represented before the 15-M is beyond the scope of this book. However, two paradigmatic examples come to mind of how the portrayal of violent behaviors were significantly limited in political situations. First is Fernando León de Aranoa's *Los lunes al sol* (2002), in which a group of chronically unemployed industrial workers deal with the ups and downs of their dire situations in an economically depressed, postindustrial Spanish society. Significantly, one of the plotlines deals with the main protagonist, Santa (Javier Bardem), a former union leader, and his having to appear in court for civil disobedience in one of the demonstrations he organized. In the end, he was symbolically sentenced for damages to repay the cost of a public lamppost in the shipyard. Despite the great amount of systemic violence all the characters suffered (e.g., one of the main characters commits suicide because of his untenable economic situation), the film refuses to depict any of them as violent or even as harboring violent intentions toward the system. Thus, Santa's plotline ended with an act of political revenge that consists in Santa vandalizing the new lamppost he was mandated by the judge to replace. And such a hardly violent action was the most the film was ready to show in terms of symbolic political violence

and/or people's rebellion. The second one that comes to mind is *Noviembre* (2003), by Achero Mañas. The film tells the story of a group of idealistic actors who want to change the world with their art. After realizing that their artistic efforts do not yield much change, they set out to up the ante by staging a more powerful political performance piece titled "Atentado" (Terrorist attack). While their performance did not put anyone in danger and was meant only to shock the audience (one of the troupe members pretended to assassinate another one with a shot to the head, simulating a typical attack by the Basque separatist group ETA during those days), it nonetheless supposed the demise of the theater company. By the end of the film, the protagonist (egged on by one the most radical members of the group) decides to perform one last time. In the middle of an opera function, in front of the symbolic representations of Spain's elites, the main character dressed as a clown bursts onto the stage. He begins a political monologue and, as he is finishing, points a toy gun at the audience. As the toy gun shoots a flower, police gun him down. Again, the use of violence coming from the system symbolically overwhelms and overpowers that emanating from the characters' rebellious tendencies. In both cases, in two very popular films of the time, the message was loud and clear: political violence would be represented on mainstream screens only as long as it did not come from symbolic representatives of the people.

18. My emphasis. Matthew I. Feinberg, "The Violence of Everyday Life: Lope de Vega's *Fuente Ovejuna* as Urban Allegory," *Revista de Estudios Hispánicos* 53 (2019): 730.

19. Feinberg, "The Violence," 746.

20. Dean Albritton, "Prime Risks: The politics of Pain and Suffering in Spanish Crisis Cinema," *Journal of Spanish Cultural Studies* 15, nos. 1–2 (2014): 102–3.

21. These front pages are accessible online. See "Hemeroteca," *El Jueves*, January 18, 2012, https://www.eljueves.es/revista/hemeroteca/2012; "Hemeroteca," *El Jueves*, March 28, 2012, https://www.eljueves.es/revista/hemeroteca/2012.

22. Bradd Epps, "Echoes and Traces," in *A Companion to Spanish Cinema*, ed. Jo Labanyi and Tatjana Pavlović (New York: Wiley-Blackwell, 2012), 69.

23. Steven Marsh, "Grotesque Comedy/Esperpento," in *Spain: Directory of World Cinema*, ed. Lorenzo J. Torre Hortelano (Bristol, UK: Intellect, 2011), 85.

24. Ramón del Valle-Inclán, *Luces de Bohemia: Esperpento* (Alicante, Spain: Biblioteca Virtual Miguel de Cervantes, 2017), 224, http://www.cervantesvirtual.com/obra/luces-de-bohemia-esperpento-875781.

25. Original: *España es una deformación grotesca de la civilización europea* [. . .] *Las imágenes más bellas en un espejo cóncavo, son absurdas.* [. . .] *Deformemos la*

expresión en el mismo espejo que nos deforma las caras y toda vida miserable de España. Valle-Inclán, 225–26.

26. Steven Marsh, *Spanish Cinema against Itself: Cosmopolitanism, Experimentation, Militancy* (Bloomington: Indiana University Press, 2020), 209.

27. Linda C. Ehrlich, "The Films of Isaki Lacuesta: Hidden Portraits, Multiple Lives," in *(Re)viewing Creative, Critical and Commercial Practices in Contemporary Spanish Cinema*, ed. Duncan Wheeler and Fernando Canet (Bristol, UK: NBN International, 2014), 433.

28. Original: *Ana: Debo ser insensible porque no me conmovió el dolor de aquellos infelices [. . .] / Rita: Yo creo que la gente del pueblo, la gente baja, es menos sensible al dolor. ¿Usted ha visto un toro herido alguna vez? ¡Impasible!"* Agustín Sánchez Vidal, "El viaje a la luna de un perro andaluz," in *Valoración actual de la obra de García Lorca: Actas del coloquio celebrado en la Casa de Velázquez* (Madrid: Editorial de la Universidad Complutense, 1988), 153.

29. Original: *Me gustaría entrar en un banco y me gustaría robarles todo el dinero y me gustaría que alguien del banco intentara impedírmelo para poderle matar [. . .]. Y me gustaría que los clientes del banco me dijeran: "muy bien hecho muchacho, lo deberíamos haber hecho nosotros mucho antes." [. . .] Pero antes de salir de la ciudad me gustaría entrar en el edificio del congreso o en el senado o en el jodido parlamento, me da igual. Entraría a tiros, cagándome en la puta con cara de malo; político que se mueva pum, pum, y pum. Y la gente: "¡Ole, Ole y Ole!" Me sacarían a hombros todas las multitudes [. . .]. [Finalmente] Mira que casualidad el palacio de justicia. Voy a cargarme a un par de jueces, pero estos no me los voy a cargar a tiros. A estos me los voy a cargar a hostias. Justicia divina. Y la gente ya loca de alegría: "¡Ahí va nuestro justiciero, venga, venga!" Y ya de paso entro en cuatro oficinas de cuatro multinacionales que yo me sé y . . . ¡eh sin especular! No quedaría nadie vivo. Y después secuestro al presidentazo de un bancazo [. . .]. Y [voy a] hacerle sufrir, torturarle [. . .]. Y ahí toda la gente [dirá]: "Está loco pero es encantador. Le queremos."* Isaki Lacuesta, dir., *Murieron por encima de sus posibilidades* (Alicorn Films, 2014), 45:11, https://www.filmin.es/pelicula/murieron-por-encima-de-sus-posibilidades.

30. Lacuesta, 32:05.

31. Lacuesta, 32:15.

32. Marc Ripley, "Housed Nowhere and Everywhere Shut In: Uncanny Dwelling in Luis Buñuel's *El ángel exterminador*," *Bulletin of Spanish Studies* 93, no. 4 (April 20, 2016): 694.

33. Ripley, 685.

34. Lacuesta, *Murieron*, 81:20.

35. Lacuesta, 82:10.

36. Lacuesta, 85:40.

37. Lacuesta, "Entrevista a Isaki Lacuesta, 'Murieron por encima de sus posibilidades,'"April 27, 2015, interview by eCartelera, 02:30, https://www.ecartelera.com/videos/entrevista-isaki-lacuesta-murieron-por-encima-de-sus-posibilidades/.

38. Mercedes Camino, "'Vivir sin ti': Motherhood, Melodrama and Españolada in Pedro Almodóvar's *Todo sobre mi madre* (1999) and *Volver* (2006)," *Bulletin of Spanish Studies* 87, no. 5 (2010): 628–29.

39. Camino, 629.

40. Pablo Sánchez León, "Universidad del Barrio. Historia: Desprecio y miedo al pueblo," lecture recorded on February 23, 2015, YouTube video, 41:50, https://www.youtube.com/watch?v=2QGYKF4fYGQ.

41. Sánchez León, 43:00.

42. My emphasis. CEOE, "Las reformas necesarias para salir de la crisis" (2013), 28. https://epoo.epimg.net/descargables/2013/08/08/ea351a703425141a122d39e3aea3f180.pdf.

43. Lacuesta, *Murieron*, 88:40.

44. Lacuesta, 89:20.

45. Lacuesta, 90:00.

46. Lacuesta, 92:30.

47. Ofelia Ferrán and Lisa Hilbink, introduction to *Legacies of Violence in Contemporary Spain: Exhuming the Past, Understanding the Present*, ed. Ofelia Ferrán and Lisa Hilbink (New York: Routledge, 2016), 7.

48. María Castejón Leorza and Rebeca Maseda García, "*Carmina o revienta* and *Carmina y amén*: Female Transgressions of Victimhood in Spanish Popular Cinema," in *Gender and Violence in Spanish Culture: From Vulnerability to Accountability*, ed. María José Gámez Fuentes and Rebeca Maseda García (New York: Peter Lang, 2017), 207.

49. Yannis Stavrakakis, "Populism and Hegemony," 542–43.

50. Pierre Ostiguy, Francisco Panizza, and Benjamin Moffitt, introduction to *Populism in Global Perspective*, ed. Pierre Ostiguy, Francisco Panizza, and Benjamin Moffitt (New York: Routledge, 2021), 3.

51. Ostiguy, Panizza, and Moffitt, introduction to *Populism in Global Perspective*, 5–6.

52. Pierre Ostiguy, "Populism: A Socio-Cultural Approach," in *The Oxford Handbook of Populism*, ed. Cristóbal Rovira Kaltwasser, Paul Taggart, Paulina Ochoa Espejo, and Pierre Ostiguy (Oxford: Oxford University Press, 2017), e-book.

53. So much so that to this date, the director Paco León, a famous actor himself and a native of Andalusia, often code switches in public appearances from his native accent to a more "acceptable" version of Andalusian and, in some instances, to a neutral "Castilianized" register. This practice is so common in Spain that it applies to all Andalusians in one way or another, from the

very public and famous, such as the iconic morning-news anchor María Teresa Campos or superstar comedian and actor Dani Rovira to the anonymous person.

54. Manuel de la Fuente, "Documenting the Indignation: Responses to the Financial Crisis in Contemporary Spanish Cinema," *Romance Quarterly* 64, no. 4 (2017): 190.

55. Paco León, dir., *Carmina o revienta* (Andy Joke, 2012), 20:55, https://www.filmin. es/pelicula/carmina-o-revienta.

56. León, 22:35.

57. Today the public persona of Carmina Barrios seems undistinguishable from the characters she has played. In this respect, not long after these two films, she would later be the protagonist of a web series, *Carmina Tube*, directed again by Paco León, in which she talks as "herself" in the style of a YouTube's influencer. There, she purports to be talking to her real-life friends, many of whom also appeared in the films analyzed. Carminism is frequently invoked. Carmina the character, the influencer, appears to have overlapped with the "real" person, as no one can distinguish who is whom. The conflation of fact and fiction is furthered by her channel's very real popularity, which reached a number of views close to actual influencers' highly viewed videos. It had almost ninety thousand subscribers, and her videos averaged views in the hundred thousands. *Carmina Tube*, YouTube channel, https://www.youtube. com/channel/UCmAyotxEDR_yAxNYm3BnlFA.

58. León, *Carmina o revienta*, 25:40.

59. León, 25:57.

60. León, 26:00.

61. León, 26:30.

62. León, 27:00.

63. León, 28:00.

64. León, 68:53.

65. León, 60:05.

66. Paco León, dir., *Carmina y amén* (Andy Joke, 2014), 64:00. https://www.filmin. es/pelicula/carmina-y-amen.

67. León, 65:30.

68. León, 65:35.

69. León, 79:30.

70. Triana-Toribio, "Spanish Cinema of the 2010s," 12.

71. According to the most reputed survey in Spain (the CIS's *Barómetro*), by December 2013, a month before Podemos was founded, 81 percent of Spaniards

thought the political situation was very bad (52 percent) or bad (29 percent), and 92 percent expressed that the political situation was either worse (42 percent) or the same (50 percent) as the previous year; more importantly, 79 percent thought that the situation would either stay the same (48 percent) or could only get worse (32 percent). Centro de Investigaciones Sociológicas, "Barómetro de diciembre 2013: Estudio 3008," http://www.cis.es/cis/export/ sites/default/-Archivos/Marginales/3000_3019/3008/es3008mar.pdf.

CHAPTER 4

1. Óscar García Agustín and Marco Briziarelli argued that Podemos attempted to export from Latin America "a new kind of Left-wing populism and a decisive embrace of mediated political communication strategies" and, to such end, the political television show *La Tuerka* (later followed by *Fort Apache*) was created; hence "*La Tuerka* hypothesis," which specifically aimed at not simply voicing "points of view traditionally excluded from the public sphere" but allowed Podemos's political tenets "to move from marginality to centrality by constructing aggregative discourses through persuasive, emotional, and rhetorically spectacular ways." Óscar García Agustín and Marco Briziarelli, "Introduction: Wind of Change: Podemos, Its Dreams and Its Politics," in *Podemos and the New Political Cycle: Left-Wing Populism and Anti-establishment Politics*, ed. Oscar García Agustín and Marco Briziarelli (Cham, Switzerland: Palgrave Macmillan, 2017), 14–15.

2. Because it is understood that the figure of Pablo Iglesias is inextricable from Podemos, and vice versa, there is no significant temporal differentiation between the two. That is, although the media persona of Iglesias precluded even the idea of founding a political party like Podemos, both were designed with the same goal in mind: the acquisition of political capital.

3. "Podemos vs. The Spanish Media," *The Listening Post*, Al Jazeera English, YouTube, May 1, 2017, video, 3:30, https://www.youtube.com/watch?v= Wzntrl-6doI&ab_channel=AlJazeeraEnglish.

4. Mediatic populism is better understood through Gianpietro Mazzoleni's definition, which describes it as the symbiotic relationship between the increasing "mediatization/marketization of political communication . . . that responds primarily to audience demands" and populist leaders who "must use the media to enhance the effectiveness of their messages and build the widest possible public support." Gianpietro Mazzoleni, "Populism and the Media," in *Twenty-First Century Populism*, ed. Daniele Albertazzi and Duncan McDonnell (London: Palgrave Macmillan, 2007), 53, 62.

5. Jorge Sola and César Rendueles, "Podemos, the Upheaval of Spanish Politics and the Challenge of Populism," *Journal of Contemporary European Studies* (2018): 7.

6. Oliver Marchart, "From Media to Mediality: Mediatic (Counter-)Apparatuses and the Concept of the Political in Communication Studies," in *Discourse Theory and Critical Media Politics*, ed. Lincoln Dahlberg and Sean Phelan (London: Palgrave Macmillan, 2011), 65.

7. Marchart, 65–66.

8. Emphasis in the original. Marchart, 66.

9. For a full discussion of the European wave of populisms or the so-called populist turn, see Carlo Ruzza and Rosa Sánchez Salgado, "The Populist Turn in EU Politics and the Intermediary Role of Civil Society Organisations," *European Politics and Society* 22, no. 4 (2021): 471–85.

10. The expression was first used by Marx in reference to the Paris Commune's political ambitions. A century later, it became the title of a famous documentary film on Trotsky's assassination in Mexico. Most significantly here, during the first congress of Podemos (or *asamblea ciudadana*, as it was called), referring to the electoral hopes of the newly founded party, Pablo Iglesias famously quoted Marx, in his usual flamboyant style: "El cielo no se toma por consenso, sino por asalto." Bernardo Marín, "'Asaltar el cielo.' ¿Quién dijo eso antes?" *El País*, October 18, 2014, https://elpais.com/politica/2014/10/18/actualidad/1413645294_999870.html.

11. As Concepción Cascajosa Virino and Vicente Rodríguez Ortega explain in their analysis of Podemos and *Game of Thrones*, before Iglesias's jump to the mainstream media, he had a solid conceptualization of television as a producer of cultural hegemony, which crystalized in the television project *La Tuerka* in November 2010. Accordingly, in his book *Disputar la democracia*, Iglesias writes: "The great media device of our time, the most important thing to establish and determine what people think (more so than education, family, or Church) is television. . . . Television shapes our aesthetic sensibility, our political opinions, our leisure and the entertainment we consume. Television teaches us the meaning of words." Concepción Cascajosa Virino and Vicente Rodríguez Ortega, "Daenerys Targaryen Will Save Spain: *Game of Thrones*, Politics, and the Public Sphere," *Television & New Media* 20, no. 5 (2019): 429–30.

12. "Ficción y poder," *Fort Apache*, HispanTV, video, 00:01, https://www.dailymotion.com/video/x3ukr6m.

13. Antonio Gómez López-Quiñones, "Introducción. En el laberinto del populismo: Algunas claves históricas y teóricas," *Arizona Journal of Hispanic Cultural Studies* 21 (2017): 121.

14. From the viewpoint of the networks—obviating the complex relationship of televisual products and their reception by audiences, it would not be unfair to claim that Iglesias's rise to fame was because his disruptive charisma was, above all, a ratings booster. At a time when the media was increasingly delegitimized, in an environment turbocharged by the crisis, Iglesias's appearances served to give the impression that some mainstream media was getting attuned to the new sociopolitical dynamics and, hence, was worthy of the public's attention (the political programming of the television channel La Sexta was the most emblematic example of this). Later, as leader of Podemos, Iglesias was an ever-refreshing part of the news cycle, who almost inevitably would guarantee a juicy headline. As his political persona grew bigger, he became an Icarus-like figure whose fall the television cameras were all too eager to catch.

15. In the self-produced documentary *Podemos: 130 días para la historia* (2015), the founding member of Podemos Jorge Moruno explains: "Behind every political argument of Pablo [Iglesias] on the media, there's a lot of hard work [made possible by a team of researchers within the party]. For a statement to sound simple and convincing when Pablo is debating in a television studio, the entire team needs to work very hard analyzing a plethora of data." Begoña Altoñano, *Podemos: 130 días para la historia*, La Barraca Producciones, YouTube, video, 15:00, https://www.youtube.com/watch?v=lg7HznCOBf4&ab_channel=LaBarracaProducciones.

16. Abigail Loxham, "Post-Crisis, Post-Feminist: Reading Ada Colau as Female Celebrity Politician in Alcaldessa (Pau Faus, 2016)," *Hispanic Research Journal* 20, no. 1 (2019): 74.

17. In *Podemos: 130 días para la historia*, in the third segment, titled "el despegue" (the takeoff), Iglesias's major television appearances between 2013 and 2015 are highlighted. In them, Iglesias talks about his precarious position as an adjunct professor confronting a high-salaried political consultant much less qualified than him; he speaks to the late prime minister Alfredo Pérez Rubalcaba in a colloquial tone about how the socialist party when in power always did way less of what it promised before getting into office; he lectures the Far Right debater Alfonso Rojo on the exact price of university tuition fees, which Rojo did not remotely know; similarly, when confronting another Far Right debater, Eduardo Inda, about his supposedly high salary as professor, Iglesias shows his quite precarious earnings and points out that he also lived in a low-income neighborhood of Madrid, the well-known working-class district of Vallecas. Ultimately, Iglesias was thus (self-)portrayed as honest and authentic, that is, of the people. Altoñano, *Podemos: 130 días*, 10:24.

18. Graeme Turner, *Ordinary People and the Media. The Demotic Turn* (London: Sage Publications, 2010), 2.
19. Turner, 3.
20. Turner, 43.
21. Ostiguy, Panizza, and Moffitt, "Introduction," 5.
22. In a tweet, Pablo Iglesias stated: "Watching *The Wire* for the second time; it is the best show in history. The city as protagonist, power as a relational force . . ." Pablo Iglesias (@Pabloiglesias), "Viendo *The Wire* por segunda vez; es la mejor serie de la historia. La ciudad protagonista, el poder como relación. . ." Twitter, 26 Feb 2016, 11.23 a.m., https://twitter.com/PabloIglesias/status/703012467874594822. On the cover of the book on *Game of Thrones* edited by Pablo Iglesias, Iglesias appears seated on the iconic "iron throne," which is the show's argumentative anchor. "Ganar o morir: Lecciones políticas en *Juego de Tronos*," Agapea, https://www.agapea.com/libros/Ganar-o-morir-Lecciones-politicas-en-Juego-de-Tronos-9788446040101-i.htm.
23. Juan Carlos Monedero, "Prólogo. Tronando por un juego: Enamorarte de un caminante de las nieves pero casarte con un Lannister," in *Ganar o morir. Lecciones políticas en* Juego de Tronos, ed. Pablo Iglesias Turrión (Madrid: Akal, 2014), 13.
24. Alejandro Torrus and Miguel Muñoz, "Pablo Iglesias: 'No soy imprescindible, soy un militante, no un macho alfa,'" *Cuartopoder*, October 19, 2014, https://www.cuartopoder.es/espana/2014/10/19/en-directo-el-debate-sobrela-organizacion-de-podemos/.
25. Although one could certainly establish legitimate comparisons between the Latin American "pink tide" leaders and Podemos's theorization of leadership, their concrete cultural practices were mostly untranslatable to the Spanish context (something indeed explicitly stated by the founding members of Podemos themselves). In this sense, when it came to cultural representation, the references to a Latin American style of leadership were untenable beyond certain xenophobically coded attacks on Iglesias, yet his alleged machismo is sadly part and parcel of most male leaderships in politics (rather than a trait specific to Iglesias's leadership).
26. As Santiago Alba Rico noted regarding Podemos's media appearances, Iglesias's articulation of a new common sense did not enter the popular realm "through 'small writings' that then begin to circulate through our [social] blood, but through sensible—audiovisual—epithets that circulate online and, above all, on television. Let us say that almost all relations of hegemony—or, in other words, all pedagogic relations—are generated today by television." Iglesias's media persona was thought under the Gramscian articulation of

the "organic intellectual" and a popular "pedagogy" that was to establish a (televisual) common sense and, eventually, a visible cultural hegemony. Santiago Alba Rico, "Podemos in Spain: Limits and Possibilities for Change," in *Spain after the Indignados/15-M Movement*, ed. Óscar Pereira-Zao and Steven L. Torres (Cham, Switzerland: Palgrave Macmillan, 2019), 84.

27. In a tweet that holds the picture of Detective Freamon from *The Wire*, Iglesias states: "Just finished *Deadwood* (a magnificent show despite being incomplete). I turn now again to The Wire: in times of confusion, one needs its reassurance." Pablo Iglesias (@Pabloiglesias), "Acabada *Deadwood* (magnífica aunque no acabe) Vuelvo a ver *The Wire*: En tiempos de incertidumbre hacen falta certezas," Twitter, February 8, 2016, 5:38 a.m., https://twitter.com/PabloIglesias/status/696402640545193984.

28. "S1E09 Freamon Follow drugs, follow money," The Wire PhD, YouTube, video, 00:01, https://www.youtube.com/watch?v=PJD_6KpBHnA.

29. "Ficción y poder," *Fort Apache*, HispanTV, 17:00.

30. Paul Julian Smith, *Dramatized Societies: Quality Television in Spain and Mexico* (Liverpool, UK: Liverpool University Press, 2016), 2.

31. The connections have indeed been made explicit by Iglesias: "In *Game of Thrones* antagonism, Schmitt's logic of friend-enemy as a fundamental aspect of the political, is absolutely central. It is in line with other tv series such as *The Wire*, *House of Cards*, or *Borgen*, but within the controlled context of fantasy, what allows for greater possibilities of theoretical analysis . . . and grants one access to key aspects of how power works." Pablo Iglesias Turrión, "Boxeo y ajedrez entre espadas y sombras," in *Ganar o morir: Lecciones políticas en* Juego de Tronos, ed. Pablo Iglesias Turrión (Madrid: Akal, 2014), 95–96.

32. Cascajosa Virino and Rodríguez Ortega, "Daenerys Targaryen Will Save Spain," 424.

33. Extract from the show *Vive Poniente*, in which famous people commented on episodes of *Game of Thrones* after they were broadcasted. "Pablo Iglesias sobre *Juego de tronos*," mandarinuelo, YouTube video, 02:30, https://www.youtube.com/watch?v=H05RN762MUs&ab_channel=mandarinuelo.

34. Iglesias Turrión, "Boxeo y ajedrez," 99.

35. Iglesias Turrión, 100.

36. In the image, Pablo Iglesias is seen gifting the DVD bundle of *Game of Thrones* to the king of Spain, Felipe VI. Andrea Sánchez, "Pablo Iglesias: 'Podemos se identifica con Khaleesi, *Infolibre*, May 16, 2015, https://www.infolibre.es/noticias/politica/2015/04/16/pablo_iglesias_quot_podemos_identifica_con_khaleesi_quot_31423_1012.html.

37. Sánchez.
38. Juan Carlos Monedero speaks of Podemos as a party with two vectors: "One was electoral, with a great media presence of its leaders, and the other was hierarchical, with an executive power that had many prerogatives (. . . [which could be defined as] 'Leninist' model). . . . [The second vector] was aimed at winning elections, allowing the Executive (initially comprised of 11 persons) to make a great number of decisions, including the altering of the order of the lists compulsorily elected through primary processes." Juan Carlos Monedero, "15M and Indignant Democracy: Legitimation Problems within Neoliberal Capitalism," in *Spain after the Indignados/15M Movement*, ed. Óscar Pereira-Zazo and Steven L. Torres (Cham, Switzerland: Springer International Publishing, 2019), 55.
39. Pablo Iglesias Turrión, "Presentación," in *Ganar o morir: Lecciones políticas en Juego de Tronos*, ed. Pablo Iglesias Turrión (Madrid: Akal, 2014), 7.
40. Emphasis in the original. Javier Franzé, "The Podemos Discourse: A Journey from Antagonism to Agonism" in *Podemos and the New Political Cycle: Left-Wing Populism and Anti-establishment Politics*, ed. Óscar García Agustín and Marco Briziarelli (Cham, Switzerland: Palgrave Macmillan, 2018), 56.
41. Marsh, *Spanish Cinema against Itself*, 6.
42. Pedro Piqueras and Pablo Iglesias, "Entrevista de Pedro Piqueras a Pablo Iglesias en tele5," February 23, 2015, MP3 audio, 17:00, https://www.ivoox.com/entrevista-pedro-piqueras-a-pablo-iglesias-en-audios-mp3_rf_4124772_1.html.
43. Antonio Maestre, "El concepto '*casta*', de Manuel Azaña a Hermann Terstch." *La Marea*, August 19, 2014, https://www.lamarea.com/2014/08/19/el-concepto-casta-un-discurso-que-se-remonta-al-siglo-xix/.
44. Joaquín Valdivielso identified the discursive resignification of the political space of "us" against "them" as populism's center of gravity. As such, he defined Podemos's populism as "a broad discursive interpellation" to the Spanish people in relation to a confronted other, to a *casta*. Joaquín Valdivielso, "The Outraged People: Laclau, Mouffe and the Podemos Hypothesis," *Constellations* 24, no. 3 (2017): 299.
45. José Álvarez Junco, "Rural and Urban Popular Culture" in *Spanish Cultural Studies: An Introduction: The Struggle for Modernity*, ed. Helen Graham and Jo Labanyi (Oxford: Oxford University Press, 1995), 82.
46. When the party tried to void the ideation of *la casta* of its ambiguity and developed the more specific idea of *la trama* (the conspiracy) in 2017, the political effect was at best much less compelling; at worst, it was ridiculed as a desperate attempt to make up for the continuous loss of electoral support after a series of bitter internal fights. The party went so far as to charter buses

(the so-called *tramabús*) with stamped images of public figures directly, indirectly, and even vaguely associated with corruption (respectively, Miguel Blesa, Esperanza Aguirre, and Juan Luís Cebrián) to no avail, which speaks to how *la casta* had an eminently populist component that la trama could not replicate and also the fact that *la casta* as a populist mental image was effective precisely because, in its ambiguity, it was not prescriptive (i.e., it did not name names), as opposed to *la trama*'s excess of concreteness and implicit political prescription.

47. Vinodh Venkatesh, "Ethics, Spectacle, and Violence in Álex de la Iglesia's *La chispa de la vida*," *Hispanófila* 178, no. 1 (2016): 24.

48. Ventakesh, 24–25.

49. Ventakesh, 27.

50. Cristina Moreiras-Menor, *La estela del tiempo: Imagen e historicidad en el cine español contemporáneo* (Frankfurt: Vervuet, 2011), 12.

51. Although no obvious straight line is intended to be drawn between cinematic reality and its political counterpart, many of De la Iglesia's most famous films follow the most important political debates of their times. For instance, broadly speaking: in *El día de la bestia* (1995) the well-known violence of terrorism and of Spanish history at large enters the screen coded as Satanism; *La comunidad* (2000) portrays the national body of Spain as a decaying corpse that wraps itself in the façade of the new millennium's modernity while its essence rots out of sight; and *Balada triste de trompeta* (2010) exemplifies much of the perverse debates of its time about the law on historical memory.

52. Núria Triana-Toribio, "Spanish Cinema of the 2010s: Back to Punk and Other Lessons from the Crisis," *Hispanic Research Journal* 20, no. 1 (2019): 18.

53. Triana-Toribio, 18.

54. Dean Albritton, "Prime Risks: The Politics of Pain and Suffering in Spanish Crisis Cinema," *Journal of Spanish Cultural Studies* 15, nos. 1–2 (2014): 104.

55. Fruela Fernández, "Podemos: Politics as a 'Task of Translation,'" *Translation Studies* 11, no. 1 (2018): 2.

56. Fernández, 6.

57. Original: *Óscar: Vivo mi vida. Soy como soy. / Óscar: Disparo. / Yuri: ¡Dispara, dispara, dispara! / Óscar: ¡No puedo¡¡Me encanta esta canción! / [. . .] / Óscar: ¡Alphonso es una leyenda! ¡Es historia de España! Y además es tu padre. / Yuri: Con más razón, hay que empezar de cero.* Álex de la Iglesia, dir., *Mi gran noche*, RTVE a la carta, Somos Cine, May 24, 2020, video, 60:21. https://www.rtve.es/alacarta/videos/somos-cine/gran-noche/4395381/.

58. So much so that Podemos's most visible performance against the old Spanish *casta*, its implementation of new political style (the so-called *nueva política*),

was blatantly copied, first, by Ciudadanos (once touted as "the right-wing version of Podemos") and later by Pedro Sánchez's second coming into politics and its regeneration of the PSOE.

59. Marco Briziarelli, "To 'Feel' and to 'Understand' Political Struggle: The National-Popular Rhetoric of Podemos," *Journal of Communication Inquiry* 40, no. 3 (2016): 300.

60. Marco Briziarelli, "Podemos' Twofold Assault on Hegemony: The Possibilities of the Post-Modern Prince and the Perils of Passive Revolution," in *Podemos and the New Political Cycle: Left-Wing Populism and Anti-establishment Politics*, ed. Óscar García Agustín and Marco Briziarelli (Cham, Switzerland: Springer International Publishing, 2018), 110.

61. That line of reasoning follows the cultural geographers Sarah Elwood and Harriet Hawkins, who analyze the essence of how images transform cultural imaginaries by asking first, "What images do in the world? How are images transformative? What kinds of social and political imaginaries can they bring into being, and what are the limits to these possible transformations?" Sarah Elwood and Harriet Hawkins, "Intradisciplinarity and Visual Politics," *Annals of the American Association of Geographers* 107, no. 1 (2017): 5.

62. Íñigo Errejón and Chantal Mouffe, *Construir pueblo: Hegemonía y radicalización de la democracia* (Barcelona: Icaria, 2015), 54.

63. Sara Martínez Guillem, "Podemos' Performative Power: Space Struggles and/ as Political Transformation," in *Podemos and the New Political Cycle: Left-wing Populism and Anti-establishment Politics*, ed. Óscar García Agustín and Marco Briziarelli (Cham, Switzerland: Springer International Publishing, 2018), 83.

64. Martínez Guillem, 84.

65. First, Podemos's own ideation of populism was not static. It was initially anchored in Íñigo Errejón's reading of Laclau's theory of (left-wing) populism but was later replaced by Pablo Iglesias's reading of Gramsci's hegemony, with a greater emphasis on building a hegemonic bloc from the Left; eventually, the latter would abandon Errejón's populist articulation of the people as a transversal marker of political identification outside the Left-Right axis. Second, all of Podemos's political conceptualizations are mostly understood as discursively engineered, largely forgetting their performative impetus or, at best, simply acknowledging the importance of performance without going into much further analysis. As such, García Agustín and Briziarelli have argued that Podemos's discursive hegemony in the media was based on "the construction of a people" through "constructing a rhetorical audience and a community that share new kinds of linguistic practices"—de facto paying no

mind to how those practices, which were visual and performative in practice, were seen when performed. García Agustín and Briziarelli, "Introduction," 14.

66. Fiona Noble, *Subversive Spanish Cinema: The Politics of Performance* (London: Bloomsbury, 2020), 6.

67. Noble, 6.

68. According to this hypothesis, Juan Carlos Mondero explained, it was fundamental to construct a "'they' (which was deemed as *la casta* or the caste, following the Italian example) and a "we" (a people under construction), thus polarizing the situation around a [Pablo Iglesias] leadership that was emptied of its specific initial demands in order to facilitate a chain of equivalencies where any disaffection with the regime could find a symbolic accommodation in the "empty signifier" represented by the leader." Juan Carlos Monedero, "15-M and Indignant Democracy: Legitimation Problems within Neoliberal Capitalism," in *Spain after the Indignados/15-M Movement*, ed. Óscar Pereira-Zazo and Steven L. Torres (Cham, Switzerland: Palgrave Macmillan, 2019), 57.

69. Amelia Jones, "'Presence' in Absentia: Experiencing Performance as Documentation." *Art Journal* 56, no. 4 (1997): 13.

70. Pablo Iglesias Turrión and Fernando León de Aranoa, "Pablo Iglesias entrevista al director de cine Fernando León de Aranoa," interview by Pablo Iglesias for the Podemos YouTube Channel, YouTube, September 17, 2020, video, 32:00, https://www.youtube.com/watch?v=L7Si5cUHZwY&feature=youtu.be&t=1931&ab_channel=PODEMOS.

71. My emphasis. Philip Auslander, "The Performativity of Performance Documentation," *PAJ: A Journal of Performance and Art* 28, no. 3 (2006): 4.

72. Martínez Guillem, "Podemos' Performative Power," 85.

73. In July 2014, the CIS's *barómetro* reflected that the three main political leaders of the country (Mariano Rajoy of the right-wing Partido Popular, Alfredo Pérez Rubalcaba of the Center-Left PSOE, and Cayo Lara of the leftist Izquierda Unida) were rated well under a 3.5 on a 10-point scale, one of the lowest ratings in the history of Spanish democracy. "Intención de voto y valoración de líderes. Barómetro del CIS de julio de 2014, *El País*, August 4, 2014, https://elpais.com/elpais/2014/08/04/media/1407160041_786585.html.

74. Iglesias Turrión and León de Aranoa, "Pablo Iglesias entrevista," video, 32:30.

75. Iglesias Turrión and León de Aranoa, 33:40.

76. Iglesias Turrión and León de Aranoa, 34:00.

77. Marsh, *Spanish Cinema against Itself*, 227.

78. Paul Julian Smith, *Spanish Visual Culture: Cinema, Television, Internet* (Manchester, UK: Manchester University Press, 2006), 9; Emmy Eklundh, *Emotions,*

Protest, Democracy: Collective Identities in Contemporary Spain (Abingdon, UK: Routledge, 2019), 11.

79. Eklundh, *Emotions, Protest, Democracy*, 11.

80. Eklundh, 12.

81. Eklundh, 223.

82. Smith, *Spanish Visual Culture*, 14.

83. Smith, 16.

84. Although the seemingly inextricable relationship of ethics and politics has been made obvious since Podemos's first electoral campaign (e.g., regarding its insistence on flying in economy class to the European Parliament or donating part of salaries to not-for-profit organizations), less attention has been paid to how such correlation was dependent on the emotional as well as the audiovisual performances of Iglesias.

85. Pablo Iglesias uttered these words inside the Spanish Parliament in his declaration as official member on January 13, 2016. Variations of this formula were used by the rest of Podemos's newly elected parliamentarians. In fact, Iglesias was not the one who captured most of the attention at the time; Carolina Bescansa did, as she brought her newborn baby to the ceremony. However, given that this chapter's object of study is centered on the figure of Iglesias, and because many of the reactions to the image of Bescansa and her baby were reflective of sexist attitudes at large rather than a direct response to her sworn statement of constitution, the analysis heavily falls on the first. Francesco Manetto and Juan José Mateo, "Podemos hace de la fórmula para prometer el cargo un mensaje político," *El País*, January 13, 2016, https://elpais.com/politica/2016/01/13/actualidad/1452685395_555063.html.

86. Smith, *Spanish Visual Culture*, 18.

87. Bill Nichols, *Introduction to Documentary* (Bloomington: Indiana University Press, 2017), 112.

88. Podemos's self-produced documentary, *PODEMOS: 130 días para la historia* (2015), is an early example of that attempt.

89. Pablo Iglesias (@Pabloiglesias) "Orgullosos de que se note lo que sentimos. Orgullosos de no olvidar de dónde venimos. Orgullosos de la gente humilde," Twitter, January 14, 2016, 3.21 a.m., https://twitter.com/pabloiglesias/status/687308500024868864.

90. *Diccionario de la Lengua Española* s.v. "humilde," Real Academia Española, https://dle.rae.es/humilde?m=form.

91. Paradoxically, the successful visualization of (an otherwise-metaphorical) retributive politics of the people greatly undermined the electoral prospects of Podemos once the party gained parliamentary representation.

CHAPTER 5

1. Given the fascist history of Spain and how tightly enmeshed Carl Schmitt is with fascism, the comparison to Podemos's vision of politics is undoubtedly polemic. Although such comparative framework here occupies little conceptual space, it is important to note that the Schmittian connection has already been explored extensively in Josh Booth and Patrick Baert's book *The Dark Side of Podemos? Carl Schmitt and Contemporary Progressive Populism*. There, the authors speak of the Schmitt-Podemos paradox of the party's first three years. During this period, the authors argue that Podemos's leaders viewed Spanish politics through the lens of what they were opposing, thinking of their political context more like Schimitt's Weimar Germany. Through that filter, Booth and Baert state that a compelling narrative was created "in which personal and political stories are woven together—a narrative that extends into both Spain's past and its future. It is a narrative that draws on cultural structures at play in Spanish politics for over a century, resulting in a patterning homologous to that which runs through Schmitt's political theory. Homology of narrative structures is the key to understanding how Schmittian ideas have managed to resonate with leaders of a progressive political party a century later." Josh Booth and Patrick Baert, *The Dark Side of Podemos? Carl Schmitt and Contemporary Progressive Populism* (Milton, UK: Routledge, 2018), 5.

2. The term *Schmittian* refers to the Schmittian connection that Booth and Baert make in their book *The Dark Side of Podemos?* and is not an assumed category for the rest of the chapter. As it was mentioned in the previous note, Schmitt has here the role of an analytical springboard when approaching how Podemos evolved institutionally. To that end, Podemos's true political impetus (Schmittian or otherwise) is less important than the party's political praxis, which is not so much influenced by a conscious implementation of Schmitt's philosophy as it is shaped by how the context of Podemos's politics lends itself to be understood in an Schmittian manner. Hence, the apparent interrelation of populism and (post)fascism is, then, above all a conceptual operation to establish the correlation of contexts from Podemos to Vox. It leaves aside deeper political-historical comparisons between populism and fascism, whose wider histories have been already thought elsewhere as in an ideological continuum, for instance, by Federico Finchelstein in *From Fascism to Populism in History* (Berkeley: University of California Press, 2017).

3. The use of *Left* is here somewhat of a misnomer, albeit a useful label. In this context, it is more akin to generalizations such as cultural progressivism than

a reference to a concrete political tradition. However, the division between Left and Right is particularly handy when it comes to differentiating leftist from rightist online content around the Podemos phenomenon. As such, the term *Left* (or *leftist*) refers to content in popular (online) culture that purports to appeal to a progressive common sense while, at the same time, not being clearly aligned with the political Right in the Spanish context.

4. Jessica Baldwin-Philippi, "The Technological Performance of Populism," *New Media & Society* 21, no. 2 (2019): 389.

5. A concrete example of how the popular disassociated from the populist could be seen in how the precarious reality fueled by a sustained fiscal austerity after the crisis was mostly assumed as unchangeable in the face of Podemos's unchanged antiausterity discourse, which evolved from the populist usage of *la casta* to the ideation of *la trama*. The unpopularity of the latter is indeed testament to that disassociation.

6. Admittedly, this is an interpretation underpinned by a conceptual framework predicated on the essential autonomy of the popular. In other words, it is the belief that in the end popular agency makes its way into politics despite efforts to control it from the top of the political food chain. Yet it should be stressed that the suggested inability to completely discipline people's political will in a democratic society does not suppose a deepening of democracy (case in point being the global wave of right-wing populisms). This interpretation (of the eventual uncontrollability of the people) is here positioned to at least offer a warning to those who see the current status quo both as a guarantor of the business-as-usual politics of liberal democracy and as an alternative to "dangerous" populisms, that is, those who think of the top-down liberal democratic order as an adequate system of checks and balances, which can be merely tweaked to quiet down popular unrest. Precisely, the theoretical argument that guides this chapter—which alleges that populist subjects cannot be controlled from above by messianic leaderships, and even their popular representations eventually escape such domination—runs counter ultimately to the desirability of any political thinking based on strong top-down hierarchies, whether be they in populism or in liberal democracy.

7. Baldwin-Philippi, "Technological," 389.

8. Noam Gal, Limor Shifman, and Zohar Kampf, "'It Gets Better': Internet Memes and the Construction of Collective Identity," *New Media & Society* 18, no. 8 (2016): 1700.

9. As a way to avoid confusion, the exact referencing to the different name changes of Podemos (first switched to Unidos Podemos, presently Unidas Podemos) is avoided whenever possible. The use of Podemos in this chapter

refers to the Podemos phenomenon unless specified otherwise. Concretely, the Podemos phenomenon refers to the impact the party had in popular culture at large, and it encapsulates the attempt by at changing the institutional structures of Spanish politics regardless of the party's eventual political alliances.

10. Limor Shifman, *Memes in Digital Culture* (Cambridge, MA: MIT Press, 2014), 15.
11. Gal, Shifman, and Kampf, "'It Gets Better,'" 1700.
12. Heidi E. Huntington, "Pepper Spray Cop and the American Dream: Using Synecdoche and Metaphor to Unlock Internet Memes' Visual Political Rhetoric," *Communication Studies* 67, no. 1 (2016): 78–79.
13. Ryan M. Milner, "Pop Polyvocality: Internet Memes, Public Participation, and the Occupy Wall Street Movement," *International Journal of Communication* 7 (2013): 2367.
14. Ryan M. Milner, *The World Made Meme: Public Conversations and Participatory Media* (Cambridge, MA: MIT Press, 2016), 157.
15. The attachment of the popular to the populist when it comes to the memetic participation in politics is not necessarily positive. In fact, concerns have been raised about how the inherent pastiche quality of memes cheapens civic conversations "when popular culture and its predominant mass commercial logics become part of political discussion." Milner, 162.
16. Milner, 164.
17. Paulo Gerbaudo, "Protest Avatars as Memetic Signifiers: Political Profile Pictures and the Construction of Collective Identity on Social Media in the 2011 Protest Wave," *Information, Communication & Society* 18, no. 8 (2015): 921.
18. Gerbaudo, 924.
19. Nicola Montesano Montessori and Esperanza Morales-López, "Multimodal Narrative as an Instrument for Social Change: Reinventing Democracy in Spain—The Case of 15-M," *Critical Approaches to Discourse Analysis across Disciplines* 7, no. 2 (2015): 211.
20. Gerbaudo, "Protest Avatars," 925.
21. Marc Tuters and S. Hagen, "(((They))) Rule: Memetic Antagonism and Nebulous Othering on 4chan," *New Media & Society* 22, no. 12 (2020): 2221.
22. See picture posted by Nazaret Castro, "Funny Anniversary Quotes," Pinterest, https://www.pinterest.es/pin/510454938995346419/.
23. El Jueves (@eljueves), "El especial El Jueves 'No hay pan para tanto chorizo' ya está en los quioscos," Twitter, March 23, 2012, 5:35 p.m., https://twitter.com/eljueves/status/183079398520537088. Seen in a still frame from a sketch uploaded to YouTube. Eitb, "Vaya Semanita-Rajoy: 'No hay pan para tanto chorizo,'" 0:02, YouTube, May 14, 2014, https://www.youtube.com/watch?v=6Sicsnt5Ryw&ab_channel=eitb.

24. Jacques Rancière, *The Politics of Aesthetics* (New York: Continuum, 2004), 9.
25. Limor Shifman, "Testimonial Rallies and the Construction of Memetic Authenticity," *European Journal of Communication* 33, no. 2 (2018): 176.
26. Shifman, 174.
27. Shifman, 180.
28. Shifman, 176.
29. These included a series of online images that had people holding signs in which it was, for instance, stated: "Single mom, grad student, unemployed, and I paid more tax last year than GE. I am the 99%. Occupy Wall Street" See "We Are The 99 Percent—Image #185,403," Know Your Meme, uploaded in 2011, https://knowyourmeme.com/photos/185403-we-are-the-99-percent.
30. Seyda Barlas Bozkus, "Pop Polyvocality and Internet Memes: A Reflection of Socio-Political Discourse of Turkish Youth in Social Media," *Global Media Journal* 6, no. 12 (2016): 47.
31. For a full list of the first memes of Iglesias (behind a tree and others), see Mari Luz Peinado, "Lo que opina Podemos de los memes de Podemos," Verne, *El País*, October 1, 2014, https://verne.elpais.com/verne/2014/10/01/articulo/1412141526_000185.html.
32. The examples are too many to be reproduced here. At that time, Twitter was the preferred social media platform for the spread of these memes. See, for instance, the parodic tweet of Iglesias behind a tree shared by Podemos's official account: Podemos (@PODEMOS), "Por muy seguros que os sintáis, alguien os estará vigilando," Twitter, August 28, 2014, 6:03 a.m., https://twitter.com/PODEMOS/status/504720854715215873. In a similar tone, Iglesias would laugh at his own memes; for instance, when he was memed as the balding but pony-tailed character of The Simpsons: Pablo Iglesias (@PabloIglesias), "Ya no hay vuelta atrás," Twitter, November 11, 2018, 6:33 p.m., https://twitter.com/PabloIglesias/status/1061522390486781952.
33. Even though Iglesias was characterized on- and offline from the beginning by his eagerness to be the center of (media) attention, the references to his perceived thirst for power only started after Podemos run in the general election of 2015. That is, it was a characterization that went hand in hand with the beginning of Podemos's institutionalization.
34. In this respect, the event that triggered the avalanche of criticisms took place in the press conference of January 2016, when Iglesias offered himself as vice president in a hypothetical Pedro Sánchez–led coalition government. Most poignantly, Iglesias justified his offering in a highly condescending manner by affirming, "La oportunidad histórica que tiene Pedro Sánchez de ser presidente del Gobierno es una sonrisa del destino que él siempre tendrá que

agradecer" (This is a historical opportunity for Pedro Sánchez to be president of Spain and is in fact, as destiny would have it, a chance he will always have to be grateful for). Luis B. García, "Pablo Iglesias ofrece un gobierno de izquierdas a Pedro Sánchez 'sin líneas rojas,'" Política, *La Vanguardia*, January 21, 2016, https://www.lavanguardia.com/politica/20160122/301592838366/pablo-iglesias-gobierno-pedro-sanchez.html.

35. Through their official Twitter accounts, prominent satiric magazines such as *El Jueves* and *El Mundo Today* parodied Iglesias as hopeless narcissist leader. See, e.g., El Jueves (@eljueves), "Pablo Iglesias discute con su propio reflejo por el liderazgo de Podemos," Twitter, March 12, 2019, 12:51 a.m., https://twitter.com/eljueves/status/1105103985361539072; El Mundo Today (@elmundotoday), "Nadie se atreve a decirle a Pablo Iglesias que es el único que queda en Podemos," Twitter, January 31, 2019, 12:59 a.m., https://twitter.com/elmundotoday/status/1178686212627947520.

36. This smear campaign was judicially investigated under the so-called *caso Villarejo*. The investigation uncovered the unholy alliance of Rajoy's Ministry of Interior, a shady group of high-ranking police commanders, and a small group of questionable journalists, whose main purpose was the fabrication of phony documents and the spreading of false rumors about political opponents (among which Pablo Iglesias and Podemos were prominent).

37. This time saw a series of remarkable events in very rapid succession that merit a brief contextualization. Podemos ran for the first time in a general election in December 2015, obtaining a total of sixty-nine seats. Although Podemos was in fact an umbrella platform for a number of smaller parties in coalition, the party at first refused to enter in a coalition with Izquierda Unida (IU) unless the latter would accept to run in the ballot under Podemos's name (a move that IU would never agree to, guaranteeing the two parties would run as separate entities). As a result, IU lost much of the leftist vote and obtained the poorest results of its history in a general election, with only two seats and less than four percent of the popular vote. The 2015 elections resulted in an extremely fragmented Parliament. Although Mariano Rajoy attained the majority of seats, he did not have enough support to form a majority government. The main consequence was the repetition of elections, which were then set for June 2016. For this election, an overambitious Podemos and a much weaker IU finally agreed on a coalition pact that changed both their names to Unidos Podemos. The pact was widely regarded as a unity front of the Left and Iglesias as his indisputable leader. Despite the hopeful environment that the coalition elicited, Unidos Podemos lost one million votes—although it only gave up one seat, given the electoral voting

system that allocates the ratio of votes to seats proportionally. These events started a major crisis that was resolved within the party with another change of name for the 2019 elections, this time Unidas Podemos (as a gesture to the much-influential Spanish feminist movement), and with the forceful exit of Íñigo Errejón and his accolades from the party.

38. Daniel Rueda Toledano, "Los legados institucionales del largo 15-M: El final del momento populista y la vía errejonista a la transversalidad," *Encrucijadas: Revista Crítica de Ciencias Sociales* 19 (2020): 13.

39. Alexandros Kioupkiolis, "Late Modern Adventures of Leftist Populism in Spain: The Case of Podemos 2014–2018," in *The Populist Radical Left in Europe*, ed. Giorgios Katasambekis and Alexandros Kioupkiolis (London: Routledge, 2019), 64.

40. Antonio Cazorla-Sánchez, "Beyond They Shall Not Pass: How the Experience of Violence Reshaped Political Values in Franco's Spain," *Journal of Contemporary History* 40, no. 3 (2005): 519.

41. José Carlos Rueda Laffond, "¿Un pasado que no cesa? Discurso patrimonial y memoria pública comunista en el franquismo y la transición española," *Revista de Estudios Sociales* 47 (2013): 20–21.

42. So much so that the mainstream PSOE was not exempted from these characterizations, especially after its former president Felipe González was forced by the circumstances to leave the leadership, which triggered the first party primaries between Joaquín Almunia and Josep Borrell. However, none was able to escape the long shadow of Felipismo; as such, all were often seen as inconsequential caricatures of the "real" Left. The satirical puppet show *Las noticias del Guiñol* emblematically and ironically caricatured the two politicians as metaphorical and actual puppets of the Spanish Left's self-defeatist impulses.

43. Kioupkiolis, "Late Modern Adventures," 64–65.

44. In a campaign against political, economic and media corruption, Podemos fleeted a bus with photographic drawings of what they considered were the main actors of a well-orchestrated conspiracy or *trama* against the Spanish people. This *tramabús* would go around Spain explaining the origins and reasons of the conspiracy. A great part of this *trama* had prominently conspired against Podemos (as it was demonstrated in what was known as the *caso Villarejo*), so while the *tramabús* was again implicitly aligning the party with the people, it did so in a perceived partisan way that distanced it from any type of populist impetus. Leonor Mayor Ortega, "Podemos fleta un autobús contra la corrupción," *La Vanguardia*, March 17, 2017, https://www.lavanguardia.com/politica/20170417/421766459530/tramabus-podemos-corrupcion.html.

45. The meme shows Venezuelan president Nicolás Maduro driving Podemos's bus, a very common association among rightist circles. PP Comunidad de Madrid (@ppmadrid), "Ya sabemos quien conduce el #TramaBUS," Twitter, April 17, 2017, 8:24 p.m., https://twitter.com/ppmadrid/status/853917016339746816. In another reference to the *tramabús*, now using *The Simpsons*, Podemos's members are portrayed as children playing absurd games inside their bus. This is an example testament to the nonpartisan nature of the criticism. Ismaël (@PassePartout__), "Nuevas imágenes del interior del #TramaBUS," Twitter, April 17, 2017, 9:32 p.m., https://twitter.com/PassePartout__/status/853934094073417728.

46. Emmanuel Rodríguez, "El 'Tramabús,' un falso debate," *Ctxt*, Tribuna, March 19, 2017, https://ctxt.es/es/20170419/Firmas/12255/tramabus-podemos-trama-instituciones-Ibex-35-iglesias.htm.

47. In a tweet in 2015, a famous meme of Errejón and Iglesias depicted the first theorizing lofty political ideas almost unintelligibly, while the second tried to bring him down to earth: El Apuntador (@quieropolonia), "Pero que solo he dicho núcleo irradiador, Pablo. Íñigo, ya está bien, eh, ya está bien. #TuiteaComoErrejón," Twitter, June 20, 2015, 7:55 a.m., https://twitter.com/quieropolonia/status/612015996556189696. A year later, the same meme showed Errejón as the child of Podemos, without any authority in the new party hierarchy. Fairlaine (@Fairlane4), "¿A Garzón también tengo que llamarle papá? Sí, es parte del acuerdo Podemos/IU. Me estáis jodiendo la infancia," Twitter, May 10, 2016, 6:38 a.m., https://twitter.com/Fairlane4/status/729772578684964864.

48. Shifman, "Testimonial Rallies," 174.

49. In the tweet, Pablo Iglesias joked about his published conflicts with Errejón and other members within the party in the language of Soviet purging: Pablo Iglesias (@Pabloiglesias), "He mandado a @CBescansa y a @ierrejon a Siberia a re-educarse por ¡disidentes!," Twitter, March 10, 2016, 5:06 a.m., https://twitter.com/PabloIglesias/status/707628640415129601. Errejón replied using the populist concept of *casta*: Íñigo Errejón (@irrejon), "@Pabloiglesias_*casta*!" Twitter, February 2, 2016, 10:46 p.m., https://twitter.com/ierrejon/status/694486974829346816.

50. Martínez Guillem, "Podemos' Performative Power," 90.

51. Late Motiv en Movistar+ (@LateMotivCero), "¿Conocéis el viral de la entrevista en la BBC interrumpida por 2 niños? Es un fake. #LateMotiv205 tiene el original gracias a @unitedunknown." Twitter, March 25, 2017, 9:14 a.m., https://twitter.com/LateMotivCero/status/841774643405049856.

52. Pablo Iglesias (@Pabloiglesias), "Sois muy grandes @LateMotivCero," Twitter, March 25, 2017, 3:49 p.m., https://twitter.com/PabloIglesias/status/841874067913363457.

53. Baldwin-Philippi, "Technological," 389.

54. Numerous tweets were posted mocking the feminist pose of the three male Podemos leaders, such as Patricia Fernández de Lis (@pflis), "Nosotras," Twitter, April 20, 2018, 3:58 a.m., https://twitter.com/pflis/status/987027780771680256.

55. For instance, the front page of *La Razón* on February 13, 2017, stated in big, bold letters: "Iglesias: Todo el poder para purgar" (Iglesias: All the power to purge). "Las portadas de los periódicos de hoy, lunes 13 de febrero de 2017," *Europapress*, Nacional, https://www.europapress.es/nacional/noticia-portadas-periodicos-hoy-lunes-13-febrero-2017-20170213000503.html. The front page of ABC on January 18, 2019, stated in similar letters across the entire masthead: "Podíamos. Errejón se rebela contra el absolutismo de Iglesias" (Yes, we could [as a play on word using the past tense of party, Podemos that translates as "we can"]. Errejón rebels against Iglesias's absolutism). "Las portadas de los periódicos de hoy, viernes 18 de enero de 2019," *Europapress*, Nacional, https://www.europapress.es/nacional/noticia-portadas-periodicos-viernes-18-enero-2019-20190118001101.html.

56. El Mundo Today (@elmundotoday), "Iglesias promete que la vicepresidencia no le va a cambiar y que seguirá siendo el mismo líder megalómano y autoritario de siempre," Twitter, January 15, 2020, 12:05 a.m., https://twitter.com/elmundotoday/status/1217070108608167936; El Jueves (@eljueves), "Pablo Iglesias remodela la cúpula de Podemos con más Pablos Iglesias," Twitter, June 10, 2019, 6:04 p.m., https://twitter.com/eljueves/status/1137993932497965056.

57. Susan Martínez Guillem, "Podemos' Performative Power: Space Struggles and/as Political Transformation," in *Podemos and the New Political Cycle: Left-Wing Populism and Anti-establishment Politics*, ed. Óscar García Agustín and Marco Briziarelli (Cham, Switzerland: Palgrave Macmillan, 2018), 84.

58. Using the famous meme of the "distracted boyfriend," Iglesias's face was photoshopped looking at the girl in red along with captions that read *vivir como la casta* (living like *la casta*), while the girl in blue looked at Iglesias with a grimace alongside captions that read *vivir como predicas* (actually doing what you preach). Julen Marmol, "Los mejores memes de Pablo Iglesias e Irene Montero tras la compra del chalé de 600,000 euros," YouTube video, May 20, 2018, https://www.youtube.com/watch?v=dUYyITg-m6o&ab_channel=JulenMarmol.

59. Representative of that criticism was a tweet posted by El Mundo Today mocking Iglesias supposedly acquired classism from his move to Galapagar: El Mundo Today (@elmundotoday), "Pablo Iglesias teme que Galapagar se llene de 'gente de Vallecas' con la subida del SMI," Twitter, January 25, 2020, 12:05 a.m., https://twitter.com/elmundotoday/status/1220694018486603778.

60. There was a famous meme of Iglesias's supposedly fake revolutionary pedigree, originally shared through WhatsApp, that mocked Che Guevara's slogan "hasta la victoria siempre" by stating instead "hasta Galapagar siempre." "Pablo Iglesias . . . Hasta Galapagar siempre," Memesvip.com, Actualidad, Memes Políticos, https://memesvip.com/memes-politicos/pablo-iglesias-hasta-galapagar-siempre/.

61. Luisa Martín Rojo and Carmelo Díaz de Frutos, "En #Sol, revolución: Paisajes lingüísticos para tomar las plazas," *Journal of Spanish Cultural Studies* 15, nos. 1–2 (2014): 164, 171–72.

EPILOGUE

1. On the one hand, the image of the Francoist *señorito*, an aristocratic landowner typical of the time, is best visually represented by the character of *señorito* Iván (Juan Diego) in Mario Camus's adapted film from Miguel Delibes's novel *Los santos inocentes* (1984). On the other, the use of *enemies* instead of *adversaries* when referring to Vox is here quite conscious. Following Mouffe's differentiation between antagonism and agonism, Vox is firmly situated both politically and ideologically as in need of an explicit antagonist, an enemy rather than an adversary. While Podemos's initial populist hypothesis necessitated of discursive antagonism (e.g., *la casta* was an enemy of the Spanish people), the party—especially, after being elected to Parliament—always understood the divisions in the political arena agonically; that is, the confrontation was always between political adversaries despite the usage of antagonism in political discourse. On the contrary, once Vox entered Parliament, Abascal's party repeatedly and emphatically declared the coalition government between Unidas Podemos and PSOE as illegitimate in essence. By all accounts, Vox regards them as enemies of the Spanish nation.

2. José Rama, Lisa Zanotti, Stuart J. Turnbull-Dugarte, and Andrés Santana, *VOX: The Rise of the Spanish Populist Radical Right* (Abingdon, UK: Routledge, 2021), 1–2.

3. Lynda Dematteo, "The Mask and the Vanity Wound. Contemporary Populism through Canetti's Insight," in *Popularisation and Populism in the Visual Arts*, ed. Anna Schoeber (New York: Routledge, 2019), 82.

4. Dematteo, 83.

5. Dematteo, 83.

6. Dematteo, 83.

7. Dematteo, 83.

8. Benjamin De Cleen and Yannis Stavrakakis, in their response to political scientist Rogers Brubaker (who argued that the people of populism and the

nation are cut from the same conceptual cloth), have in my opinion made the most convincing case for the theoretical separation between populism and nationalism: "Characteristic of populism, we argue, is that it interpellates citizens as members of 'the people,' considered as an underdog, and opposed along a vertical down/up axis to 'the elite,' conceived as a small and illegitimately powerful and privileged group. Nationalism, by contrast, interpellates people as members of 'the nation' conceived as a limited and sovereign community that exists through time and is tied to a certain territory, with the nation being discursively constructed along a horizontal in/out axis that distinguishes (which should not be confused with 'opposes') members from non-members, and the own nation from other nations." Benjamin De Cleen and Yannis Stavrakakis, "How Should We Analyze the Connections between Populism and Nationalism? A Response to Rogers Brubaker," *Nations and Nationalism* 26 (2020): 315.

9. As the historian Agustín Cuadrado explains, the term was originally coined by Amando de Miguel in his book *Sociología del franquismo* in 1975, while Antonio López Pina and Eduardo López Aranguren a year later theoretically fleshed it out in their book *La cultura política de la España de Franco.* Agustín Cuadrado, "Presencias y ausencias en la representación del espacio familiar: La gran familia franquista frente a la familia democrática," *Hispanic Research Journal* 15, no. 3 (2014): 249. Yet much more recently, it was Pablo Iglesias, via his love for renowned novelist Manuel Vázquez Montalbán, who reentered the term into the post-15-M political era. *FortApache,* "La mitificación del franquismo sociológico-Pablo Iglesias," YouTube video, posted December 6, 2015, https://www.youtube.com/watch?v=ZtmyECWFJsE.

10. This double conceptualization of Vox's antagonism as both national (in terms of its Spanishness) and nationalist (following a more general nationalist framing of the people) justifies here the usage of the term *national(ist).*

11. Rama et al., *VOX,* 118.

12. Rama et al., *VOX,* 120.

13. Enzo Traverso, *The New Faces of Fascism. Populism and the Far Right,* trans. David Broder (London: Verso, 2019), 4.

14. Traverso, 6.

15. Traverso, 7.

16. Traverso, 33.

17. In a tweet by Vox's leader Santiago Abascal calling all Spaniards to demonstrate against the PSOE–Unidas Podemos coalition government, the Spanish flag is featured most prominently: Santiago Abascal (@Santi_ABASCAL), "¡A LA CALLE! Este gobierno nos está matando con su incompetencia frente al

virus y nos está arruinando con sus medidas totalitarias y absurdas. El lunes obliguemos a los mafiosos a dimitir. En coche y con la bandera de la libertad, la de España. #CaravanaLibertad," Twitter, October 9, 2020, 10:46 p.m., https://twitter.com/Santi_ABASCAL/status/1314532690180407296.

18. Lena Tahmassian, "Carl Schmitt and the Basque Conflict: From the Design of Francoism to Spanish Democracy," *Journal of Spanish Cultural Studies* 13, no. 1 (2012): 61.

19. Luís Angosto-Ferrández, "Mausoleums, National Flags and Regime Crises: Comparing Spain and Venezuela," *Politics, Religion & Ideology* 19, no. 4 (2018): 486.

20. Pablo Sánchez León, "The Study of Nation and Patria as Communities of Identity: Theory, Historiography, and Methodology from the Spanish Case," *Genealogy* 4, no. 23 (2020): 7.

21. Angosto-Ferrández, "Mausoleums, National Flags and Regime Crises," 486.

22. Juan Francisco Fuentes, "Totalitarian Language: Creating Symbols to Destroy Words," *Contributions to the History of Concepts* 8, no. 2 (2013): 55–56.

23. Walter Benjamin, "Theories of German Fascism," *New German Critique: An Interdisciplinary Journal of German Studies* 17 (Spring 1979): 128.

24. Robert Paxton, *The Anatomy of Fascism* (New York: Vintage Books, 2004), 17.

25. Antonio López Pina and Eduardo López Aranguren, *La cultura política de la España de Franco* (Madrid: Taurus, 1976), 214.

26. Jo Labanyi, "Musical Battles: Populism and Hegemony in the Early Francoist Folkloric Film Musical," in *Constructing Identity in Contemporary Spain: Theoretical Debates and Cultural Practices*, ed. Jo Labanyi (Oxford: Oxford University Press, 2002), 208.

27. Labanyi, 208.

28. It is not until the end of 2017, in response to the Catalan crisis, that the party started to have some relevance by garnering increasing media attention through a series of viral political campaigns on social media. Before, Vox had been mostly considered a fringe party of the extreme Right.

29. Stuart J. Turnbull-Dugarte, "Explaining the End of Spanish Exceptionalism and Electoral Support for VOX," *Research and Politics* 1, no. 8 (April–June 2019): 6.

30. Turnbull-Dugarte, 6.

31. In tweet by Vox during the first months of pandemic lockdown, the party was promoting a vote of no confidence against the PSOE–Unidas Podemos coalition government. Its reasons were justified as a question of national security that concerned Spain's national unity: Vox (@VOX_es), "#MociónSeptiembre contra: El Gobierno de Sánchez e Iglesias. La mafia separatista. Las élites globalistas. Y a favor de: La prosperidad, el trabajo y la libertad de los españoles.

La unidad de España. Nuestras fronteras y nuestra civilización," Twitter, July 29, 2020, 10:45 p.m., https://twitter.com/VOX_es/status/1288455609126445057.

32. In a tweet by Vox for the 2019 electoral campaign, Vigo Mortensen's character in the film *Lord of the Rings* was shown fighting multiple symbols heterogeneously and almost randomly associated with the Spanish Left (from the rainbow flag to Catalan pro-independence flags or the communist hammer and sickle): Vox (@VOX_es), "¡Qué comience la batalla! #PorEspaña," Twitter, April 28, 2019, 7:09 p.m., https://twitter.com/VOX_es/status/1122427641750011904.

33. Vox (@VOX_es), "Con estos memes que movéis por Whatsapp no nos extraña que tengamos a todos los demás partidos, a los podemitas y separatistas tan asustados," Instagram, November 26, 2018, https://www.instagram.com/p/Bq09mfjgNr4/.

34. As referred to in the previous chapter, Josh Booth and Patrick Baert's book *The Dark Side of Podemos? Carl Schmitt and Contemporary Progressive Populism* most prominently developed the Podemos-Schmitt connection.

35. Alison Ribeiro de Menezes, "Memory as Disruption: Entanglements of Memory and Crisis in Contemporary Spain," *Bulletin of Hispanic Studies* 94, no. 8 (2017): 899.

CONCLUSION

1. Susan Sontag, *Against Interpretation and Other Essays* (New York: Picador, 2001), 14.

2. Sontag, 15.

3. Sontag, 16.

4. Sontag, 15–16.

5. The picture was made famous in a tweet by *La Vanguardia* announcing that "Pablo Iglesias gets rid of his ponytail after leaving politics," which linked to Pedro Vallín's article, the journalist who got the image and the scoop about Iglesias's change of look: La Vanguardia (@LaVanguardia), "Pablo Iglesias se corta la coleta tras dejar la política," Twitter, May 12, 2021, 10:03 p.m., https://twitter.com/LaVanguardia/status/1392450262237855744.

6. Luis Casal, "La foto 'revolucionaria' de Pablo Iglesias y el mensaje oculto que lanza con el libro que sostiene," *El Español*, May 13, 2021, https://www.elespanol.com/reportajes/20210513/revolucionaria-pablo-iglesias-mensaje-oculto-lanza-sostiene/580693599_0.html.

BIBLIOGRAPHY

Alba Rico, Santiago. "Podemos in Spain: Limits and Possibilities for Change." In *Spain after the Indignados/15M Movement*, edited by Óscar Pereira-Zazo and Steven L. Torres, 75–87. Cham, Switzerland: Springer International Publishing, 2019. https://doi.org/10.1007/978-3-030-19435-2_4.

Albritton, Dean. "Prime Risks: The Politics of Pain and Suffering in Spanish Crisis Cinema." *Journal of Spanish Cultural Studies* 15, nos. 1–2 (2014): 101–15. https://doi.org/10.1080/14636204.2014.931663.

Alegre Zahonero, Luis. "'Populism' as the Task of Constructing a People for Change." In *Spain after the Indignados/15M Movement*, edited by Óscar Pereira-Zazo and Steven L. Torres, 65–74. Cham, Switzerland: Springer International Publishing, 2019. https://doi.org/10.1007/978-3-030-19435-2_3.

Alvarado Jódar, Alejandro, and Concha Barquero Artés. "Un despertar revulsivo: Prácticas colaborativas en el documental sobre el 15-M." *Fonseca* 6 (2013): 304–24.

Alvarez, Marta. "De la reivindicación a la ira: Espacios de crisis en el cine español contemporáneo." *Iberoamericana* 18, no. 69 (2018): 81–102. https://doi.org/10.18441/ibam.18.2018.69.81-102.

Álvarez Junco, José. "Rural and Urban Popular Culture." In *Spanish Cultural Studies: An Introduction, the Struggle for Modernity*, Helen Graham, and Jo Labanyi, 82–90. Oxford: Oxford University Press, 1995.

Amador, Alfonso, dir. *50 días de mayo (Ensayo para una revolución)*. Valencia, Spain: Lovers Film, 2012.

Angosto-Ferrández, Luis F. "Mausoleums, National Flags and Regime Crises: Comparing Spain and Venezuela." *Politics, Religion & Ideology* 19, no. 4 (2018): 471–93. https://doi.org/10.1080/21567689.2018.1537606.

Antentas, Josep Maria. "Spain: The Indignados Rebellion of 2011 in Perspective." *Labor History* 56, no. 2 (2015): 136–60. https://doi.org/10.1080/00 23656X.2015.1029813.

Araüna, Núria, and Laia Quílez Esteve. "Crisis económica, transformación política y expresión documental: Crónica del anhelo (más que del cambio)." *Journal of Spanish Cultural Studies* 19, no. 4 (2018): 427–43. https://doi.org/10.1 080/14636204.2018.1524992.

Auslander, Philip. "The Performativity of Performance Documentation." *PAJ: A Journal of Performance and Art* 28, no. 3 (2006): 1–10. https://doi.org/10.1162/ pajj.2006.28.3.1.

Baldwin-Philippi, Jessica. "The Technological Performance of Populism." *New Media & Society* 21, no. 2 (2019): 376–97. https://doi. org/10.1177/1461444818797591.

Barlas Bozkus, Seyda. "Pop Polyvocality and Internet Memes: A Reflection of Socio-Political Discourse of Turkish Youth in Social Media." *Global Media Journal* 6, no. 12 (2016): 44–74.

Benjamin, Walter. "Theories of German Fascism." *New German Critique* 17 (1979): 120–28.

Bernabé, Daniel. *La distancia del presente: Auge y crisis de la democracia española (2010–2020).* Madrid: Akal, 2020.

Booth, Josh, and Patrick Baert. *The Dark Side of Podemos? Carl Schmitt and Contemporary Progressive Populism.* Milton, UK: Routledge, 2018. https://doi. org/10.4324/9781351212557.

Briziarelli, Marco. "Podemos' Twofold Assault on Hegemony: The Possibilities of the Post-Modern Prince and the Perils of Passive Revolution." In *Podemos and the New Political Cycle*, edited by Óscar García Agustín and Marco Briziarelli, 97–122. Cham, Switzerland: Springer International Publishing, 2018. https://doi.org/10.1007/978-3-319-63432-6_5.

———. "To 'Feel' and to 'Understand' Political Struggle: The National-Popular Rhetoric of Podemos." *Journal of Communication Inquiry* 40, no. 3 (2016): 287–304. https://doi.org/10.1177/0196859916634084.

Cameron, Bryan. "Crowd Control: Populism, Public Assembly, Institutional Crises, and Pere Portabella's Informe General II. El Nuevo Rapto de Europa." *Arizona Journal of Hispanic Cultural Studies* 21, no. 1 (2017): 159–85. https://doi.org/10.1353/hcs.2017.0009.

———. "Spain in Crisis: 15-M and the Culture of Indignation." *Journal of Spanish Cultural Studies* 15, no. 1–2 (2014): 1–11. https://doi.org/10.1080/146362 04.2014.1002601.

Camino, Mercedes. "'Vivir sin ti': Motherhood, Melodrama and Españolada in Pedro Almodóvar's *Todo sobre mi madre* (1999) and *Volver* (2006)." *Bulletin of Spanish Studies* 87, no. 5 (2010): 625–42. https://doi.org/10.1080/14753820.2010.493062.

Carpentier, Nico. *Media and Participation: A Site of Ideological-Democratic Struggle*. Bristol, UK: Intellect, 2011. https://doi.org/10.26530/OAPEN_606390.

Castejón Leorza, María, and Rebeca Maseda García. "*Carmina o revienta* and *Carmina y amén*: Female Transgressions of Victimhood in Spanish Popular Cinema." In *Gender and Violence in Spanish Culture: From Vulnerability to Accountability*, edited by María José Gámez Fuentes and Rebeca Maseda, 195–212. New York: Peter Lang, 2017.

Castells, Manuel. *Networks of Outrage and Hope: Social Movements in the Internet Age*. Cambridge, UK: Polity Press, 2015.

Cazorla-Sánchez, Antonio. "Beyond They Shall Not Pass: How the Experience of Violence Reshaped Political Values in Franco's Spain." *Journal of Contemporary History* 40, no. 3 (2005): 503–20. https://doi.org/10.1177/0022009405054.

Collado Campaña, Francisco, and José Francisco Jiménez Díaz. "Discursos políticos ante la crisis económica: Estudio del líder del PSOE." *Barataria-Revista Castellano-Manchega de Ciencias Sociales*, no. 14 (2012): 41–57. https://doi.org/10.20932/barataria.voi14.100.

Cuadrado, Agustín. "Presencias y ausencias en la representación del espacio familiar: La gran familia franquista frente a la familia democrática." *Hispanic Research Journal* 15, no. 3 (2014): 240–55. https://doi.org/10.1179/1468273714Z.00000000088.

Davies, Ann. "The Spanish Femme Fatale and the Cinematic Negotiation of Spanishness." *Studies in Hispanic Cinemas* 1, no. 1 (2004): 5–16. https://doi.org/10.1386/shci.1.1.5/0.

De Cleen, Benjamin, and Yannis Stavrakakis. "How Should We Analyze the Connections between Populism and Nationalism: A Response to Rogers Brubaker." *Nations and Nationalism* 26, no. 2 (2020): 314–22. https://doi.org/10.1111/nana.12575.

De la Fuente, Manuel. "Documenting the Indignation: Responses to the 2008 Financial Crisis in Contemporary Spanish Cinema." *Romance Quarterly* 64, no. 4 (2017): 185–95. https://doi.org/10.1080/08831157.2017.1356155.

De la Iglesia, Alex, dir. *Mi gran noche*. Madrid: Canal+ España, Enrique Cerezo Producciones Cinematográficas SA, Telefónica Studios, Televisión Española, 2015.

Dematteo, Lynda. "The Mask and the Vanity Wound: Contemporary Populism through Canetti's Insight." In *Popularisation and Populism in the Visual Arts*, edited by Anna Schober, 80–93. London: Routledge, 2019.

Díez García, Rubén, and Enrique Laraña. *Democracia, dignidad y movimientos sociales: El surgimiento de la cultura cívica y la irrupción de los "indignados" en la vida pública.* Madrid: Centro de Investigaciones Sociológicas, 2017.

Ehrlich, Linda C. "The Films of Isaki Lacuesta: Hidden Portraits, Multiple Lives." In *(Re)viewing Creative, Critical and Commercial Practices in Contemporary Spanish Cinema*, edited by Duncan Wheeler, 119–30. Bristol, UK: NBN International, 2014.

Eklundh, Emmy. *Emotions, Protest, Democracy: Collective Identities in Contemporary Spain.* Abingdon, UK: Routledge 2019.

Elwood, Sarah, and Harriet Hawkins. "Intradisciplinarity and Visual Politics." *Annals of the American Association of Geographers* 107, no. 1 (2017): 4–13. https://doi.org/10.1080/24694452.2016.1230413.

Epps, Brad. "Echoes and Traces: Catalan Cinema, or Cinema in Catalonia." In *A Companion to Spanish Cinema*, edited by Jo Labanyi and Tatjana Pavlović, 50–80. New York: Wiley-Blackwell, 2012. https://doi.org/10.1002/9781118322765. ch3.

Errejón, Íñigo, and Chantal Mouffe. *Construir pueblo: Hegemonía y radicalización de la democracia.* Barcelona: Icaria, 2015.

Estrada, Isabel. "Re-politicizing Documentary Footage from the Transición in Spain: Images, Representation and the Digital Age." *Bulletin of Spanish Visual Studies* 2, no. 2 (2018): 267–83. https://doi.org/10.1080/24741604.2018.15 07534.

Evinson, Katryn. "The Generative Politics of Presentism in Post-15M Spain." *boundary 2* 48, no. 3 (2021): 169–90. https://doi.org/10.1215/01903659-9155789.

Faber, Sebastiaan. "Salvados como periodismo populista: En busca de un sujeto nacional-popular." *Arizona Journal of Hispanic Cultural Studies* 21, no. 1 (2017): 235–62. https://doi.org/10.1353/hcs.2017.0012.

Feenstra, Ramón A. *Kidnapped Democracy.* London: Rowman & Littlefield International, 2019.

Feenstra, Ramón A., Simon Tormey, Andreu Casero-Ripollés, and John Keane. *Refiguring Democracy: The Spanish Political Laboratory.* London: Routledge, 2017. https://doi.org/10.4324/9781315160733.

Feinberg, Matthew I. "The Violence of Everyday Life: Lope de Vega's Fuente Ovejuna as Urban Allegory." *Revista de Estudios Hispánicos* 53, no. 2 (2019): 727–51. https://doi.org/10.1353/rvs.2019.0033.

Fernández, Fruela. "Podemos: Politics as a 'Task of Translation.'" *Translation Studies* 11, no. 1 (2018): 1–16. https://doi.org/10.1080/14781700.2017.1373695.

Fernández-Savater, Amador. "Emborronar la CT (del 'No a la guerra' al 15-M)." In *CT o la cultura de la transición: Crítica a 35 años de cultura española*, edited by Guillem Martínez, 37–52. Barcelona: Debolsillo, 2016.

———. "El nacimiento de un nuevo poder social." *Hispanic Review* 80, no. 4 (2012): 667–81. https://doi.org/10.1353/hir.2012.0038.

Fernández Segado, Francisco. "El estado de excepción en el derecho constitucional español: Ed. Revista de Derecho Privado. Madrid, 1978 (J. L. Hernández Conesa)." *Documentación Administrativa* 179 (June 1978): 463–82. http://ezproxy.library.usyd.edu.au/login?url=https://www.proquest.com/scholarly-journals/el-estado-de-excepción-en-derecho-constitucional/docview/2012168151/se-2.

Ferrán, Ofelia, and Lisa Hilbink. Introduction to *Legacies of Violence in Contemporary Spain: Exhuming the Past, Understanding the Present*, edited by Ofelia Ferrán and Lisa Hilbink, 1–22. London: Routledge, 2016. https://doi.org/10.4324/9781315725109.

Finchelstein, Federico. *From Fascism to Populism in History*. Berkeley: University of California Press, 2017. https://doi.org/10.1525/j.ctv1wxr8b.

Flesher Fominaya, Cristina. "Debunking Spontaneity: Spain's 15-M/Indignados as Autonomous Movement." *Social Movement Studies* 14, no. 2 (2015): 142–63. https://doi.org/10.1080/14742837.2014.945075.

———. *Democracy Reloaded: Inside Spain's Political Laboratory from 15-M to Podemos*. New York: Oxford University Press, 2020.

———. *Social Movements and Globalization: How Protests, Occupations and Uprisings Are Changing the World*. Basingstoke, UK: Palgrave Macmillan, 2014.

Franzé, Javier. "The Podemos Discourse: A Journey from Antagonism to Agonism." In *Podemos and the New Political Cycle*, edited by Óscar García Agustín and Marco Briziarelli, 49–74. Cham, Switzerland: Springer International Publishing, 2018. https://doi.org/10.1007/978-3-319-63432-6_3.

Fuentes, Juan Francisco. "Totalitarian Language: Creating Symbols to Destroy Words." *Contributions to the History of Concepts* 8, no. 2 (2013): 45–66. https://doi.org/10.3167/choc.2013.080203.

Gal, Noam, Limor Shifman, and Zohar Kampf. "'It Gets Better': Internet Memes and the Construction of Collective Identity." *New Media & Society* 18, no. 8 (2016): 1698–1714. https://doi.org/10.1177/1461444814568784.

García Agustín, Óscar. "The Aesthetics of Social Movements in Spain." In *Street Art of Resistance*, edited by Sarah H. Awad and Brady Wagoner, 325–48.

Cham, Switzerland: Springer International Publishing, 2017. https://doi. org/10.1007/978-3-319-63330-5_14.

García Agustín, Óscar, and Marco Briziarelli. "Introduction: Wind of Change: Podemos, Its Dreams and Its Politics." In *Podemos and the New Political Cycle*, 3–22. Cham, Switzerland: Springer International Publishing, 2017. https://doi.org/10.1007/978-3-319-63432-6_1.

Gerbaudo, Paolo. "Feeds from the Square: Live Streaming, Live Tweeting and the Self-Representation of Protest Camps." In *Protest Camps in International Context: Spaces, Infrastructures and Media of Resistance*, edited by Gavin Brown, Anna Feigenbaum, Fabian Frenzel, and Patrick McCurdy, 91–108. Bristol, UK: Policy Press, 2017.

———. "Protest Avatars as Memetic Signifiers: Political Profile Pictures and the Construction of Collective Identity on Social Media in the 2011 Protest Wave." *Information, Communication & Society* 18, no. 8 (2015): 916–29. https:// doi.org/10.1080/1369118X.2015.1043316.

Godoy, Carmina, Isabel Casado, Lucía Ballesteros, and María Sánchez. "La representación visual de los 'indignados': Aproximación a un análisis visual sobre la caracterización de los participantes del movimiento 15-M." *Nómadas* 47, no. 1 (2016): https://doi.org/10.5209/rev_NOMA.2016.v47. n1.52393.

Gómez López-Quiñones, Antonio. "Introducción. En el laberinto del populismo: Algunas claves históricas y teóricas." *Arizona Journal of Hispanic Cultural Studies* 21 (2017): 105–35. https://doi.org/10.1353/hcs.2017.0007.

Grattan, Laura. "Populism, Race, and Radical Imagination." In *Populism in Global Perspective*, edited by Pierre Ostiguy, Francisco Panizza, and Benjamin Moffitt, 136–54. London: Routledge, 2020.

Huntington, Heidi E. "Pepper Spray Cop and the American Dream: Using Synecdoche and Metaphor to Unlock Internet Memes' Visual Political Rhetoric." *Communication Studies* 67, no. 1 (2016): 77–93. https://doi.org/10.10 80/10510974.2015.1087414.

Jones, Amelia. "'Presence' in Absentia: Experiencing Performance as Documentation." *Art Journal* 56, no. 4 (1997): 11–18. https://doi.org/10.1080/00 043249.1997.10791844.

Kantara, Argyro. "Populism as Mainstream Politicians' Political Style during the 2012 Greek Election Campaign." In *Discursive Approaches to Populism across Disciplines*, 405–31. Cham, Switzerland: Springer International Publishing, 2020. https://doi.org/10.1007/978-3-030-55038-7_15.

Kioupkiolis, Alexandros. "Late Modern Adventures of Leftist Populism in Spain: The Case of Podemos 2014–2018." In *The Populist Radical Left in*

Europe, edited by Giorgos Katsambekis and Alexandros Kioupkiolis, 47–72. Abingdon, UK: Routledge, 2019.

Kornetis, Kostis. "'Is There a Future in This Past?' Analyzing 15M's Intricate Relation to the Transición." *Journal of Spanish Cultural Studies* 15, nos. 1–2 (2014): 83–98. https://doi.org/10.1080/14636204.2014.938432.

Labanyi, Jo. "Musical Battles: Populism and Hegemony in the Early Francoist Folkloric Film Musical." In *Constructing Identity in Contemporary Spain: Theoretical Debates and Cultural Practice*, edited by Jo Labanyi, 206–21. Oxford: Oxford University Press, 2002.

López Pina, Antonio, and Eduardo López Aranguren. *La cultura política de la España de Franco*. Madrid: Taurus, 1976.

Iglesias Turrión, Pablo. "Boxeo y ajedrez entre espadas y sombras." In *Ganar o morir: Lecciones políticas en* Juego de Tronos, edited by Pablo Iglesias Turrión, 5–11. Madrid: Akal, 2014.

———. "Presentación." In *Ganar o morir: Lecciones políticas en* Juego de Tronos, edited by Pablo Iglesias Turrión, 93–110. Madrid: Akal, 2014.

Laclau, Ernesto. *On Populist Reason*. London: Verso, 2005.

Lacuesta, Isaki, dir. *Murieron por encima de sus posibilidades.* Girona, Spain: Alicorn Films, 2014.

León, Paco, dir. *Carmina o revienta.* Seville, Spain: Andy Joke, 2012.

———. *Carmina y amén.* Seville, Spain: Andy Joke, 2014.

Loxham, Abigail. "Post-Crisis, Post-Feminist: Reading Ada Colau as Female Celebrity Politician in Alcaldessa (Pau Faus, 2016)." *Hispanic Research Journal* 20, no. 1 (2019): 73–86. https://doi.org/10.1080/14682737.2019.1584478.

Marchart, Oliver. "From Media to Mediality: Mediatic (Counter-)Apparatuses and the Concept of the Political in Communication Studies." In *Discourse Theory and Critical Media Politics*, edited by Lincoln Dahlberg and Sean Phelan, 64–81. London: Palgrave Macmillan, 2011. https://doi.org/10.1057/9780230343511_3.

Marino, Angela (Marino Segura). *Populism and Performance in the Bolivarian Revolution of Venezuela*. Evanston, IL: Northwestern University Press, 2018.

Marsh, Steven. "Grotesque Comedy/Esperpento." In *Spain: Directory of World Cinema*, edited by Lorenzo J. Torres Hortelano, 84–103. Bristol, UK: Intellect, 2011.

———. *Spanish Cinema against Itself: Cosmopolitanism, Experimentation, Militancy.* Bloomington: Indiana University Press, 2020.

Martín Rojo, Luisa, and Carmelo Díaz de Frutos. "En #Sol, revolución: Paisajes lingüísticos para tomar las plazas." *Journal of Spanish Cultural Studies* 15, nos. 1–2 (2014): 163–86. https://doi.org/10.1080/14636204.2014.982889.

Martínez, Guillem. "El concepto CT." In *CT o la cultura de la transición: Crítica a 35 años de cultura española*, edited by Guillem Martínez, 13–24. Barcelona: Debolsillo, 2016.

Martínez, Miguel. *Squatters in the Capitalist City: Housing, Justice, and Urban Politics*. New York: Routledge, 2020.

Martínez García, José Saturnino. *Estructura social y desigualdad en España*. Madrid: Los Libros de la Catarata, 2013.

Martínez Guillem, Susana. "Podemos' Performative Power: Space Struggles and/as Political Transformation." In *Podemos and the New Political Cycle*, edited by Óscar García Agustín and Marco Briziarelli, 75–94. Cham, Switzerland: Springer International Publishing, 2017. https://doi. org/10.1007/978-3-319-63432-6_4.

Mazzoleni, Gianpietro. "Populism and the Media." In *Twenty-First Century Populism: The Spectre of Western European Democracy*, edited by Daniele Albertazzi and Duncan McDonnell, 49–64. London: Palgrave Macmillan, 2007.

McGuigan, Jim. *Cool Capitalism*. London: Pluto, 2009.

———. *Neoliberal Culture*. London: Palgrave Macmillan, 2016. https://doi. org/10.1057/9781137466464.

Medina, Alberto. "De flujos, lugares y peceras: Mutaciones y permutaciones del 'cualquiera' en el 15M." *Journal of Spanish Cultural Studies* 16, no. 3 (2015): 293–316. https://doi.org/10.1080/14636204.2015.1103363.

Milner, Ryan M. "Pop Polyvocality: Internet Memes, Public Participation, and the Occupy Wall Street Movement." *International Journal of Communication* 7 (2013): 2357–90.

———. *The World Made Meme: Public Conversations and Participatory Media*. Cambridge, MA: MIT Press, 2016.

Moffitt, Benjamin. *The Global Rise of Populism: Performance, Political Style, and Representation*. Stanford, CA: Stanford University Press, 2016.

Moffitt, Benjamin, and Simon Tormey. "Rethinking Populism: Politics, Mediatisation and Political Style." *Political Studies* 62, no. 2 (2014): 381–97. https://doi.org/10.1111/1467-9248.12032.

Monedero, Juan Carlos. "15M and Indignant Democracy: Legitimation Problems within Neoliberal Capitalism." In *Spain after the Indignados/15M Movement*, edited by Óscar Pereira-Zazo and Steven L. Torres, 21–63. Cham, Switzerland: Springer International Publishing, 2019. https://doi. org/10.1007/978-3-030-19435-2_2.

———. "Prólogo. Tronando por un juego: Enamorarte de un caminante de las nieves pero casarte con un Lannister." In *Ganar o morir: Lecciones políticas en Juego de Tronos*, edited by Pablo Iglesias Turrión, 13–31. Madrid: Akal, 2014.

Montagut, Marta, and Nereida Carrillo. "Estrategias de espectacularización en las tertulias políticas televisivas: Caso de la cobertura de las elecciones municipales de Barcelona de 2015." *El Profesional de la Información* 26, no. 4 (2017): 621–29. https://doi.org/10.3145/epi.2017.jul.06.

Montesano Montessori, Nicola, and Esperanza Morales-López. "Multimodal Narrative as an Instrument for Social Change: Reinventing Democracy in Spain—The Case of 15-M." *Critical Approaches to Discourse Analysis across Disciplines* 7, no. 2 (2015): 200–221.

Morán Conesa, Adriano, dir. *La Plaza: La gestación del movimiento 15-M*. Madrid: 93 Metros, 2011.

Moreiras-Menor, Cristina. *La estela del tiempo: Imagen e historicidad en el cine español contemporáneo*. Frankfurt: Vervuert Verlagsgesellschaft, 2011. https://doi.org/10.31819/9783954870448.

Moreno-Caballud, Luis. *Cultures of Anyone: Studies on Cultural Democratization in the Spanish Neoliberal Crisis*. Translated by Linda L. Grabner-Coronel. Liverpool, UK: Liverpool University Press, 2015.

Morgan, Marcus. "A Cultural Sociology of Populism." *International Journal of Politics, Culture, and Society* 35, no. 2 (2020): 179–99. https://doi.org/10.1007/s10767-020-09366-4.

Mouffe, Chantal. "Deliberative Democracy or Agonistic Pluralism?" *Social Research* 66, no. 3 (1999): 745–58.

———. *For a Left Populism*. London: Verso, 2018.

Mudde, Cas, and Cristóbal Rovira Kaltwasser. "Populism." In *The Oxford Handbook of Political Ideologies*, edited by Michael Freeden and Marc Stears. Oxford: Oxford University Press, 2013. https://doi.org/10.1093/oxfordhb/9780199585977.013.0026.

Nichols, Bill. *Introduction to Documentary*. Bloomington: Indiana University Press, 2017.

Noble, Fiona. *Subversive Spanish Cinema: The Politics of Performance*. London: Bloomsbury, 2020.

Nöth, Winfried. "Visual Semiotics: Key Features and an Application to Picture Ads." In *The SAGE Handbook of Visual Research Methods*, edited by Eric Margolis and Luc. Pauwels, 298–315. London: SAGE Publications, 2011. https://doi.org/10.4135/9781446268278.n16.

Ostiguy, Pierre. "Populism: A Socio-Cultural Approach." In *The Oxford Handbook of Populism*, edited by Cristóbal Rovira Kaltwasser, Paul A. Taggart, Paulina Ochoa Espejo, and Pierre Ostiguy, 73–98. Oxford: Oxford University Press, 2017. https://doi.org/10.1093/oxfordhb/9780198803560.013.3.

Ostiguy, Pierre, and Benjamin Moffitt. "Who Would Identify with an 'Empty Signifier'? The Relational, Performative Approach to Populism." In *Populism in Global Perspective: A Performative and Discursive Approach*, edited by Pierre Ostiguy, Francisco Panizza, and Benjamin Moffitt, 47–72. New York: Routledge, 2021.

Ostiguy, Pierre, Benjamin Moffitt, and Francisco Panizza. Introduction to *Populism in Global Perspective: A Performative and Discursive Approach*, edited by Pierre Ostiguy, Francisco Panizza, and Benjamin Moffitt, 1–18. New York: Routledge, 2021.

Ott, Brian L., and Robert L. Mack. *Critical Media Studies: An Introduction*. 2nd ed. Hoboken, NJ: Wiley, 2014.

Panizza, Francisco. "Introduction: Populism and the Mirror of Democracy." In *Populism and the Mirror of Democracy*, 1–31. London: Verso, 2005.

Paxton, Robert. *The Anatomy of Fascism*. New York: Vintage Books, 2004.

Pereira-Zazo, Óscar, and Steven L. Torres. "Introduction: After the 15M." In *Spain after the Indignados/15M Movement*, edited by Óscar Pereira-Zazo and Steven L. Torres, 1–17. Cham, Switzerland: Springer International Publishing, 2019. https://doi.org/10.1007/978-3-030-19435-2_1.

Pérez-Agote, Alfonso. "The 15M Movement and the Crisis of Conventional Politics." In *Crisis and Social Mobilization in Contemporary Spain*, edited by Ignacia Perugorría and Benjamín Tejerina, 140–66. London: Routledge, 2018. https://doi.org/10.4324/9781315574875-8.

Perugorría, Ignacia, and Benjamín Tejerina. "Politics of the Encounter: Cognition, Emotions, and Networks in the Spanish 15M." *Current Sociology* 61, no. 4 (2013): 424–42. https://doi.org/10.1177/0011392113479743.

Portabella, Pere, dir. *Informe General II: El nuevo rapto de Europa.* Barcelona: Films 59, 2016.

Rama, José, Lisa Zanotti, Stuart J. Turnbull-Dugarte, and Andrés Santana. *Vox: The Rise of the Spanish Populist Radical Right*. Abingdon, UK: Routledge, 2021.

Ramírez Blanco, Julia. *Artistic Utopias of Revolt Claremont Road, Reclaim the Streets, and the City of Sol*. Cham, Switzerland: Springer International Publishing, 2018. https://doi.org/10.1007/978-3-319-71422-6.

Rancière, Jacques. *Dissensus: On Politics and Aesthetics*. Translated by Steve Corcoran. London: Continuum, 2010.

———. *The Politics of Aesthetics*. New York: Continuum, 2004.

Ribeiro de Menezes, Alison. "Memory as Disruption: Entanglements of Memory and Crisis in Contemporary Spain." *Bulletin of Hispanic Studies* 94, no. 8 (2017): 883–901. https://doi.org/10.3828/bhs.2017.54.

Ripley, Marc. "Housed Nowhere and Everywhere Shut In: Uncanny Dwelling in Luis Buñuel's El Ángel Exterminador." *Bulletin of Spanish Studies* 93, no. 4 (2016): 679–95. https://doi.org/10.1080/14753820.2016.1178508.

Robles, José Manuel, Rubén Díez, Antón R. Castromil, Arturo Rodríguez, and Mildred Cruz. "El Movimiento 15-M en los medios y en las redes: Un análisis de sus estrategias comunicativas." *Empiria* 32 (2015): 37–61. https://doi.org/10.5944/empiria.32.2015.15308.

Rubio-Pueyo, Vicente. "A Populist Experiment in Spanish Political Culture? On the Cultural Politics of Podemos." *Boundary* 2 48, no. 3 (2021): 145–68. https://doi.org/10.1215/01903659-9155775.

Rueda Laffond, Jose Carlos. "¿Un pasado que no cesa? Discurso patrimonial y memoria pública comunista en el franquismo y la transición española." *Revista de Estudios Sociales* 47 (2013): 12–24. https://doi.org/10.7440/res47.2013.01.

Rueda Toledano, Daniel. "Los legados institucionales del largo 15-M: El final del momento populista y la vía errejonista a la transversalidad." *Encrucijadas* 19 (2020): 1–25.

Ruzza, Carlo, and Rosa Sanchez Salgado. "The Populist Turn in EU Politics and the Intermediary Role of Civil Society Organisations." *European Politics and Society* 22, no. 4 (2021): 471–85. https://doi.org/10.1080/23745118.2020.1801180.

Sánchez León, Pablo. "Pueblo, oligarquía, clase media y plebe: Combinaciones para pensar históricamente el populismo en la España contemporánea." *Arizona Journal of Hispanic Cultural Studies* 21, no. 1 (2017): 137–58. https://doi.org/10.1353/hcs.2017.0008.

———. "The Study of Nation and Patria as Communities of Identity: Theory, Historiography, and Methodology from the Spanish Case." *Genealogy* 4, no. 1 (2020): 1–23. https://doi.org/10.3390/genealogy4010023.

Sánchez Vidal, Agustín. "El viaje a la luna de un perro andaluz." In *Valoración actual de la obra de García Lorca: Actas del coloquio celebrado en la Casa de Velázquez*, 141–62. Madrid: Editorial de la Universidad Complutense, 1988.

Seguín, Bécquer. "Introduction: A Decade of Indignation." *boundary* 2 48, no. 3 (2021): 1–6. https://doi.org/10.1215/01903659-9155689.

———. "Podemos and Its Critics." *Radical Philosophy* 193 (September–October 2015): 9–19.

Serrano Azcona, Carlos, dir. *Banderas falsas*. Madrid: Estar Ahí Cinema, 2012.

Sevilla-Buitrago, Álvaro. "Outraged Spatialities: The Production of Public Space in the #spanishrevolution." *ACME: An International E-journal for Critical Geographies* 14, no. 1 (2015): 90–103.

Shifman, Limor. *Memes in Digital Culture*. Cambridge, MA: MIT Press, 2014.

———. "Testimonial Rallies and the Construction of Memetic Authenticity." *European Journal of Communication* 33, no. 2 (2018): 172–84. https://doi.org/10.1177/0267323118760320.

Smith, Paul Julian. *Dramatized Societies: Quality Television in Spain and Mexico*. Liverpool, UK: Liverpool University Press, 2016.

———. *Spanish Visual Culture. Cinema, Television, Internet*. Manchester, UK: Manchester University Press 2006.

Sola, Jorge, and César Rendueles. "Podemos, the Upheaval of Spanish Politics and the Challenge of Populism." *Journal of Contemporary European Studies* 26, no. 1 (2018): 99–116. https://doi.org/10.1080/14782804.2017.1304899.

Sontag, Susan. *Against Interpretation and Other Essays*. New York: Picador, 2001.

Stavrakakis, Yannis. "Populism and Hegemony." In *The Oxford Handbook of Populism*, edited by Cristóbal Rovira Kaltwasser, Paul A. Taggart, Paulina Ochoa Espejo, and Pierre Ostiguy, 535–53. Oxford: Oxford University Press, 2017. https://doi.org/10.1093/oxfordhb/9780198803560.013.26.

Tahmassian, Lena. "Carl Schmitt and the Basque Conflict: From the Design of Francoism to Spanish Democracy." *Journal of Spanish Cultural Studies* 13, no. 1 (2012): 59–81. https://doi.org/10.1080/14636204.2012.740257.

Taibo, Carlos. *Nada será como antes: Sobre el Movimiento 15-M*. Madrid: Los Libros de la Catarata, 2011.

Thomas, Sarah. "Primed for Suffering: Gender, Subjectivity, and Spectatorship in Spanish Crisis Cinema." *boundary 2* 48, no. 3 (2021): 215–51. https://doi.org/10.1215/01903659-9155817.

Toret Medina, Javier. *Tecnopolítica y 15M: La potencia de las multitudes conectadas. Un estudio sobre la gestación y explosión del 15M*. Barcelona: Editorial UOC, 2015.

Torelló Oliver, Josep, and Jaume Duran Castells. "Informe general (1976) de Pere Portabella: Un estado de la cuestión cinematográfica sobre la Transición española." *Archivos de la Filmoteca* 73 (2017): 213–23.

Traverso, Enzo. *The New Faces of Fascism: Populism and the Far Right*. London: Verso, 2019.

Triana-Toribio, Núria. "Spanish Cinema of the 2010s: Back to Punk and Other Lessons from the Crisis." *Hispanic Research Journal* 20, no. 1 (2019): 10–25. https://doi.org/10.1080/14682737.2019.1584464.

Turnbull-Dugarte, Stuart J. "Explaining the End of Spanish Exceptionalism and Electoral Support for Vox." *Research & Politics* 6, no. 2 (2019): 1–8. https://doi.org/10.1177/2053168019851680.

Turner, Graeme. *Ordinary People and the Media: The Demotic Turn*. Los Angeles: SAGE Publications, 2010.

Tuters, M., and S. Hagen. "(((They))) Rule: Memetic Antagonism and Nebulous Othering on 4chan." *New Media & Society* 22, no. 12 (2020): 2218–37. https://doi.org/10.1177/1461444819888746.

Valdivielso, Joaquín. "The Outraged People. Laclau, Mouffe and the Podemos Hypothesis." *Constellations* 24, no. 3 (2017): 296–309. https://doi. org/10.1111/1467-8675.12287.

Valle-Inclán, Ramón del. *Luces de Bohemia: Esperpento.* Alicante, Spain: Biblioteca Virtual Miguel de Cervantes, 2017. http://www.cervantesvirtual. com/obra/luces-de-bohemia-esperpento-875781/.

Venkatesh, Vinodh. "Ethics, Spectacle, and Violence in Álex de La Iglesia's *La chispa de la vida.*" *Hispanófila* 178, no. 1 (2016): 21–35. https://doi.org/10.1353/ hsf.2016.0057.

Vidal Pelaz López, José, and Jorge Lafuente Del Cano. "Presentación: El centro político en la Transición y los problemas de España." *Memoria y Civilización* 23 (2020): 289–95.

Vilaseca, Stephen Luis. "The 15-M Movement: Formed by and Formative of Counter-Mapping and Spatial Activism." *Journal of Spanish Cultural Studies* 15, nos. 1–2 (2014): 119–39. https://doi.org/10.1080/14636204.2014.931653.

Villacañas de Castro, Luis S. "Chavs, chonis, y el nuevo socialismo (si lo hubiera)." *Res Pública: Revista de Filosofía Política* 29 (2013): 88–98.

Villarmea Álvarez, Iván. "Rostros y espacios de la austeridad en los cines ibéricos (2007–2016)." *Iberoamericana* 18, no. 69 (2018): 13–36. https://doi. org/10.18441/ibam.18.2018.69.13-36.

Virino, Concepción Cascajosa, and Vicente Rodríguez Ortega. "Daenerys Targaryen Will Save Spain: *Game of Thrones*, Politics, and the Public Sphere." *Television & New Media* 20, no. 5 (2019): 423–42. https://doi. org/10.1177/1527476418770748.

Weymans, Wim. "From Marianne to Louise: Three Ways of Representing the (European) People in Democratic Societies." In *Popularisation and Populism in the Visual Arts: Attraction Images*, edited by Anna Schober, 31–45. London: Routledge, 2019. https://doi.org/10.4324/9780429467882-3.

White, Jerry. "The Changing of the Age. Pere Portabella on *Informe General II.*" *Cinema Scope*, no. 67 (2016). https://jawabsoal. live/baca-https-cinema-scope.com/cinema-scope-online/ general-report-ii-new-abduction-europe-pere-portabella-spain-wavelengths/.

Wilhelmi, Gonzalo. *Romper el consenso: La izquierda radical en la Transición española (1975–1982).* Madrid: Siglo XXI, 2016.

INDEX

Numbers in *italic* refer to images.

www.ingramcontent.com/pod-product-compliance
Lightning Source LLC
Chambersburg PA
CBHW030356270326
41926CB00009B/1126